875

LOCOMOTION

LOCOMOTION

A World Survey of Railway Traction

O. S. Nock
B.Sc., C.Eng., F.I.C.E., F.I.Mech.E.

Routledge & Kegan Paul   London

*First published in 1975
by Routledge & Kegan Paul Ltd
Broadway House, 68–74 Carter Lane,
London EC4V 5EL
Text set in Monophoto Ionic
and printed in Great Britain by
BAS Printers Limited, Wallop, Hampshire
© O. S. Nock 1975
No part of this book may be reproduced in
any form without permission from the
publisher, except for the quotation of brief
passages in criticism*

ISBN 0 7100 8222 3 (c)

Contents

	Preface	vii
1	The prelude to locomotives	1
2	Twenty-five years to Rainhill	10
3	Steam rail-power and the first alternative	22
4	Europe and America	33
5	The development of speed	43
6	Climbing steep gradients	56
7	In search of efficiency	67
8	The elements of speed	80
9	Problem of the commuters	96
10	The world of the narrower gauges	110
11	Worldwide technical advances: 1900–14	124
12	Articulated locomotive development	142
13	Rack railways	154
14	Main line electrification	163
15	Steam: moving towards the climax	176
16	Inception and early development of the diesel	190

17	**The zenith of steam: 1935–45**	201
18	**The ultimate in articulation**	217
19	**The superseding of steam**	229
20	**High-speed electrics**	243
21	**The belt-conveyor railways**	256
22	**The Great Anniversary and a look ahead**	268
	Bibliography	278
	Acknowledgments	280

Preface

To write a book on the history of railway traction, covering no less than 175 years of momentous evolution is to follow humbly in the path of some of the greatest historians of the industrial world, British, French and American, some of whose works are mentioned in the bibliography. In casting my own net worldwide I have been constantly aware of the erudition and depth of detail in research that some of these earlier works display. It has helped me enormously in tracing the broad outlines of development, and the way in which events in far distant parts of the world are linked. In making personal visits to many railways, the locomotive practice of which has made significant contributions to the development as a whole, I have been able to talk to men who have participated, and themselves influenced design, and whose knowledge extends far back into history. There are British engineers who have worked in the Argentine, Burma, China and West Africa; Austrian, French and Swiss locomotive men who have accompanied me over their railways, and many within the British Commonwealth who have shown me with pride their workshops, running sheds and on-line operation.

Over the years I have had the privilege of meeting some of the greatest British locomotive engineers of the last fifty years personally: F. W. Hawksworth of the GWR, whose major experience ranged from the detail designing of *The Great Bear* to the introduction of the first British gas turbine locomotive; H. G. Ivatt of the LMS, who made so massive a contribution to diesel-electric traction; Sir Nigel Gresley; R. A. Riddles; S. B. Warder, who made the historic decision to adopt 25,000-volt a.c. traction; and 'Garratt' Williams, of Beyer, Peacock. But perhaps my most treasured recollections are those of the late Sir William Stanier, for his personal friendship as well as his technical backing of my work. Behind these giants of the locomotive world are many, in all parts of the world, who by their friendship, and simple devotion to the job, have indirectly helped to write this book, and in addition to those who have been so ready to explain the technicalities of their profession, I remember with gratitude the running inspectors, drivers and firemen with whom I have ridden on steam, diesel and electric locomotives, in fair weather and foul, in extremes of heat and cold, and with every one of whom a love of locomotives was a bond that no difference of language, creed or colour could break. I recall, no less, occasions when the descendants of some, long passed on, have welcomed me in their homes, like the son and surviving daughters of the great C. J. Bowen-Cooke, of the London and North Western Railway, and Swindon men rich in their memories of G. J. Churchward.

In a book of this kind, however, there is little room for personal reminiscence, and in the more professional side of the work I must express my indebtedness to the records of the Institutions of Civil, and of Mechanical Engineers, and to the transactions of learned societies in France and America. No less am I indebted to the files of distinguished journals such as *Engineer*, *Engineering*, *Railway Gazette* and *Railway Engineer*, in Great Britain; to *Railway Mechanical Engineer* in the USA, and to *Revue Générale des Chemins de Fer* in France. On more recent topics the journal of the Association Française des Amis de Chemin de Fer, and its distinguished editor Daniel Caire, have been most helpful.

It would be manifestly impossible to mention all those who, over a period of more than forty years, have given most generously of their help in my railway quests and investigations, but a few I must mention specially. There is Derek S. Barrie, formerly Chairman and General Manager of the Eastern Region of British Railways; the late C. A. Cardew, Assistant Chief Mechanical Engineer of the New South Wales Government Railways; Ray Corley, formerly of Canadian General Electric; Maurice Crane, of Beyer, Peacock & Co.; Sam Ell, who had charge of dynamometer car testing at Swindon; R. H. Kindig, of Denver, Colorado; the late R. A. Smeddle, Chief Mechanical and Electrical Engineer, Western Region, British Railways; Jack Taylor of the Victorian Railways, at one time United Kingdom Representative of the Railways of Australia; H. Uematsu, of Tokyo; Baron Gérard Vuillet, and Trevor A. Wright, General Manager of the Rhodesia Railways. To all of them, and to countless others of my personal friends, my best thanks are due.

Silver Cedars, O. S. Nock
High Bannerdown,
Batheaston, Bath

The prelude to locomotives

The wheel is one of the greatest inventions of all time. Its origin goes back into the mists of antiquity; but the development of the tracks on which it ran to enable heavier loads to be handled by either man or beast is a matter of history that is recent compared to that of the evolution of the wheel itself. Although this is a book primarily about traction, one can never cease to be mindful of the track on which the wheels run, and the stages by which the medieval wagon-ways developed into a 'road' substantial enough to carry a locomotive form an important prelude to the introduction of mechanical locomotion. Several times in its history the progress of the locomotive, whether steam, diesel or electric, has been halted because its potentiality had run ahead of the load-carrying capacity of the track. There are instances of conflict between civil and locomotive engineers, often because those responsible for track and bridges took an ultra-cautious view of the capacity of their own structures, and road bed. This attitude stemmed possibly from the aftermath of the famous affair on the Penydaren plateway in 1804, which was in some ways more significant than the winning of Samuel Homfray's bet. But I am anticipating. There was railway traction – of a kind – decades before the days of Trevithick.

The ancients had found that by making tracks solid and relatively smooth, beasts of burden, or teams of human slaves, could draw heavier loads, and the tracks were made with the materials most readily to hand, such as blocks of stone. Then the need was felt for some means of guiding the wheels, and the stone-ways were developed in certain places into rut-ways in which the running surface was flanked by stones placed at a higher level. Next came the Iron Age when the tracks formerly made of stone blocks began to give place to 'plateways' and forged angle sections took the place of the old rut-ways. Up to this time, how-

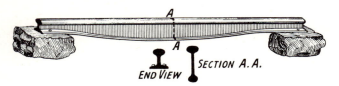

William Jessop's patent 'edge' rail of 1789.

ever, no appreciable development had taken place in the running surface of the wheel itself, which in profile was quite flat. The eighteenth century however brought rapid development. It was Ralph Allen, the English West Country magnate, who first introduced flanged wheels, in 1733, on the wagon-way built to convey stone from his quarries at Prior Park, Bath, to the River Avon. The rails were planed from timber logs, and were 6 in. wide by 5 in. deep, and the wheels of his trucks were entirely of wood. The earliest known instance of iron rails – no more than a forged angle section laid along the top of the wooden rail – was at Whitehaven Colliery, Cumberland, in 1738. But the foundation of all modern railway practice was laid in 1789 when William Jessop invented and patented his 'edge' rail, on which flanged wheels ran on the upper surface of a specially forged section, that obviated the need for continuous support from underneath.

The potentialities of steam, as a means of traction on rails, were first evolved in a somewhat roundabout way. Before the end of the seventeenth century a Frenchman, Dionysius Papin, had built what is believed to be one of the earliest cylinders with a piston working in it, and in Dartmouth, Thomas Newcomen had a development of this engine working while the last of the Stuart monarchs was on the throne of Great Britain. Newcomen used his engines for pumping in the tin mines of Cornwall, though of course it was an easy mechanical transition from pumping water and raising minerals from the mines to hauling small trucks along the wagon-ways. The Newcomen engines were nevertheless not very efficient, though even before James Watt had made his important contribution of the separate condenser, and cut the steam consumption by more than one half, there were others working to use steam for transport. In 1763, two years before Watt's development, a Frenchman, Cugnot by name, constructed a model of a steam carriage, and six years later had advanced sufficiently to build a full-sized engine intended to run on the ordinary roads. It ran at 3 or 4 mph, but had to stop every quarter of an hour to get up steam. In England William Murdoch followed in 1784, but none of these 'steam carriages' had any lasting significance. They were faithfully and amusingly portrayed by the artists of the day, more in ridicule than anything else, because in speed and haulage capacity they could easily be outclassed by any self-respecting horse!

On the railways of the late eighteenth century the development of the track was in advance of motive power. The improvements wrought by Jessop, and others, had made things easier for horses, and also in those locations where human 'push-power' was used, and a pattern emerged

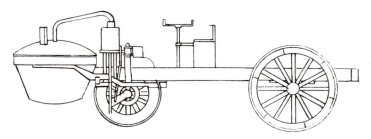

Cugnot's engine of 1769.

The prelude to locomotives

The Newcastle coal wagon, 1773.

that less enterprising minds imagined would be adequate for very many years. Horses were considered to be the prime source of motive power on level or moderately graded lines, while on steep inclines cable haulage was being introduced, from carefully sited stationary steam engine houses. It so happened that many of the early rail or wagon-ways were in the hilly country of north-eastern England, and no little skill was shown in the layouts to use gravity to its fullest extent. The natural flow was for the loaded wagons to pass from the high inland regions to seaports, and they progressed by gravity. The horses then drew the empty wagons back over all but the steepest inclines. Even so, it was rarely possible to make the entire loaded journeys by gravity, and rather than use locally based horses for short journeys, the horses stayed with the trains throughout the loaded run. These trains included one or more wagons, known as dandy cars, in which the horses travelled when the train was running by gravity. It did not take the intelligent horses long to know the places along the routes where they ceased pulling, and once unhitched they could not get into the dandies quickly enough. Contemporary observers said that most of them thoroughly enjoyed their rides.

Watt's steam engines may have revolutionized the pumping operations in tin mines and elsewhere, but even as a stationary plant, with the important addition of the separate condenser, they were unwieldy and not over-efficient. One can understand that a man of Watt's retiring and rather timid outlook would be content with relatively low steam pressures. He and his partner Matthew Boulton built up a good business, but it was one that could not have been developed towards any form of locomotion. Even before the turn of the century Boulton and Watt had a serious rival in Cornwall in Richard Trevithick, a man as opposite in temperament to Watt as it would be possible to imagine. Trevithick was as venturesome as Watt was timid. He judged that by using steam at much higher pressure he would be able to have much smaller cylinders, and instead of the separate condenser, he exhausted the steam after use into the atmosphere. From the noise of the exhaust steam escaping his engines became known as 'puffers'. Not content with capturing some of the Cornish business from Boulton and Watt, Trevithick turned his attention to the steam carriage, and by using relatively high pressure steam, he was able to stride ahead of anything Murdoch and the earlier pioneers had done, though often with disconcerting and destructive results.

Trevithick's restless, ebullient nature led him to plunge in with little in the way of premeditation. There was the eventful run of his first road carriage on New Year's Eve, 1801, with his friend and partner, Andrew Vivian. They were careering down a road near Camborne when they came unexpectedly to a gully in the road, and the whole thing turned over. Instead of taking normal precautions after such a mishap, they pushed the engine under a shelter outside a hotel, left it, and treated themselves to a sumptuous meal. In the meantime the fire in the engine evaporated all the water in the boiler, heated the boiler itself red hot, and set the wooden framing of the carriage on fire. The whole thing went up in flames, burnt down the shelter too, and it was only when the fire looked like spreading to the hotel that anyone noticed something was wrong. Another trial, in London in 1803, ended with the road carriage crashing into a garden wall at night, and tearing down six or seven yards of railing! To Trevithick these adventures were all part of the game. His rivals made much of the danger of his work, and particularly of the risks run in using high pressure steam. The bursting of a boiler at Greenwich in September 1803 caused much shaking of heads and mutterings of 'I told you so'.

But Trevithick was not to be stayed, and in that same autumn of 1803 he met the man who, more by accident than anything else, was to help in writing the first page in the history of steam railways – Samuel Homfray, a prominent South Wales ironmaster. As a keen and successful businessman he appreciated the merits of Trevithick's high pressure engine, to such an extent indeed that he was admitted to a half share in the patent rights. But he and Trevithick were drawn together equally in their love of sport, and inclination to 'have a go' in any novelty. Now there was an old

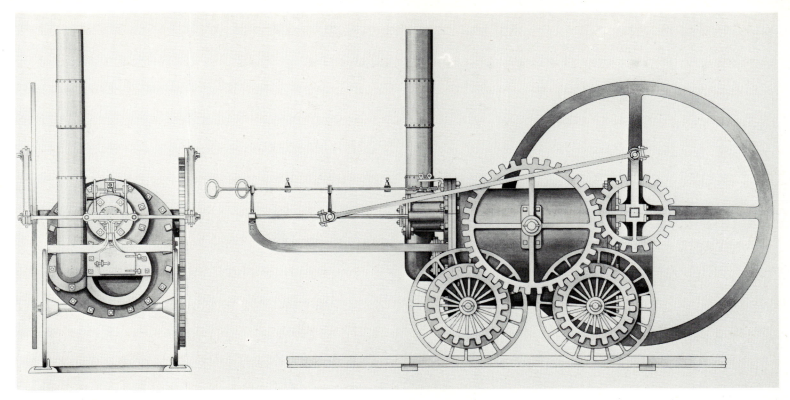

Trevithick's Coalbrookdale locomotive of 1803.

plateway from Homfray's Penydaren Works to the canal at Abercynon, and Trevithick suggested that his development of the road carriage might be extended to haulage of loads on the plateway. Homfray was delighted with the idea, in full knowledge of the mishaps that had attended Trevithick's earlier experiments in this direction. The news got round that a 'tram wagon' was under construction, and some of Homfray's fellow ironmasters were frankly sceptical. One of them, Anthony Hill of the Plymouth ironworks, made a bet of 500 guineas even money that Trevithick's tram wagon could not haul a pay load of 10 tons over the 9¾ miles from the Penydaren Works to the Abercynon Basin. No time was set. It was simply and solely the haulage of a load.

Trevithick threw himself heart and soul into the building of what proved to be the first ever railway locomotive. It was a most remarkable machine. The single cylinder, 4¾ in. diameter by 3 ft stroke, was horizontal and contained within the boiler barrel, extending somewhat at the front end. The piston rod went well forward, like a trombone, and the connecting rod, which was about 7 ft long, drove on to a crank mounted on a shaft just in rear of the boiler. From this crankshaft the drive on to the wheels was through gearing, one set on each side of the boiler. On one side only was the huge flywheel, about 6 ft in diameter. The wheels had no flanges, because the locomotive was

The great run on the Penydaren tramway in 1804: from the original painting by Terence Cuneo.

The prelude to locomotives

designed to run on a plateway. But although this consideration was taken into account, little else of preliminary investigation was made, and on the appointed day, Tuesday, 21 February 1804, they set out gaily only to find some large rocks in the way, and having to cut down trees to clear a path. The account of the first locomotive run, as told in Trevithick's own words and spelling, cannot be bettered:

> Yesterday we proceeded on our journey with the engine; we carry'd ten tons of Iron, five waggons, and 70 men riding on them the whole of the journey. Its above 9 miles which we perform'd in 4 hours & 4 Mints, but we had to cut down som trees and remove som Large rocks out of road. The engine while working, went nearly 5 miles pr hour; there was no water put into the boiler from the time we started untill we arriv'd at our journey's end. The coal consumed was 2 Hund^d. On our return home, abt 4 miles from the shipping place of the Iron, one of the small bolts that fastened the axel to the boiler broak, and let all the water out of the boiler, which prevented the engine returning untill this evening. The Gentleman that bet five Hund^d Guineas against it, rid the whole of the journey with us and is satisfyde that he have lost the bet. We shall continue to work on the road, and shall take forty tons the next journey. The publick untill now call'd mee a schemeing fellow but now their tone is much alter'd.

Nevertheless, although the run was a great personal triumph for Trevithick, it had no immediate effects in South Wales. His great friend Davies Giddy was not able to be present on the actual day, but in the following month when he went to Penydaren he found that the great weight of the locomotive had broken a large number of the iron plates, and finished a report with the words 'on the whole the Experiment was considered as a failure'. Worse than this, Anthony Hill persistently refused to pay the bet. He argued that after the time the bet was made 'some of the train plates that was in the tunnel were removed to get the road in the middle of the arch'. Trevithick wrote to Giddy:

> I expect Mr. Homfray will be forced to take steps that will force him to pay. As soon as I return from here their will be another tryal, and some person will be calld to testify its effects, and then I expect their will be a law suite immidly. The Travelling engine is now working a hammer.

Referring back to the damage done to the track during the run of 21 February 1804, there is considerable doubt as to how the locomotive was guided. The drawing of it in the Science Museum, London, shows plain wheels; and although this is not the *original* drawing, most erudite historians consider it to be a reliable representation of the locomotive as it ran on the famous trial. The driver rode on a truck propelled in front of the chimney, and controlled it by the pull-out handle extending furthest forward. A locomotive of similar design was built in 1805, by John Whinfield of Gateshead, and intended for use at Wylam Colliery. It differed from the Penydaren locomotive in having the crankshaft at the forward end of the boiler, and the cylinder at the rear end. This locomotive was intended to run on wooden edge rails, and from the original drawing, which is preserved in the Science Museum, London, it can be seen that it definitely had flanged wheels. But it was a heavy and cumbersome thing weighing $4\frac{1}{2}$ tons, and on its trials did such damage to the wooden rails that it was never put into service.

So, despite all the dash and enterprise of Trevithick and his friends, the first attempts at locomotive haulage on rails ground to a halt. Not for the last time in railway history the motive power men strode verily decades ahead of those responsible for the track. A less volatile man than Trevithick might have retraced his steps, possibly designing a track that would carry his locomotives, or alternatively modifying or improving his designs to suit the rather primitive 'roads' then existing. But Trevithick already had many other interests, and apart from a brief reappearance, when the *Catch-me-who-can* made its exhibition runs in London in 1808, he disappears from the railway scene. It was his sons and grandsons who carried the name and fame of Trevithick into the railway world of the twentieth century, with no fewer than four of his grandsons simultaneously holding positions of eminence on railways in England, India, Egypt and Japan.

Before concluding this account of the earliest days, and passing on to the more sustained development that led eventually to the Rainhill Trials of 1829, more than a brief mention must be made of the *Catch-me-who-can*, because practically everything surrounding it typifies the sporting temperament of Trevithick. On 8 July 1808 *The Times* had a paragraph:

> We are credibly informed that there is a Steam Engine now preparing to run against any mare, horse, or gelding that may be produced at the next October Meeting at Newmarket; the wagers at present are stated to be 10,000 1; the engine is the favourite. The extraordinary effects of mechanical powers is already known to the world; but the novelty, singularity and powerful application against time and speed has created admiration in the minds of every scientific man. TREVITHICK, the proprietor and patentee of the engine, has been applied to by several distinguished personages to exhibit this engine to the public, prior to its being sent to Newmarket; we have not heard this gentleman's determination yet; its greatest speed will be 20 miles in one hour, and its lowest rate will never be less than 15 miles.

As it turned out the demonstration in London was the only running the *Catch-me-who-can* ever did. The intriguing name was given to the engine by the sister of Davies Giddy,

Trevithick's London locomotive of 1808, the *Catch-me-who-can*.

8 The prelude to locomotives

and from a letter of Trevithick's dated 28 July 1808, it seems that he had profited from the experience of damaged track with his earlier locomotives, particularly as this new one was reputed to weigh 8 tons. He wrote to Giddy:

> I have yours of the 24th and intend putting the inscription on the engine which you sent me. Abt 4 or 5 days since I tryd the engine which worked exceedingly well, but the ground was very soft, and the engine, abt 8 tons, which sunk the timber under the rails, and broake a great number of them, since when I have taken up the whole of the timber and Iron, and have laid Balk of from 12 to 14 In Square, down in the ground, and have nearley all the road laid again, which now appair to be very firm, as we prove every part as we lay down, by running the engine over it by hand. I hope that it will all be compleat by the end of this week.

Detailed information about the locomotive seems to be negligible. From the sketch on the admission card to the enclosure, on open ground near Russell Square, it appears to have been much neater than either of its two predecessors. The cylinder was at the rear end of the boiler with its axis vertical, with connecting rod driving directly on to cranks on the main rear axle, without any gearing, or flywheel. The leading pair of wheels under the forward end of the boiler did not appear to be coupled in any way to the driven trailing pair. Contemporary accounts of the actual running are again almost non-existent; but in 1847 a letter appeared in the *Mechanics Magazine* which throws some authoritative light on the event, and more significantly, why nothing more was heard of the *Catch-me-who-can*:

Mr. Trevithick's New Road Experiments in 1808.
Sir,
    Observing that it is stated in your last number, under the head of 'Twenty-one Years' Retrospect of the Railway System', that 'the greatest speed of Trevithick's engine was five miles an hour', I think it is due to the memory of that extraordinary man to declare that about the year 1808 he laid down a circular railway in a field adjoining the New Road, near or at the spot now forming the southern half of Euston Square; that he placed a locomotive engine, weighing about 10 tons, on that railway, on which I rode, with my watch in hand at a rate of 12 miles an hour; that Mr. Trevithick then gave his opinion that it would go 20 miles an hour, or more, on a straight railway; that the engine was exhibited at one shilling admittance, including a ride for the few who were not too timid; that it ran for some weeks, when a rail broke and occasioned the engine to fly off in a tangent and overturn, the ground being very soft at the time.
    Mr. Trevithick having expended all his means in erecting the works and inclosure, and the shillings not having come in fast enough to pay current expenses, the engine was not set again on the rail.
    I am, Sir, your obedient servant,
        John Isaac Hawkins,
        Civil Engineer.

And so, with *Catch-me-who-can* lying on her side in the mud the prelude to the commercial use of locomotives was virtually over.

2 Twenty-five years to Rainhill

While Trevithick's locomotives were leaving trails of destruction in their wakes, other men were beginning a more cautious approach to railway traction, with more regard for the problem as a whole. Although no contemporary account mentions it specifically, it could certainly be inferred that a degree of wheel-slip was experienced with the very narrow unflanged wheels of the Penydaren locomotive, and Trevithick's 'Newcastle' locomotive wrought such destruction on its trials at Gateshead that it never did any useful work. Nevertheless it was in northeastern England that the next development and the first real success of steam traction took place. The places where the increased hauling power of steam could be used to advantage were for the most part in hilly country; gradients had to be climbed, and it was at the Middleton Colliery near Leeds that in 1811 the Viewer, John Blenkinsop, devised the rack rail and cogged driving wheel. It was probably the first instance of railway traction being considered as a whole – the locomotive in its true relation to the track. Three years earlier Trevithick was no more than improvising when he rebuilt the circular track in London used to display the *Catch-me-who-can*.

Blenkinsop designed a form of track specifically to carry locomotives, and to obviate the evils of wheel-slip. To what extent Blenkinsop was limited in the weight he could put upon the track we do not know, but he had the rack drive to depend upon rather than the adhesion of a smooth wheel upon smooth rails, or plates. Apart from the rack drive, Blenkinsop's engine had many points of similarity to those of Trevithick, but by using two cylinders instead of one he was able to dispense with the heavy flywheel. The boiler was oval in cross-section, and had a single large flue, while the framing of the locomotive consisted of two large rectangular baulks of timber running

Blenkinsop's locomotive of 1812.

from end to end. The admission of steam to the cylinders was controlled by hand-operated cocks, as in Trevithick's locomotives. This was interesting, because in 1802 Matthew Murray, a partner in the firm of Murray, Fenton and Wood who had built the locomotive, had invented the slide valve, which for three-quarters of a century was to prove the standard form of steam distribution in locomotive cylinders. It was Murray also who had suggested the use of two cylinders instead of one. The first Blenkinsop engine was completed early in 1812, and named *Prince Regent*. It can well be claimed as the first commercially successful railway locomotive. In early trials it hauled a load of 89 tons, and later proved capable of hauling 110 tons at a speed of $3\frac{1}{2}$ mph.

By the end of 1813 there were four Blenkinsop locomotives working on the Middleton Colliery railway, and the system was installed on the Kenton and Coxlodge wagon-way near Newcastle-on-Tyne, also in 1813. Locomotive haulage on this latter line was however shortlived, due it is thought to prejudice on the part of a newly appointed high official who had interests in horse traction! But at Middleton Colliery the Blenkinsop engines continued in service for more than twenty years, and their performance provided evidence in favour of steam traction when the Liverpool and Manchester Railway was under construction in 1829. So far as ordinary haulage was concerned, the rack drive on the Middleton Colliery railway remained the only one of its kind. Trevithick's 'Newcastle' locomotive of 1805 had been built to the order of Christopher Blackett, owner of the Wylam Colliery, and after the disappointment over its failure, or rather its destructive ways, the prospects of steam traction on Tyneside had remained in abeyance, until Blackett went to Leeds and saw the Blenkinsop engines at work. In 1809, however, he had relaid the five miles of the Wylam Colliery line with plate rails, and could not justify the early replacement of this equipment with the cogged edge rails of the Blenkinsop system; but in view of the advantages to be derived from steam traction, which were very evident on the Middleton Colliery railway, he turned again to Trevithick's engine. As constructed in 1805 it had already been proved too heavy and destructive, and William Hedley, the Viewer at Wylam Colliery in 1812, carried out some experiments to determine the relation between the weight of a locomotive and the load it could haul. As a result he determined that a locomotive of a weight that would not damage the track and which could haul a satisfactory paying load seemed possible, without resorting to the cogged rail of Blenkinsop.

Hedley's locomotive of 1813, constructed at Wylam, was in its machinery a blend of the practice of Trevithick and Matthew Murray. It had a boiler with return flue, like the 'Newcastle' locomotive of 1805, with a firedoor at the same end as the chimney, but with two cylinders. For the first time these were placed outside the boiler, with their axes vertical, and driving through oscillating beams. But one of the most interesting features was that to distribute the weight on the rails the locomotive was carried on eight wheels, the axles of which were all driven through a system of gearing. It seems that only one was built like this, and Hedley subsequently attained a degree of reliability with his famous *Puffing Billy* of 1815, which was similar to the 1813 type but ran on no more than four wheels. It was in service at Wylam Colliery for many years afterwards, and is now preserved. Before passing on to subsequent developments three 'firsts' in the history of the locomotive must be noted:

1804, Trevithick built the first to haul a load.
1812, Blenkinsop built the first commercially successful locomotive.

William Hedley's *Puffing Billy* of 1815 at work.

1813, Hedley produced the first successful locomotive to operate on a smooth rail.

Then came George Stephenson. One cannot begin to comment upon the work of this man, who became a veritable colossus in the field of railways and steam traction upon them, without pondering over the astonishing difference between his early life and education compared to those of the six men who had preceded him in making contributions to the development of steam power, and to its use for traction in some form. Newcomen, Watt, Trevithick, Murray, Blenkinsop and Hedley were all men of some status; but while Hedley was building his first locomotives at Wylam Colliery, Stephenson was no more than a humble enginewright. Success came to him no more than gradually; but it was success based on steadfastness and

Twenty-five years to Rainhill

The *Wylam Dilly* of 1813.

perseverance in outlook, and a vision of the future development of railways that put him leagues ahead of all the eminent men who had contributed so far. Despite his humble birth he had none of the timidity of Watt, nor yet the dashing enterprise of Trevithick. Entirely self-taught he steered an unswervingly honest, middle course, studying closely what had gone before and making improvements one by one.

Killingworth Colliery, where George Stephenson was enginewright, is only a few miles from Wylam, and he had plenty of opportunity for getting to know what Hedley was doing. His first locomotive, built in 1814, was something of a synthesis of the work of Blenkinsop and Hedley, having the two cylinders on the centre line of the boiler, and a drive to the wheels through gearing. The boiler had a single flue. Ralph Dodds, Viewer at Killingworth Colliery, was interested in Stephenson's work, and in 1815 they took out a joint patent for an improved locomotive that carried the development one step nearer to the final form. By using a direct drive from a transverse horizontal scale beam attached to the piston rod by a crank on the driving axle, the need for gearing was eliminated. Each cylinder drove one axle, but to keep the correct relation between the cranks – at right angles – and so ensure continuity of smooth drive, the axles were connected by a chain working over sprocket wheels. There was, of course, nothing new in the direct drive, if the sketch of the *Catch-me-who-can* on the admission card to Trevithick's London railway can be accepted as evidence. But Dodds and Stephenson were the first to use *two* cylinders in this way, and to couple the axles by a chain.

The chain connection was, however, no more than an expedient, though provided for in the Dodds and Stephenson patent of 1815. The more far-reaching alternative was to crank the driving axles and have a solid coupling rod between them to maintain correct relation. The intention was to crank the axle at its mid-point, and have the coupling rod beneath the boiler; but this feature was not actually applied in the Killingworth locomotive of 1815. Many years later, Robert Stephenson in a narrative of his father's inventions said that the reason for its abandonment was because 'the mechanical skill of the country was not equal to the task of forging crank axles of the soundness and strength necessary to stand the jars incident to locomotive work'. Nevertheless the principle was established and patented. It was only one of the several important developments taking place at Killingworth during the ten years between 1815 and the opening of the Stockton and Darlington Railway. With Stephenson's locomotives coming into regular use at Killingworth Colliery, the track began to suffer. It was having to carry greater weights than any previously foreseen, and Stephenson secured the collaboration of William Losh in improving the methods of fixing and jointing the rails. These latter, of cast iron, were made in short lengths, involving many joints; and Stephenson and Losh together patented a form of scarfed joint, that went some way towards avoiding the bumps previously occasioned in passing over a rail joint.

Stephenson went a great deal further. Even with the improvements wrought by his collaboration with Losh, the rail tracks were still inclined to be uneven, and locomotives with four or six wheels solidly supported on the frames of that era would not always have all the wheels resting on the rails. So Losh and Stephenson between them devised a novel and ingenious method of individual suspension. The boiler was carried on cylinders fixed by flanges to the underside of the barrel and projecting a few inches into it. They were open at the top to the water in the boiler, and contained solid pistons of the customary kind. The piston rods, extending downwards, rested on the

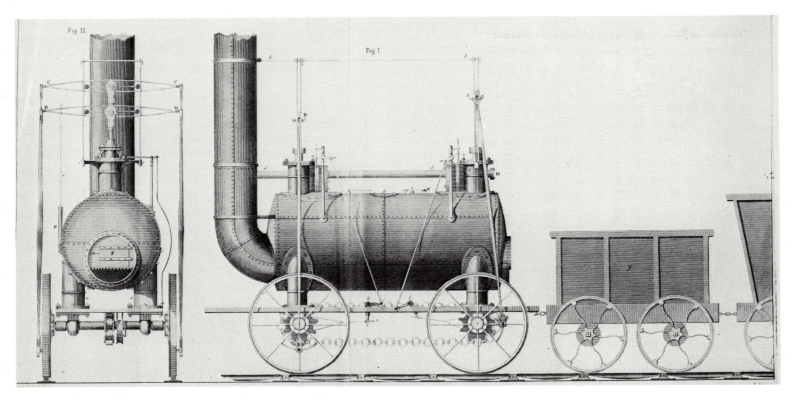

axles, and were free to move up and down, as the wheels adjusted themselves to the inequalities in the track. Nicholas Wood, the distinguished mining engineer who succeeded Dodds as Viewer at Killingworth, commented in 1822: 'The engine is therefore, as it were, supported upon springs of the most exquisite elasticity by which the various and unavoidable inequalities of the road are never felt.'

As originally built the Killingworth engines did not steam freely. The steam having done its work was allowed to escape to the chimney, but with a single flue there was not sufficient draught to maintain the rapidity of combustion to keep the engine constantly working. In his classic work of 1825, *Treatise on Rail Roads*, Nicholas Wood wrote:

> To effect a greater rapidity or to increase the draught of the chimney, Mr. Stephenson thought that by

left
George Stephenson's colliery locomotive of 1820.

Locomotion No. 1 of the Stockton and Darlington Railway, 1825.

causing the steam to escape into the chimney through a pipe with its end turned upwards, the velocity of the current would be accelerated, and such was the effect; but in remedying one evil another has been produced, which, though objectionable in some places, was not considered as objectionable on a private Rail-road. . . .

This, of course, was the strong puffing noise of the exhaust. But by experimenting with the size of the single flue in the boiler, it was found that with a much larger diameter it was possible to get enough steam for all current requirements without resorting to the 'trumpet', as Wood calls it, and the noise nuisance was eliminated. In so doing however the seeds were sown for one of the greatest controversies in early locomotive history: 'Who invented the blastpipe?'

In the meantime the prowess of the Killingworth type of locomotive was becoming well known. It was adopted for

Twenty-five years to Rainhill

the Hetton Colliery railway, and visitors from as far as the USA came to see them at work. How George Stephenson came to be appointed Engineer of the Stockton and Darlington Railway is outside the present narrative; but the first locomotive to be used on a public railway, *Locomotion No. 1*, was in all essentials an improved Killingworth type. The invaluable feature of the coupling rod, included in the Dodds and Stephenson patent of 1815, had been incorporated for some time, but in duplicate, outside the wheels, working on crank bosses on the wheels themselves. On the Stockton and Darlington Railway, at its inception in September 1825, steam traction was used only for freight traffic and to the limited extent possible, with only one locomotive on the strength at the outset. And after all the excitement and glamour of the opening on 27 September 1825, the heat and burden of the day to day work passed on to the devoted foreman of locomotives, Timothy Hackworth.

Now Hackworth had been with Hedley, at Wylam Colliery, when the earliest steam locomotives in Northumberland had been built. How he resigned his appointment there and became associated with George Stephenson is another matter; but from 1825 onwards he had the job of keeping the Stockton and Darlington Railway running and, with more locomotives of the Killingworth type arriving from the works of the newly established firm of Robert Stephenson & Co. in Newcastle, it was not proving an easy task. The Killingworth engines, with their soft and quiet exhaust, may have been adequate for the work of a private colliery railway, but on the much longer hauls of the Stockton and Darlington they were regularly running short of steam. Furthermore, the workmanship was often not of the best and mechanical failures were frequent. Hackworth had a very trying time in keeping the locomotives serviceable, and there were periods when mostly all of the haulage of the coal trains was done by horses. George Stephenson was away for much of the time, engaged on preparations for the Liverpool and Manchester Railway, while Robert Stephenson was in America. The flood tide of enthusiasm for locomotives which had been so evident at the time of the opening of the railway was very much on the ebb, and the abandonment of their use was being openly canvassed. At this period of crisis Timothy Hackworth sought permission to build a locomotive of his own design, and this being granted he eventually produced one of the most significant machines in the early history of railways.

The outstanding need on the Stockton and Darlington Railway was for much greater and more consistent steaming capacity. This Hackworth furnished with a larger boiler, including the double return flue, and by inclusion of the blastpipe which Stephenson had used in his early Killingworth engines but had abandoned largely in the cause of noise abatement. The double flue meant that the fireman had to ride on a tender propelled in front of the engine while the driver was at the opposite end of the boiler. Hackworth placed the cylinders on either side of the boiler and drove on the rearmost of three coupled axles. The wheels were of Hackworth's distinctive 'plug' type, built up in cast sections mounted upon a central hub. At that time there was no machinery capable of turning a wheel of such diameter. Such was the *Royal George* put on to the road in September 1827, and taking up regular work two months later. It was a great success, and undoubtedly saved the day for the steam locomotive on the Stockton and Darlington Railway.

Nevertheless, prejudice against locomotives remained strong, and the Stephensons, father and son, were having to fight tooth and nail to ward off the threat of cable traction being adopted for the entire traffic of the Liverpool and Manchester Railway, then under construction. In January 1829 a deputation of two eminent engineers was

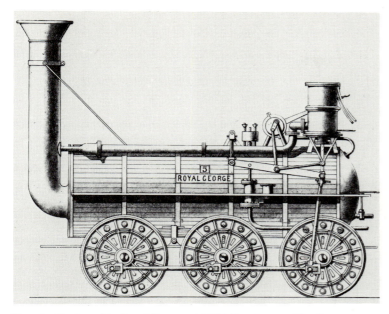

Timothy Hackworth's *Royal George* of 1827, Stockton and Darlington Railway.

sent to Darlington by the directors of the Liverpool and Manchester to observe and report upon methods of railway traction. There they were able to see all three methods: cable haulage on the steep inclines in the neighbourhood of Bishop Auckland; horses drawing some of the coal trains and all the passenger coaches, and of course Hackworth's locomotives. Despite the relatively sound performance of the *Royal George* and other locomotives that had been somewhat rebuilt by Hackworth, both engineers, independently, reported in favour of cable traction for the Liverpool and Manchester Railway. It was a critical moment for the steam locomotive. But for the tremendous vigour and debating skill of Robert Stephenson the day could have been lost, and the development of the locomotive retarded by many years.

As soon as the report was published Robert Stephenson fairly waded into it, and showed by his own knowledge of the Stockton and Darlington Railway how 'facts' had been misrepresented – perhaps unintentionally – to the advantage of cable traction and to the detriment of locomotives, and ultimately the directors of the Liverpool and Manchester Railway were persuaded to stage the famous Rainhill Trials, to determine the most suitable type of steam locomotive to work their line. A stretch of level track $1\tfrac{3}{4}$ miles long was set for the trials. One eighth of a mile at each end was allowed for accelerating to full speed, and for stopping, and this left one and a half miles to be run at full speed. Each competing locomotive was required to haul a load of three times its own weight at a speed of not less than 10 mph, and to make ten double trips, or 35 miles in all – equal to the distance from Liverpool to Manchester. The test was actually more arduous than a straightforward run of 35 miles, because it included stopping and restarting twenty times, and making half the journey in reverse. After the completion of this 35 mile test a fresh supply of fuel and water had to be taken on, and the test repeated in the same conditions. To anyone connected with the working of steam locomotives the constant stopping and restarting, and alternations of forward and reverse travelling, could provide the most severe test of steaming ability in its complete prevention of any steady and continuous production of steam.

Although there were five entrants for the prize offered by the directors, only two proved to be serious contestants, the *Sanspareil*, built by Timothy Hackworth, and the *Rocket*, by Robert Stephenson. Not for the last time in locomotive history a competitive trial ended in acrimony.

Hackworth was certainly at a disadvantage from the start. As a servant of the Stockton and Darlington Railway, paying for his engine out of his own pocket, he was virtually competing against his own masters. Worse still, he had to get some parts of his engine made by Robert Stephenson & Co. at Newcastle; and while it would perhaps be unfair to suggest that the Forth Street Works did not take as much care in manufacturing his cylinders as they might have done the fact remains that one cylinder failed during the test, and severely crippled the performance of the locomotive. The *Sanspareil* was nevertheless rather apart from Hackworth's usual style of construction, which for many

The *Rocket*; photograph of the replica built to the order of Henry Ford.

right
Hackworth's *Sanspareil*, as preserved today.

years after Rainhill followed the style of the *Royal George*. The *Sanspareil* was a four-wheeled engine, with all Hackworth's usual features, including return flue boiler, and the blastpipe. Until the cylinder burst, however, the engine did well, hauling a load of 25 tons, and running up to 15 mph; but after running 25 miles the mishap occurred, and although Hackworth tried to carry on his case was hopeless. Naturally he had every cause to be disappointed, and indeed angry, in that the failure was not due to any defect in design, but entirely due to faulty manufacture.

The *Rocket* on the other hand turned in a faultless performance. Unlike the *Sanspareil*, although carried on four wheels, only one axle was driven, and it set the precedent of having the 'carrying' wheels of considerably smaller diameter than the drivers. It was a complaint of the defeated competitors that the total weight of the *Rocket* was not borne equally on the two axles, though in this respect Robert Stephenson was anticipating later standard practice in having the maximum possible weight on the driving axle, or axles, to secure good adhesion. But the most important feature of the *Rocket*, and a novelty in 1829, was the boiler with a separate firebox, and a barrel with a series of small tubes instead of the hitherto customary one large flue. This innovation had been suggested, strangely enough, by a non-technical man, Henry Booth, the Secretary of the Liverpool and Manchester Railway. It was so effective that it became the standard form of locomotive boiler for as long as there was steam traction. The *Rocket* did not have a blastpipe, but instead had the steam exhausted through two duction pipes, one from each cylinder, and leading into the base of the chimney. It only needs to be added that the locomotive fulfilled all the test conditions, and carried off the £500 prize. Having so done, Robert Stephenson detached his load, and with the engine running light made an exhibition run at nearly 20 mph.

3 Steam rail-power and the first alternative

The construction of the *Rocket* and its successful performance in the Rainhill Trials certainly represented a milestone in the development of railway traction; but so far as details of design are concerned it was no more than transitory. To those becoming familiar with the early locomotives of north-eastern England the most obvious change was in the position of the cylinders, high up at the rear end of the boiler and inclined steeply downwards, instead of vertically, as hitherto. This arrangement had been anticipated by Robert Stephenson on the *Lancashire Witch*, a freight engine built for the Bolton and Leigh Railway in 1828, and one of the first fruits of the metamorphosis wrought in the working of the firm of Robert Stephenson & Co. after Stephenson's return from America, and assumption of direct control of the locomotive building activity. But the *Lancashire Witch* was a slow-moving 0-4-0, and although its working was a great improvement upon that of the older Killingworth type, its other defects did not become apparent until the cylinder arrangement came to be embodied in a fast-running passenger engine like the *Rocket*.

On the Liverpool and Manchester Railway in ordinary service it was found that the *Rocket* developed a jerky, swaying action, because of the unbalanced inertia effects of the reciprocating pistons, and the movement of the connecting rods. Robert Stephenson was quick enough to realize the nature of the trouble, and he attempted to cure it by rebuilding the engine with the cylinders in a more nearly horizontal position, and this arrangement was followed in a number of additional engines built by his firm for the Liverpool and Manchester Railway. Although the undesirable motion was thereby much reduced, it was not eliminated, and it was attributed as much to the distance apart of the cylinders as to their position on the

The *Lancashire Witch* of 1828, by Stephenson for the Bolton and Leigh Railway.

Steam rail-power and the first alternative

boiler. The fact that the cranks had to be at right-angles to each other instead of diametrically opposite, to avoid the trouble of an engine stopping with the cranks on dead centre, increased the unbalancing effect. The Liverpool and Manchester Railway purchased a number of locomotives of the modified 'Rocket' type in 1830 for the opening of the railway. They all had a single pair of driving wheels, and cylinders at the rear no more than slightly inclined from the horizontal. There was no question of standardization. The first four, named *Meteor*, *Comet*, *Dart* and *Arrow*, were definitely of the 'Rocket' type. The next two, the *Phoenix* and the *North Star*, were slightly larger, while the last two, the *Northumbrian* and the *Majestic*, incorporated many improvements, all attained within a year of the production of the prototype *Rocket* that ran at Rainhill.

In adopting Booth's suggestion of the multi-tubular boiler, Robert Stephenson had brought the firebox outside the cylindrical shell of the boiler itself in a separate casing attached at the rear, and this arrangement had been followed in the next six engines of the type built for the Liverpool and Manchester Railway; but in the *Northumbrian* the firebox was made an integral part of the boiler. In this respect the new engine was a veritable patriarch, for the form of its boiler and firebox determined the standard arrangement that was followed in most respects throughout the history of steam traction. In another notable respect the *Northumbrian* was both a pioneer and a precursor. From the early days at Wylam and Killingworth, when locomotives were built on a framing consisting of two large baulks of timber, the framing had tended to be a matter of 'bits and pieces' – plates here, angles there, connected up somewhat haphazardly. In the *Northumbrian*, however, Robert Stephenson for the first time used a continuous wrought iron frame consisting of plates arranged vertically. This arrangement, instead of the previous flat plates, gave greatly increased strength, and was of course the origin of the traditionally British inside plate frame.

Nevertheless, although the *Northumbrian* and the *Majestic* represented such an advance upon both the original and the modified versions of the *Rocket*, they, in turn, were no more than a quickly passing phase. Robert Stephenson, still concerned about the unbalancing effect of outside cylinders, decided to try a radical change in design. Not only did he turn the machinery end for end, as it were, putting the cylinders at the forward end and the driving wheels at the rear, but for the first time the cylinders were placed inside, beneath the smokebox, with the drive on to a cranked axle just ahead of the firebox. Manufacturing methods had advanced sufficiently for him to venture upon a cranked driving axle, while the disposition of the axles enabled a greater proportion of the total engine weight to rest on the driving axle giving the locomotive greater and more reliable tractive power than that of the *Northumbrian*. The frames, which were continuous from end to end of the locomotive, were outside, with attachments – forerunners of the later horn guides – bolted on and extending downwards to carry the axleboxes. This notable engine was named *Planet*, and it arrived from Stephenson's works at Newcastle early in October 1830.

At once it demonstrated a marked superiority over all the outside cylinder locomotives already on the line, and on 4 December 1830 it hauled a gross load of 80 tons from Liverpool to Manchester in 2 hr. 54 min. including three stops for watering and oiling. The run was not entirely unassisted, because additional engines were employed to get this relatively big load up the Whiston 'inclined plane'. It is notable, however, that this run was the first occasion on which merchandise had been conveyed. The pay load of freight was 51 tons. It is nevertheless significant of the emphasis originally placed on passenger haulage on the

Liverpool and Manchester Railway: the improved 'Rocket' type locomotive, *Northumbrian*, by Robert Stephenson, 1830.

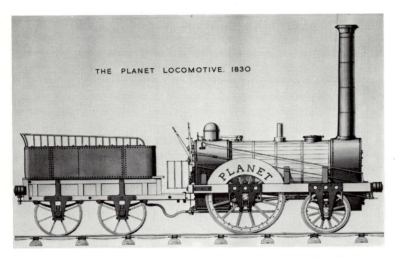

The *Planet*, of 1830, by Stephenson. First locomotive with inside cylinders.

Liverpool and Manchester Railway that all the earliest locomotives were single-wheelers, either of the 0-2-2 or, in the case of the *Planet*, 2-2-0 type. It is reported that on an early trial this latter engine, working light, ran the 30 miles from Liverpool to Manchester in one hour, with one brief intermediate stop for oiling and examination. The directors were so impressed with the performance of this engine that the design was immediately adopted as a standard, to be imposed on other manufacturers than Stephenson, who might tender for the supply of further locomotives. By that time indeed other makers were coming into the field, notably Bury, Curtis and Kennedy. Of this firm Edward Bury became a most persistent and aggressive competitor of the Stephensons, in his advocacy of a different type of framing and machinery layout. In 1830 this firm produced a remarkable engine, the *Liverpool*, but for some time it was not allowed to be tried on the Liverpool and Manchester Railway.

Designed in its essentials by James Kennedy, it was a four-coupled machine, and although stated to be a goods engine had wheels of the unprecedented size, at that time, of 6 ft diameter. But its principal distinction when compared to the *Planet* was that the frames were inside the wheels, and of the bar instead of the plate type. This gave it a distinctly spidery appearance from outside, and led to some prejudiced opinions of it, when Bury urged the Liverpool and Manchester Railway Board to give it a trial. George Stephenson in particular was vehement in its condemnation. Recalling no doubt his earlier experiences at Killingworth he stigmatized the inside bearings for the axles as unsafe, and strongly criticized the large diameter of the driving wheels. His views led indeed to a decision by the Board not to accept any locomotive with a wheel larger than 5 ft, for the time being at any rate – this being the diameter of the driving wheels of the *Planet*. There can be little doubt however that the Stephensons, father and son, realized that in Bury's firm there was arising a strong competitor, and they had good reason for opposition. The *Liverpool* provided the first example of the distinctive and picturesque 'haystack' type of firebox, which can be seen on the preserved Furness Railway 0-4-0 *Coppernob* today. Opposition or not, the work of Bury, Curtis and Kennedy brought a third style of locomotive design into the early railway scene, the other two being the Stephensons', and Hackworth with his return flue type boilers, and the fireman propelled on a tender in front.

In 1831 Robert Stephenson & Co. began building an 0-4-0 variant of the 'Planet' type, for goods work on the Liverpool and Manchester Railway. These had outside frames, and when Bury secured an order for a similar engine he was instructed to make the frames likewise. The frames

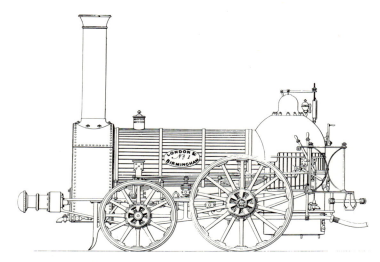

Edward Bury's 2-2-0 passenger locomotive of 1837 for the London and Birmingham Railway.

were of what is known as the 'sandwich' type, consisting of a stout plank of timber held between two wrought iron plates. In respect of the frames, however, these two Stephenson 0-4-0s had 'belt and braces', with inside bar frames, or stays, extending between the cylinders and the firebox. These inside frames did not carry any of the weight and provided bearings only for the driving axle. They were intended as a safeguard in case of a breakage of the driving axle, which would keep the wheels in line and prevent a derailment. George Stephenson had a horror of broken crank axles, and this feature of the design was undoubtedly due to his apprehensions. With the need to line up four bearings on the crank axle, however, it required some fine workmanship both in erection and maintenance. Excellent though the 'Planet' type locomotives were for hauling a load, their increased weight, with $5\frac{1}{2}$ tons on the driving axle, proved excessive for the very light permanent way. This was not altogether surprising, for in two years from Rainhill the weight of locomotives had more than doubled, from the $4\frac{1}{2}$ tons of the *Rocket* to the 10 tons of the 0-4-0 'Planet' type, named *Samson*.

Even before the question of locomotive size came up before the Board of the Liverpool and Manchester Railway, in 1832, Robert Stephenson had considered the addition of a third pair of wheels to the 2-2-0 'Planet' type, and at Newcastle a drawing had been prepared for a similar addition to the 0-4-0. So eventuated the famous *Patentee* engine of 1834, the first ever 2-2-2. It is scarcely possible to over-emphasize the influence this design had upon locomotive development both in Great Britain and overseas. Ironically enough, however, while it virtually determined the design of the British express passenger engine for the ensuing fifty years, the *Patentee* itself was the very last supplied by Robert Stephenson & Co. to the Liverpool and Manchester Railway. But while other makers moved into what had originally been an exclusive Stephenson preserve, the fame of both father and son led to their being consulted over numerous projects, most of which resulted in good business for the Forth Street Works in Newcastle. The six-wheeled locomotive was produced with the 2-2-2, 0-4-2 and 0-6-0 wheel arrangements during the 1830s, though Bury adhered rigidly to his bar-framed four-wheelers, and Hackworth produced ever larger versions of his ponderous 0-6-0s with a tender at each end, for use on trains limited to a maximum speed of 6 mph.

In this chapter I am concerned only with developments within the United Kingdom, though before the end of the 1830s there had been much activity overseas. With the end of the brief Stephenson monopoly of locomotive power on the Liverpool and Manchester Railway, one or two highly

Stephenson's 2-2-2 locomotive *Patentee*, for the Liverpool and Manchester Railway, 1834.

unorthodox designs were tried – none stranger, for the year 1833, than the *Experiment* built by Sharp, Roberts & Co., having vertical cylinders, and a drive through a large bell crank. This firm, which achieved such a notable record in later years, seems to have got off to a very shaky start, and three 2-2-0 locomotives of generally similar design supplied to the Dublin and Kingstown Railway in 1834 proved failures due to the pitching action that made them positively dangerous at passenger train speed. There would be little point in mentioning them at all, but for the part the Dublin and Kingstown Railway, and its motive power, played indirectly towards the subsequent development of British locomotive practice. Also in 1834, and continuing with the 2-2-0 type of locomotive, the Dublin and Kingstown ordered three outside cylindered engines from George Forrester, of Liverpool, which were important in one respect in being the first ever to have horizontal outside cylinders. A further example of the same design was supplied to the Liverpool and Manchester Railway, and others subsequently to the London and Greenwich line. But the combination of outside cylinders with a very short wheelbase produced a strong swaying action at speed, and earned for them the nickname of 'boxers'.

It was in another respect altogether that Forrester's 'boxers' had an influence for the future, quite unconnected with their original usage. They had a combination of inside and outside frames. The driving axle, just ahead of the firebox as in the 'Planet' type, had inside frames, but the leading axle was supported in a composite arrangement depending upon the outside frame, that included not only the horn guides for the leading axle, but the support for the cylinder and the crosshead guide. The significance of this form of construction was not apparent until some ten years later, and then in quite a different connection; because by the mid-1830s it was only Edward Bury who was persisting with the 2-2-0 type for main line working. Already the traffic developing on the railways of Great Britain was requiring larger locomotives. Equally, while the first flush of popular enthusiasm for steam operated railways was giving place to a growing view of the new form of transport as a field for investment, and to some a means of 'getting rich quick', the novelty of travel was being tempered by an awareness of its shortcomings from an amenity point of view. Clouds of smoke and steam, and the emission of red hot cinders and smuts, often made conditions unpleasant in the open and semi-open carriages of the day, while even in the enclosed first-class coaches, designed in the style of an old time stage coach, cinders lodging

Forrester's 2-2-0 for the Dublin and Kingstown Railway, 1834.

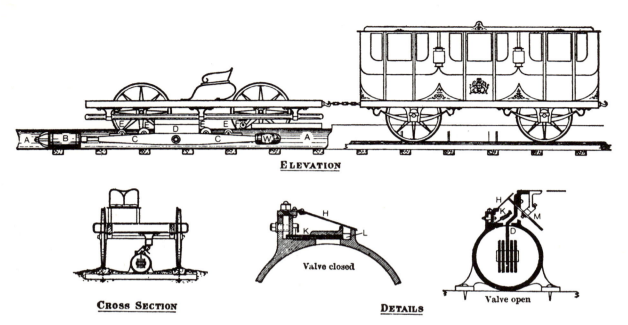

The atmospheric system of traction: pictorial diagrams.

A A Continuous pipe fixed between the rails.
B   Piston.
C C Iron plates connected to the piston.
D   Plate connecting apparatus to carriage.
E   Metal rollers to open the continuous valve.
F   Roller attached to carriage for closing the valve.
H   Weather valve.*
K   Continuous airtight valve hinged at left.
L   Composition for sealing valve.
M   Roller attached to carriage for opening weather valve.*
W   Counterweight to piston.

* These complications do not appear to have been in use on the South Devon Railway.

amongst the luggage piled on the roofs sometimes started fires.

Before railway history had proceeded ten years beyond Rainhill, there were men becoming interested in forms of traction other than steam. It was in 1833 that Isambard Kingdom Brunel first became associated with the project of building a railway between Bristol and London. How the network of lines on the exceptional 7 ft gauge extended was one of the phenomena of the age, and in 1836 Brunel was down in the West Country surveying a route for the continuation of the line from Exeter to Plymouth. All his routes had so far been laid out for fast running, with good alignments and easy gradients, and his first proposals for the South Devon line were in much the same style, with tremendous engineering works in getting a good line through the hilly country of the South Hams. It was not justified on economic grounds, and a new survey for a line of minimum cost involved quite exceptional gradients and incessant curvature. At that stage in the development of the steam locomotive such a line seemed altogether impracticable. It would have been equally impracticable on what was intended as a fast express route to incur the delays of changing from locomotive to cable traction on the steep inclines. While the problem was in gestation, Clegg and the Samuda brothers laid an experimental length of what was termed a 'pneumatic railway' over 1¼ miles of what eventually became the West London Railway.

Midway between the rails ran a pipe 9 in. in diameter which could be exhausted ahead of a travelling carriage, by a steam operated pumping engine, but the key feature of the invention was a narrow continuous slot along the top of the pipe sealed by a hinged leather flap valve. This was continuous along the line, and was so designed as to be opened by the piston arm of the travelling carriage and to reseal afterwards. On the little test track in west London the inventors succeeded in hauling a load of 5 tons at 30 mph up a gradient of 1 in 120. The news of this experimental installation spread like wildfire. Some of the most eminent engineers of the day went to see it, and were duly impressed – none more so than the directors of the Dublin and Kingstown Railway whose experiences with steam locomotives in the shape of George Forrester's 'boxers' had not been of the happiest. They decided to give the 'atmospheric', as it was called, a trial on a short branch line between Kingstown and Dalkey. The Samuda brothers secured the contract for the equipment, and built on a much more lavish scale than the little experimental section in London. Unfortunately the speed of the trains was entirely governed by the work of the engineman in the pumping station about three miles from one end of the line; and the pump was so large that if he chose to run it at anything like full power the speeds were alarming. On one occasion someone forgot to couple the motive carriage to the rest of the train, and before anyone in authority realized what was happening, the sole occupant of that carriage was being whirled along at about 80 mph.

But although the control methods on the Kingstown and Dalkey branch were virtually non-existent, and because of the power built into the pump the whole system was inherently dangerous, the possibilities for hauling normal railway loads swiftly up steep gradients were amply evident. William Cubitt was so impressed that he recommended the atmospheric, and installed it on the London and Croydon Railway. Monsieur C. F. Mallet of the French public works department advocated its general adoption for railways in France, while a Board of Trade enquiry reported favourably. Such capacity for climbing hills was just what Brunel needed for the South Devon line, and he went for it in a big way, backing his recommendation with considerable personal investment. Alone among the eminent railway engineers of the day, the Stephensons flatly opposed it. Old George, with characteristic bluntness, denounced it as a 'humbug', while Robert, after careful study of the installation in Ireland, made a closely reasoned report listing all its likely disadvantages. Brunel, however, was not to be deterred, and he committed the South Devon Railway to its adoption throughout the 52 miles between Exeter and Plymouth. This line included 20 level miles round the coast through Dawlish and Teignmouth to Newton Abbot before the very hilly section of the route was reached.

The line was built for atmospheric propulsion, and west of Newton Abbot, in the tumbled but not really mountainous country, Brunel went ahead regardless of hill or dale. It would seem that with very little extra constructional costs he could have got a much better route; but with the power of the atmospheric gradients mattered little. It was certainly not the gradients that brought about the downfall of the system, and a shattering blow to the reputation of Brunel. On the level stretches of line beside the estuary of the Exe, and beneath the red cliffs of Dawlish and Teignmouth, rats and the sea air wreaked such havoc on the leather flap that it failed to seal the pipe, and all the power in the world could not create sufficient vacuum to draw the trains along. The system had been brought into operation between Exeter and Newton Abbot in the autumn of 1847, and in favourable conditions speeds up to 64 mph were attained. But the winter was very trying, and despite every possible remedial action then and during the ensuing spring, Brunel had to admit defeat, and to recommend scrapping the entire plant in June 1848. The installation on the Croydon dropped unobtrusively out of the picture, and except for certain local instances of cable traction on steep gradients, the steam locomotive was left in undisputed possession on the railways of the United Kingdom for upwards of forty years.

It was perhaps ironic that some of the finest examples of the basic Stephenson 'Patentee' type were, by 1840, to be found on Brunel's 7 ft gauge Great Western Railway, though the first of these came into their possession incidentally rather than by direct specification. In carrying the British side of the story forward to the 1840s, however, I have jumped ahead of the important developments that were beginning in North America. A distinguished author, John H. White, Jr, in his book *The American Locomotive* has written:

> It is not surprising that the first locomotives in this country were imported from Britain, but it is surprising how quickly they were found unsuitable for American roads and how quickly our rural nation launched its own locomotive establishments. This is not to say that we are not enormously indebted to the British builders. It was the British who perfected the basic design of the locomotive and introduced the separate firebox, multi-tubular boiler, direct connection to the wheels, blast pipe and other fundamental features that remained with the steam locomotive to the end of its production. American improvements – mainly in running gears – were hardly as fundamental or as far reaching as the work of the British designers who had perfected their basic design by 1830.

This is indeed a most generous tribute, because the earliest British exports to North America, however basic their fundamental design, were not particularly successful in service, as I shall relate in the next chapter.

4 Europe and America

Reports of the working of steam locomotives in the north of England, and particularly on the Stockton and Darlington Railway, had been studied with much interest in the USA, and in 1828 the Delaware and Hudson Canal Company entrusted a young engineer, Horatio Allen, with the task of procuring rails in England for their railroad, and also purchasing locomotives. He ordered one from Robert Stephenson & Co. and three from Foster and Rastrick of Stourbridge. There is a certain mystery about the Stephenson engine. Many years afterwards Allen said it was a prototype of the *Rocket*; but since it had a twin flue and not a multi-tubular boiler it would seem to have been more like the *Lancashire Witch*. It is however notable as the first locomotive to be exported to America. The first of the Rastrick engines however achieved a much greater fame, for this was none other than the *Stourbridge Lion*. In design it was typical of British practice at the time, having vertical cylinders on each side of the boiler at the rear end and driving through the oscillating scale-beam mechanism.

At this same period the fame of the Stockton and Darlington Railway, and of the Forth Street Works of Robert Stephenson & Co., had also attracted attention in France, and at the end of the year 1827, Marc Séguin, and other French engineers, paid a visit to England. Séguin and his brother were associated with the plan to build a railway between Lyons and St Étienne, and as a result two locomotives of Stephenson design were obtained. These were of the same broad type then in use in England except that the cylinders were mounted low down, with their axes vertical, but between the forward and rear pairs of wheels. These two locomotives were used as a pattern for future development, and in building further locomotives of his own Séguin made railway history. Finding the Stephenson locomotives somewhat deficient in steaming power in conditions of continuous working, he designed a boiler of his own including no fewer than forty-three small firetubes. In conception this design actually preceded the *Rocket* by about eighteen months, and on this ground Séguin could claim priority of the idea over Henry Booth, except that the French engine incorporating Séguin's design was not completed until two months after Rainhill. There is no evidence to suggest that one idea was taken from the other. The concept of the multi-tubular boiler most likely occurred to Booth and Séguin quite independently of each other, and while Séguin was the first to think of it Robert Stephenson was the first to have such a boiler in service.

While steam traction was introduced in France and America at much the same time, at first it was only in the USA that there was any appreciable development; and there it was very important. The circumstances in which railways were built were quite different from those in Great Britain. Although locomotive prowess was constantly tending to outstrip the carrying capabilities of the track, the British road beds were most solidly constructed. George Stephenson considered that the maximum steepness of gradient that a steam locomotive could be expected to climb was 1 in 330, and in consequence great expense was incurred in laying out almost level lines. On the Liverpool and Manchester Railway, where there were sharp ascents of 1 in 91 from Huyton Quarry up to Rainhill, and in the westbound direction from St Helens Junction up to Lea Green, engines were kept standing by to assist the through trains. There was ample money available for capital investment in railways, and the British steam locomotive developed in a way that the fine, level roads permitted. In America the earliest railways were built for colonizing purposes. Money was scarce, materials and equipment at first had to be imported, and tracks and alignments were built in the cheapest way possible – with sharp curves, steep

Camden and Amboy Railroad: the 0-4-0 locomotive *Stevens* built by Robert Stephenson & Co. in 1831.

gradients, and rails of the flat-bottomed Vignoles type, spiked directly down to timbers no more than roughly shaped from freshly hewn trees. These cross timbers, which came to furnish the standard form of track all over the world, were, more often than not, simply laid on the surface of the ground, with little in the way of a prepared road bed beneath them.

In such conditions of working the short wheelbased British four-wheelers, and the later six-wheelers with a relatively stiff wheelbase, did not prove satisfactory. The case of the *John Bull* may be specially mentioned, because its immediate history started a chain of development that had the most far-reaching results. The *John Bull* was a 0-4-0 with inside cylinders built by Robert Stephenson & Co.

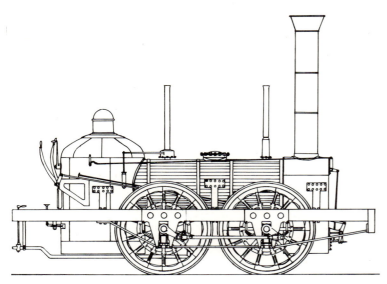

One of the earliest Stephenson locomotives built for the USA: the *John Bull* of 1831.

in 1831 for the Camden and Amboy Railroad and Transportation Company. It was contemporary with another 0-4-0 built for the Mohawk and Hudson Railroad, except that the *John Bull* had a special type of firebox specified by Stevens of New York. But both the *John Bull* and the Mohawk and Hudson engine had the short fixed wheelbase of the 'Planet' type; and although the records of Robert Stephenson & Co. show that many locomotives of the 'Planet' type, both 2-2-0 and 0-4-0, were supplied to America between the years 1831 and 1836, it was a case of necessity rather than choice so far as the Americans were concerned, because at that time their own manufacturers could not meet the demand. In all these locomotives the suspension was at four points, and on twisting uneven track they did not ride well, often derailed, and sometimes broke axles. In 1831 John B. Jervis of the West Point Foundry tried what was then a quite novel form of locomotive suspension. It was simply the principle of the three-legged stool which will stand firmly on any ground, however uneven.

He built a new locomotive for the Mohawk and Hudson Railroad, called the *Experiment*, which was of the 4-2-0 type. There was a pair of driving wheels in rear of the firebox, and the front end was carried on a short wheelbase swivelling bogie. The three-point suspension was at the main bearings of the driving axle in rear, and at the point of support of the swivelling bogie in the front. It was a very small, lightly built locomotive weighing no more than 7 tons, and although Jervis achieved an immediate success in the excellent tracking qualities the boiler would not steam freely, and within a few months of running it had to be rebuilt. But in his form of suspension Jervis had fairly started something, and gradually the leading bogie became a standard feature of most American locomotives. The Stephenson engine supplied to the Mohawk and Hudson Railroad in 1831, which was of the plain, unadulterated 'Planet' type, steamed well enough and had great tractive power; but it was found too heavy and stiff for light American tracks, and in 1833 it was so rebuilt as to be virtually unrecognizable. Only the boiler and cylinders beneath the smokebox remained. Jervis changed her into a 4-2-0 of similar machinery layout to the *Experiment* with a leading bogie, a single pair of driving wheels behind the firebox, and a drive from the inside cylinders through an intermediate jack shaft. The two massive wooden baulk frames remained. To add a spice of confusion with the Camden and Amboy locomotive previously mentioned this Jervis rebuild was named the *John Bull*!

From a very early date in American railway history it was the manufacturers of locomotives, rather than members of the railway staffs, who governed design practice, and of this there is no more outstanding example than Matthias W. Baldwin. He made a careful study of the earliest British locomotives exported by Stephensons, and before long he was in business on his own. The Baldwin locomotive works was established in Philadelphia in 1833, and 4-2-0 locomotives carefully designed to suit American conditions were soon being produced. For a time British locomotives continued to be imported, because the rapid spread of railways in the USA was faster than could be coped with by American manufacturers. At one time it was considered that railway progress there was more rapid and far-reaching than in Great Britain. Stephensons built their first bogie engine for America in 1833 to the order of the Saratoga and Schenectady Railroad. This had a 'Planet' type boiler, but the wheel arrangement was in the Baldwin style, with a single pair of driving wheels in rear of the firebox and a leading bogie with wheels 2 ft 8 in. diameter. From drawings it appeared as though the bogie was supported at each side, and that the central pin, on which it pivoted, took little or no weight, as in the earliest Baldwin 4-2-0s.

In chapter 3 I have referred to the celebrated patent 2-2-2 locomotive of Robert Stephenson, which, because of its long fixed wheelbase, made little or no headway in America. But between 1834 and 1837 the firm supplied the first steam locomotives to run in three more European countries, to Belgium and Germany in 1835, and to Russia in 1836. All these locomotives were variants of the 'Patentee' type, with one exception all 2-2-2. One of the three ordered by the Belgian government was a 0-4-2, and the order for this was transferred, by Stephensons, to the firm of Tayleur & Co., later to become the Vulcan Foundry. The British type of locomotive had a much more lasting run of success on the well built and easily graded first lines in Europe, though even here there was competition from America. Ross Winans built an engine named the *Columbus* for the Leipzig and Dresden Railway in 1837, and then in 1838 William Norris began his very successful exporting of the 4-2-0 type to Europe, including England. The Norris 4-2-0 was a remarkable job. There was little variation in detail design in the examples supplied to Austria, England, Germany and Italy. They differed from the British exports to America, and the earliest American adaptations from them, in having outside cylinders, with the valve chests on the top, and all the valve gear outside.

This was a notable departure, because following the

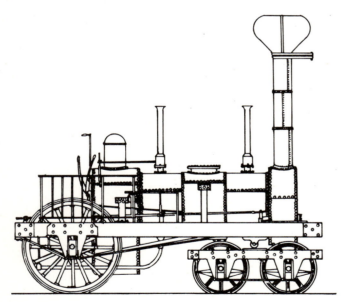

Adapting locomotives to the American tracks: the *Brother Jonathan*, the first 4-2-0 built in the USA, at West Point Foundry, in 1832, and modified as shown in 1833.

experience with the *Rocket* and the 'Northumbrian' type on the Liverpool and Manchester all British locomotives had been uniformly of the inside cylinder type to secure steadiness of running. This of course was more important in Great Britain, where the speed of running with passenger trains was rapidly on the increase. It was of no consequence at that early stage in America, and Norris's plan of having outside cylinders placed in an inclined position on the side of the smokebox left the underside clear for the support of the leading bogie. The boiler had the haystack type of firebox, and the positioning of the single driving axle ahead of the firebox, instead of in rear in Baldwin's arrangement, threw a maximum weight on to the driving axle, and made locomotives of this type suitable for heavy haulage by the standards of the day, which otherwise might have rendered a single driving wheel engine useless. No greater vindication of the Norris type could be imagined than the use of the English imports on the Lickey Incline, of all places, on the Birmingham and Gloucester line of the Midland Railway, where the gradient is of the exceptional steepness of 1 in 37. The question of dealing with steep inclines is discussed in more detail in a following chapter.

Before even the Norris 4-2-0 locomotive had reached the full flowering of its development there were other Americans who felt that something more in the way of adhesion was needed than a single pair of driving wheels. It was the lightness of the early tracks, and the relative roughness of the road beds that had originally retarded development, because by the late 1830s British locomotives intended for freight service were uniformly of the four-coupled type, and it was only the fast passenger engines that were built as 2-2-2s, or in some cases as 2-2-0s. In America, in 1836, H. R.

Model of one of the celebrated Norris 4-2-0 locomotives: the *Austria* built in 1838.

Europe and America 37

Campbell patented a locomotive of the 4-4-0 type. It was intended to be a kind of 'universal provider' – a standard type that could be used for anything, passenger, freight and shunting alike, and it is remarkable to recall how successful it did become. It was appropriately known as the 'American' type of locomotive, and until the latter years of the nineteenth century there was little except it on the vast network of railways that spread all over the USA. Campbell's engine was a giant for its time, yet it was not typical of what followed. It had the 'Planet' type of boiler, with the deep firebox between the two coupled axles. The cylinders were inside, and all the valve gear discreetly hidden. Its general aspect was contemporary British rather than American.

From this beginning, however, the true 'American' type was evolved. This had outside cylinders driving on to the leading pair of coupled wheels, inside valve gear, and the earliest of them had a very short wheelbased bogie. At the rear end to maintain the important feature of three-point suspension, the springing of the coupled axles was connected by a compensating beam pivoted at its mid-point to a bracket suspended from the main frames. The three points of suspension were thus the pivot points of the compensating beam at each side at the rear end, and the pivot point of the bogie beneath the smokebox. Some of the earliest of these American 4-4-0s were very long and ungainly looking, because the coupled wheels were carried on axles situated fore and aft of the firebox, and practically the whole length of the boiler barrel intervened between the leading coupled axle and the bogie beneath the smokebox. As in Great Britain and on the continent of Europe, no protection was at first provided for the enginemen. They were completely exposed to the elements, though when cabs came to be introduced in America, they were at once of a large and commodious design, instead of the plain weatherboards provided for British enginemen. Nevertheless it must be recorded that in Great Britain although engine crews had to run at speeds considerably higher than anywhere else in the world the majority of them took most unkindly to the introduction of cabs, and complained that they could not see!

The evolution of the steam locomotive, from primitive early designs like the *Locomotion*, the *Lancashire Witch*, the Liverpool and Manchester 0-2-2s and American engines like the *Stourbridge Lion*, to the more elegant creations of the later 1830s, was accompanied by a rapid spread of a fashion for decoration. It is true that the competitors at

The first-ever 4-4-0: H. R. Campbell's patent locomotive of 1836. Campbell was Chief Engineer of the Philadelphia, Germantown and Norristown Railway, and the locomotive was built at Brooks's Works, Philadelphia.

A typical 'American' type 4-4-0, built by the Rogers Locomotive Works *circa* 1850, with elaborate floral and other decorations on its panels and parts not subject to heating.

Rainhill were smartly painted in distinctive colours, but for the most part locomotives were regarded as work-a-day pieces of functional machinery. This situation did not last for long, and one finds Brunel writing of the broad gauge *North Star*:

> ... and lastly let me call your attention to the appearance. We have a splendid engine of Stephenson's. It would be a beautiful ornament in the most elegant drawing room and we have another of Quaker-like simplicity carried even to shabbyness but very possibly as good an engine, but the difference in the care bestowed by the engineman, the favour in which it is held by others and even oneself not to mention the public, is striking – a plain young lady however amiable is apt to be neglected ....

With such instigation from Brunel the locomotives of the Great Western Railway became some of the most ornate in Great Britain, though they came to be far outclassed by the early locomotives in the USA. There was an important difference in principle. In the United Kingdom the styles of painting were decided on a company basis, with variations in some of the larger concerns for different areas, or the spheres of influence of the various maintenance centres, whereas in the USA the painting styles were usually decided by the manufacturer, as much to advertise his products as anything else. On the American railways there were no resident engineers of the status of Robert Stephenson – manufacturer though he also was – of Daniel Gooch on the Great Western, or Trevithick's son, Francis, on the Grand Junction. The American manufacturers like Baldwin, Rogers and Norris, had beautifully executed coloured lithographs made of their standard products, and would go to a railway administration and say, in as many

Europe and America 39

words: 'How would you like a few like this', displaying one or more of their coloured lithographs. The locomotives themselves were decorated with ornamental scroll work on the cab panels, and on the tenders; the boiler mountings were highly embellished, and some builders even went to the extent of adorning their favourite designs with inset paintings of scenes along the route, and the brass work with representations of animals or birds, as on some ornamental fire screen in the drawing-room.

Mention of Brunel introduces the vexed question of rail gauges. In Great Britain George Stephenson argued vehemently for complete uniformity of rail gauge, basing all his work on the rail gauges in the colliery lines of Northumberland and Durham. When new railways further afield were projected he said that although they were then a long way apart the time was not far off when they would all be joined up. Brunel on the other hand considered that the gauge of the colliery railways was far too restrictive and instead of 4 ft 8½ in. he proposed 7 ft for the Great Western. His advocacy carried the Board with him, and so there eventuated the great confrontation that led to the setting up of a Royal Commission on Rail Gauges. Similar variations marked the early development of railways in North America, and some of the early gauges varied from 4 ft 3 in. to 5 ft 6 in. At the time of the Royal Commission on Rail Gauges in the United Kingdom one of the strongest arguments put forward for complete uniformity of gauge was the crippling inconvenience that could occur in times of war, when troops and supplies would have to be moved rapidly, and over routes that could differ from the normal channels of civilian traffic. This difficulty was experienced in full measure during the American Civil War, when one of the lines having a non-standard gauge, the Louisville and Nashville, was in the thick of the fighting. This railroad was laid to the 5 ft 0 in. gauge, but although much damaged during the fast moving campaigns, reconstruction took place on the 5 ft gauge, and it was not until 1886 that it became standard. In Europe the standard Stephensonian gauge was used except in Russia and Spain.

The American 4-2-0 type created by Jervis and Matthias Baldwin, had a striking counterpart that became very popular in Europe. In the early 1840s an engineer named Thomas Russell Crampton was employed in the locomotive department of the Great Western Railway at Swindon. That famous establishment was then steeped in the practice of Brunel's 7 ft gauge, but Crampton looking further afield felt that to get stability of running at high speed on the Stephensonian gauge required a locomotive with a low centre of gravity. To what extent he was aware of Baldwin's early work in the USA we do not know, but assured of a solid, relatively straight road bed in England and on the continent of Europe, he took out a patent for a heavy express locomotive with a single pair of huge driving wheels located at the extreme rear end, and only the smaller carrying wheels forward. Two locomotives of this basic design were built by Messrs Tulk and Ley, of the Lowca Works, Whitehaven, Cumberland, for the Liège and Namur Railway, but in the most striking contrast to prevailing American practice, the suspension was at no fewer than *five* points. The four carrying wheels in front were not mounted on a bogie, but each had their own independent laminated springs. Against this the suspension of the driving wheel axleboxes was compensated, one against the other, transversely, by a large laminated spring across the footplate with its central buckle supported on a massive casting bolted to the back of the boiler.

Crampton managed to secure orders for some of his patent locomotives from English and Scottish railways, but they never achieved any great degree of popularity. They were certainly massive and solid riding – too much so, in fact.

Nuremberg and Fürth Railway: the first locomotive to run in Germany, a model of the Stephenson-built *Der Adler*.

A picturesque German example of the Crampton 'stern-wheeler' type: the *Badenia* of 1863. As was so often the case with continental locomotives the valve gear was outside the frames.

They had not the ease and freedom of action that is essential in a fast express locomotive. They rode 'hard' and damaged the track. But though Crampton won little success on English railways, and none at all on the line of his earlier association, the development was far otherwise in France and Germany. Crampton locomotives in their hundreds were supplied to the Northern, Eastern and Paris, Lyons and Mediterranean Railways, and to some of the state railways in southern Germany. The name became a word in the French language, in which *prendre le Crampton* was a standard phrase for 'to go by train'. While the tracks were good the speeds were not high, and those mighty old 'stern-wheelers' jogged along pleasantly enough. They are remembered with affection, and it is in France rather than in England that one of them has been preserved as a national relic, in the newly established railway museum at Mulhouse, in Alsace. The tracking qualities of locomotives had a great influence upon the development of railway speed, as will be discussed in detail in the next chapter.

Europe and America

The development of speed

In the ten years that followed the trials on the Liverpool and Manchester Railway, when so much work was done towards the development of the steam locomotive, not a great deal was heard about its increasing capacity for speed. In Great Britain there was great activity in railway building; but at first it was only Brunel – and he not a locomotive engineer at all – who seemed to realize the importance of accelerated service. When he was incurring some criticism over the expense of building so straight and level a line he remarked: 'I shall not attempt to argue with those who consider any increase in speed unnecessary. The public will always prefer that conveyance which is the most perfect; and speed, within reasonable limits, is a material ingredient in perfection of travelling.'

He was convinced that high speed could be attained more safely on a wider gauge than that of the Stephensons, and this was the basis of his advocacy of so wide a gauge as 7 ft. When the confrontation between the Great Western and the other railways came to the point of the setting up of a Royal Commission, it is interesting to find in the mass of evidence presented that it was not until men of the Great Western were called that there was any detailed reference to the speed of travel.

The commission commenced its sittings in the summer of 1845, and by that time the fundamental British passenger locomotive, consisting of variations on the Stephenson 'Patentee' type 2-2-2 had been joined by two others that were to play a considerable part, though not as it turned out in the realm of speed. These were Robert Stephenson's 'long-boiler' type, and the Alexander Allan design sometimes referred to as 'Old Crewe'. The picture in Great Britain was completed by Edward Bury's bar-framed four-wheelers, and Timothy Hackworth's double-ended freight 0-6-0s on the Stockton and Darlington. Neither of these

One of the Hackworth 'return flue' 0-6-0 goods engines, fired from the chimney end: Stockton and Darlington Railway.

A long-boilered Stephenson 4-2-0 on the Southern Division of the London and North Western Railway.

latter need be considered in relation to the development of high speed. The long-boilered Stephensons and the Allan group are important in bringing a revival of outside cylinders, though not all the former were so equipped. Robert Stephenson was concerned with the improvement in thermal efficiency of his engines, and by lengthening the boiler he aimed to get more complete combustion of the fuel, and to eliminate the throwing out of hot cinders. On the other hand, the lengthening of the tubes meant that the draught from the smokebox had to be increased to order to facilitate the necessary rate of combustion in the firebox, though so far as speed was concerned the long-boilered engines were soon found to have a much more serious disadvantage.

At the time the early railways in Great Britain were equipped no very great increase in the size of locomotives or coaching stock was foreseen; and while some of the major running sheds like Camden Town on the London and Birmingham were fitted with turntables, in many places the only way to turn an engine was to uncouple it from its tender and run it on to one of the short turntables that were used for transferring carriages from one line to another. Stephenson had good reason for keeping the wheelbase of his long-boilered engines very short, and he did so by placing all the wheels ahead of the firebox. The Americans had no such difficulty. From the outset they did not adopt turntables except as the centre point of large roundhouses. With plenty of space in a virgin countryside they laid out

Y tracks on which locomotives could be run from either direction on the main running lines. The stem of the Y could be extended as necessary when the overall length of locomotives and their tenders increased. One result of the short wheelbase of the Stephenson long-boilered engines was that they were apt to become very unsteady when running at any speed. Although this tendency could be checked to some extent by firm coupling to the tender, the tenders themselves were usually so short and so light as to be practically incapable of providing any steadying influence. In consequence derailments, sometimes with loss of life, were not infrequent.

On the other hand the locomotives derived from Stephenson's earlier design, the 'Patentee', ran well, though in fuel consumption perhaps not so economically. They did particularly well on the broad gauge lines of the Great Western, and before that critical decade after Rainhill was ended, Daniel Gooch was able to report that they were frequently running at 60 mph. This was an astonishing advance, seeing that speeds of 20 mph were considered rather wonderful when the passenger service on the Liverpool and Manchester Railway was first introduced. The factors that enabled the Great Western to do this are important. It is true that the tractive machinery was good. They steamed freely, and the workmanship put into cylinders, valves, wheels and axles was the best of its day; and certainly the wide gauge gave them stability in a lateral sense. But equally the design of the frames made them easy riding on the track. These were of the outside 'sandwich' type originated by Robert Stephenson. The wood forming the 'meat' of the sandwich was ash at first, but in later years this was changed to oak to give greater strength. While this form of construction gave a degree of flexibility in riding, it also had an adverse effect on the many bolts that were needed to clamp the sandwich together. Furthermore, when this design of frame was perpetuated into the latter part of the nineteenth century, with oak as the standard 'meat', the acid in the wood caused corrosion of the bolts, and teak had to be substituted.

Sandwich frames were a great boon in the heyday of the broad gauge. To secure the utmost strength and rigidity of track Brunel designed his distinctive 'baulk' road, in which his rails of 'bridge' section were laid on continuous longitudinal timbers. It was rigid enough – too rigid in fact! – and locomotives and carriages rode very hard upon it. Had it not been for the inherent flexibility of the sandwich frames the broad gauge express locomotives would have been very harsh and uncomfortable to ride. As it was, at the time of the Royal Commission on Rail Gauges they proved incomparably the fastest in the country, and at that time, of course, that meant the whole world. Daniel Gooch had been appointed Locomotive Superintendent in 1837, when he was no more than 21 years of age, and with him there was no question of purchasing locomotives of manufacturers' standard types. From his early experience with the first engines from Stephensons he worked out an entirely new design, based it is true upon the 'Patentee' concept, but much larger, and embodying the fruits of his experience in running the first engines. The first of Gooch's own engines to arrive from the makers was the *Firefly*, in March 1840, and she did indeed make locomotive history. It was the first time that a railway locomotive superintendent had laid down the complete specification, requiring the builders to work strictly to his drawings and instructions, and it set the pattern that was to be followed in the United Kingdom throughout the era of steam traction.

Technically, the *Firefly* was an inside cylinder 2-2-2, with the Stephenson type of sandwich frames, but with a much larger boiler, and a firebox rising high in the form of a haystack and clad with copper. All Brunel's wishes about handsome appearance were carried out *in excelsis* on this epoch-marking locomotive. The outside lagging of the boiler barrel was in polished wooden slats; the sandwich frames were painted a rich red brown, and the tender panels were finished in the dark Brunswick green that became the standard engine colour of the Great Western for more than a hundred years afterwards. But the *Firefly* was not only a beautiful engine to behold. She arrived from the makers just in time for the ceremonial opening of the line from Paddington to Reading. On the return journey the 36 miles were covered in 45 minutes, with a maximum speed of 58 mph on the run. This was good enough, and amply confirmed the faith the company had in its youthful locomotive superintendent. Many more engines of the *Firefly* class were ordered, and one of the most remarkable performances that had been seen on any railway took place on 1 May 1844, when the Bristol and Exeter Railway was opened throughout. This line, though at first independent, was a close associate of the Great Western. Brunel was the engineer, and Gooch had certain responsibilities for locomotive power.

At that time opposition to the broad gauge was mounting to fever heat, and the Great Western and the Bristol and Exeter between them determined to make the occasion of the opening an opportunity for demonstrating the immense technical superiority that they had already achieved. Not only was the through run to Exeter, $193\frac{3}{4}$ miles, the longest that had ever been attempted anywhere, but it was made with one engine throughout, one of the latest of the 'Firefly' class, the *Actaeon*. The run was to be made in five hours, at an astonishing average, for that period, of 39 mph; but as the programme provided for various stops, to pick up distinguished guests, take water, and so on, the running average would need to be considerably higher. Daniel Gooch, then 28 years of age, drove the engine himself, and leaving Paddington at 7.30 a.m. he steamed triumphantly into Exeter on the stroke of 12.30 p.m. That however was not good enough for the Great Western. The return train, with the same engine and Gooch still driving, left Exeter at 5.20 p.m. Care was taken to keep the line clear, and after an amazing run they reached Paddington at 10 p.m. – *twenty minutes early*, and an overall average, including stops, of $41\frac{1}{2}$ mph. Gooch wrote in his diary:

> It was a hard day's work for me, as apart from driving the engine 387 miles, I had to be out early in the morning to see that all was right for the trip, and while at Exeter was busy with matters connected with the opening, so that my only chance of sitting down was for the hour we were at dinner. Next day my back ached so that I could hardly walk. Mr Brunel wrote me a very handsome letter, thanking me for all I had done, and all were very much pleased.

When the Royal Commission on gauges was set up all the earlier evidence given by numerous protagonists of the narrow gauge was quite unconnected with speed of travel. It was not until Daniel Gooch was called that any questions of technical achievement were raised. Trial runs made for the benefit of the commissioners, between Paddington and Didcot on the one hand, and between Darlington and York on the other, show the great superiority of the Great Western 'Firefly' class over Stephenson's long-boilered type, one of which derailed itself in the course of a trial run. Despite this, however, the decision went against the broad gauge, chiefly on the grounds that it was used by only one group of lines against the rest of Great Britain; and while the Great Western, by way of some quite sensational running, strove to cast the decision of the gauge commissioners into their teeth a renewed awareness of what was going on between Paddington and Bristol led to some interesting developments on the north-going lines, particularly on the London and North Western, which was formed in 1846 by an amalgamation of the London and Birmingham with the Grand Junction. Until that time neither constituent had been famed, either for enterprising train services or for the tractive capacity of its locomotives; but a profound change was to take place in the ensuing ten years.

On the Great Western itself, far from resting on the laurels of what Gooch had done with the *Actaeon* in 1844, and what the sister engine *Ixion* had done in the gauge trials, authority was given for the construction of a new 'colossal' locomotive, and the tremendous advance in size and power over the 'Firefly' class can be seen in Table 5.1 which shows comparative dimensions.

Table 5.1

Engine	Cylinders dia.	stroke	Driving wheel diameter
Firefly	15¾ in.	18 in.	7 ft
Great Western	18 in.	24 in.	8 ft

In June 1846 Gooch took the *Great Western* for a trial run to Exeter and back, and the total running times for the journey of 193¾ miles were 208 minutes going down, and 211 minutes on the return – respective average speeds of 55·8 and 55·2 mph. Nothing remotely to touch this had been made on any narrow gauge line, or anywhere else in the world for that matter, and as if this had not been enough Gooch had run the *Great Western* from Paddington to Didcot, 53 miles, in 47 minutes start to stop, an *average* speed of 67 mph. This astonishing feat was quoted in a letter from Gooch himself to the Institution of Civil Engineers, in June 1846. But I must pass on from the Great Western to the London and North Western Railway.

Until the time of amalgamation traffic working on the London and Birmingham Railway had been somewhat bogged down by the commitment of the Board to the locomotives of Edward Bury, who was in the anomalous position of being for many years both contractor and locomotive superintendent. The situation was hamstrung by having to work the ever-increasing traffic with nothing larger than small bar-framed four-wheelers, so undersized for the job that some trains needed *four* locomotives. When the amalgamation took place, Bury was at once replaced, in the Southern Division, by a man of very different stamp, James Edward McConnell, who had been Locomotive Superintendent of the Birmingham and Gloucester, and had under his care the little Norris 4-2-0 imports from the USA for working on the Lickey Incline. McConnell had no time for small underpowered engines, and while he was formulating his designs for new standard locomotives, a large miscellany of types was added to the stock between the years 1846 and 1848, ranging from Cramptons and long-boilered Stephensons to various more conventional 2-2-2s. One of the most interesting and significant of the latter, because of its subsequent influence, not only on the LNWR but far wider afield, were two express engines from E. B. Wilson & Co. of Leeds, of the 'Jenny Lind' type. This had become a standard product of the firm ever since their celebrated designer David Joy had produced it in response to an urgent request from the Brighton Railway in 1846.

The *Jenny Lind* itself was indeed a pace-setter. It was an abnegation of the idea that a narrow gauge express engine must have a low centre of gravity if it was to run fast and safely. Joy's engine had outside frames for the leading and trailing wheels, but inside frames for the driving wheels, which were 6 ft diameter. On the good track of the London

A 'Jenny Lind' type 2-2-2 built by E. B. Wilson & Co. of Leeds. The *Will Shakspere* of the Oxford, Worcester and Wolverhampton Railway.

and Birmingham line the 'Jenny Linds' rode easily and well, in total contrast to the Cramptons, and to the swaying of the long-boilered Stephensons. But even by the standards of 1848 they were not large engines, with a cylinder horsepower roughly equal to that of the Great Western 'Fireflys', but with considerably less boiler capacity. Although there were only two of them among the 145 engines of various types added to the stock in the years 1846–8, they gave McConnell the clue to the future, and in 1851 there appeared the first of the 2-2-2 express locomotives by which he will always be famous. These engines, with 7 ft diameter driving wheels, had inside frames throughout, and a completely straight running plate. Like the 'Jenny Linds' they had a relatively long wheelbase that eliminated the dangerous yawing action of the long-boilered Stephensons, and a *high* centre of gravity. David Joy records in his diary how 'they rode like a swing', and were consequently light on the track. Technically they had a large boiler, of straightforward design, but incorporated the best proportions of the day, and the steam pressure was the high figure of 150 lb. per sq. in.

Technicalities apart, the origin of their celebrated nickname must be recalled. The first of them took the road just about the time that Mrs Amelia Bloomer was trying to introduce reforms in ladies dress, and the late Colonel Kitson Clark, a former President of the Institution of Mechanical Engineers, once said: 'McConnell cleared away the decent skirting of an outside frame, and exhibited the whole of his wheels to the gaze of the traveller, who recognised, and named, a "Bloomer".' Certainly those splendid engines have never been known by any other name. The original series, with 7 ft driving wheels, became the standard express engines of the Southern Division. They were very fast and free runners, and one can well imagine that if they had been available at the time of the gauge trials the result could well have been in favour of the narrow gauge, on all counts. The success of the 'Bloomers' was such that the directors began thinking in terms of a two hour service between London and Birmingham, involving an overall average speed of 56 mph in 1851! McConnell was authorized to build some special engines in readiness for the job; but in the event the situation in the country became so unsettled that this very enterprising train service was not proceeded with. But McConnell, as well as Daniel Gooch, had shown the way to higher speed.

Rivalry with the broad gauge was also taken up on the Northern Division, where Francis, a son of the great Richard Trevithick, was Locomotive Superintendent, with his headquarters at Crewe. He was a placid, easy-going individual, very different from his father who had a volcanic temperament; but once in his life he seems to have been thoroughly roused, when Daniel Gooch followed his 'colossal' 2-2-2 *Great Western* by the *Iron Duke* of 1847, a huge 4-2-2 with 8 ft driving wheels, and reputedly capable of running at nearly 80 mph. Trevithick set out to surpass this with a 2-2-2 having driving wheels of no less than 8 ft 6 in. diameter. The resulting engine was something of a freak in its original condition, when, to keep the centre of gravity low, the boiler was slung underneath the driving axle. A tale persisted for some time that this engine had attained a speed of 117 mph, but this must be regarded as the purest fiction. The *Cornwall*, for such it was named, did no useful work in its original condition; but the curious outside framing and those great driving wheels have been preserved for posterity. The engine was rebuilt as an orthodox 2-2-2 by F. W. Webb; subsequent chief mechanical engineers of the LNWR used her for hauling their private saloon, and she is now preserved in the railway museum at York.

Francis Trevithick may have been the titular head of

A McConnell 'Bloomer' 2-2-2 on the Southern Division of the LNWR.

Crewe Works, but the man who carried the real heat and burden of the day was his foreman of locomotives, Alexander Allan. In chapter 3 of this book I referred to the 2-2-0 outside cylinder locomotives built by George Forrester of Liverpool for service in Ireland, which by their ungainly action earned the nickname of 'boxers'. Allan was in Forrester's service at the time when these engines were built, and the experience was duly 'pigeon-holed' in his receptive mind. In 1840 he transferred to the Grand Junction Railway, under W. B. Buddicom, at a time when considerable trouble was being experienced with broken crank axles. The engines concerned were traditional 2-2-2s of the period, with outside frames and inside cylinders. These engines, which were variants of the Stephenson 'Patentee', were excellent on a relatively straight road, but at its northern extremity the Grand

The development of speed

One of Daniel Gooch's broad gauge 8 ft 4-2-2s, the *Lord of the Isles*, Great Western Railway. Note the shelter on the back of the tender for the travelling porter.

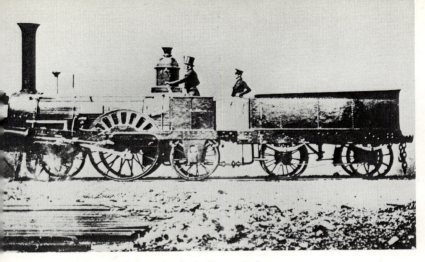

A Buddicom 2-2-2 on the Paris–Rouen Railway.

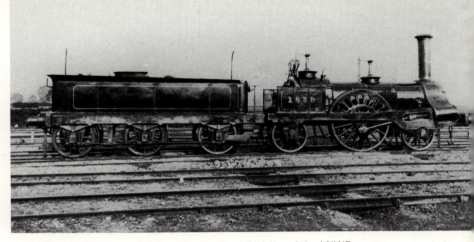

The Alexander Allan type 2-2-2 on the Northern Division of the LNWR: note similarity to the Buddicom engine.

Junction made a Y connection to the Liverpool and Manchester Railway at Newton Junction, by rather sharp curves. The old 2-2-2s took unkindly to these curves and suffered accordingly. Allan obtained Buddicom's permission to rebuild one of these engines with outside cylinders and a plain crank axle. In so doing he followed to some extent the precedent of the Forrester 'boxers', by fitting the outside cylinders in a section of outside framing; but he carried the main framing also through to the front end, and made a very strong and secure job by fixing the cylinders to both framings. This arrangement became the prototype of many hundreds of locomotives in Great Britain and overseas.

A feature of Allan's locomotives was the valve gear. From the primitive early methods of regulating the supply of steam to the cylinders, a degree of finality had been attained in 1841, when Robert Stephenson, visiting the Locomotive Superintendent of the North Midland Railway at Derby, is recorded as saying: 'There is no occasion to try any further at scheming valve motions; one of our people has now hit on a plan that beats all the other valve motions.' This was the celebrated Link Motion. There has been much controversy as to who was the actual inventor; the invention was subsequently claimed by several members of the staff; but it has always been known as the Stephenson Link Motion, as originating in the firm rather that with Robert Stephenson personally. It gave a beautiful distribution of the steam, and was used to the very end of the steam era in Great Britain. On the LNWR, engines so fitted were known as 'curved links', to distinguish them from the many fitted with Alexander Allan's variant, which used straight links. This was another very successful gear, if anything even more accurate than the Stephenson, though having the mechanical disadvantage of a few more

The development of speed

A Stephenson-built 2-4-0 for the Great Western Railway of Canada, 5 ft 6 in. gauge, built 1856.

working parts. McConnell's engines on the LNWR used the Stephenson link motion though the many locomotives built at Crewe during the same period naturally had the Allan gear.

Another important feature that enabled locomotives of this period to attain higher speeds with greater safety was the introduction of various means of balancing the reciprocating parts of the pistons, crossheads and rods. Because the cranks of a two cylinder engine were at right angles to each other there was an inherent lack of balance in the motion. Attempts were made to balance one piston by the action of another, as was later done on large twentieth-century locomotives that needed four cylinders to provide the necessary tractive power. But in the mid 1840s the means proposed in this direction were complicated. It was William Fernihough, Locomotive Superintendent of the Eastern Counties Railway, who found the answer, by putting weights in the periphery of the driving wheels to provide the necessary counterbalancing effect to the reciprocating action of the pistons. This was a technique adopted generally, though as later chapters of this book will show it began to have serious side effects on the track and underline bridges where very large and heavy modern locomotives were concerned. So far as the 1850s were concerned, Gooch, on the Great Western, and McConnell in the Southern Division of the London and North Western had each produced locomotives that could be safely run up to speeds of at least 70 mph though at that stage the means of stopping them had not progressed so rapidly as the means for making them go!

6 Climbing steep gradients

By the mid-1840s the tractive power of locomotives had increased to such an extent that steep gradients were no longer thought to be insurmountable with ordinary rail traction. It is true that on one of the major projects over which George Stephenson was consulted in his advancing years, the line between Lancaster and Carlisle, he recommended a circuitous route round the coast of Cumberland rather than go through the Westmorland fell country. But his advice was not accepted, and his one-time pupil, Joseph Locke, took the line by the famous route over Shap summit, including a 4½ mile gradient of 1 in 75. Furthermore on the Scottish continuation of the route there was the equally steep but much longer Beattock Bank in Dumfriesshire. These steeply graded routes were brought into operation in 1846 and 1848 respectively; but before that a much more venturesome project was under active consideration in Europe. This latter was the far-famed Semmering line, part of an Austrian main route from Vienna to Trieste, which was eventually to have long gradients of 1 in 40. It may well be asked, what had happened in a mere fifteen years from the opening of the Liverpool and Manchester Railway to cause so profound a change in outlook.

Without extending the survey to the large 2-2-2 express locomotives on the broad gauge Great Western Railway, the basic dimensions of the *Rocket* and the *Planet*, with those of Alexander Allan's 'Old Crewe' type, with which the line over Shap was opened, may be compared as in Table 6.1. In other words Allan's 2-2-2 of 1845 had roughly eight times the tractive power of the *Rocket*, and five times that of the *Planet*. Furthermore, Allan's 2-4-0s, which were used for goods and mixed traffic work, had wheels of only 5 ft diameter, and an increased tractive effort in consequence of 7,600 lb. If not the fastest these engines were among the most reliable of the day; and yet by the year

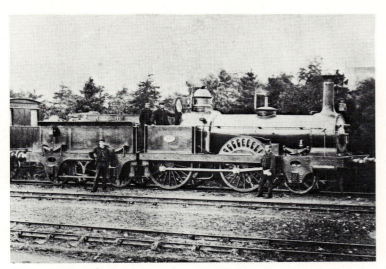

The basic Allan 2-2-2 developed into the 2-4-0 type for mixed traffic and hill climbing: a Scottish example.

Table 6.1

Locomotive	*Rocket*	*Planet*	Allan 2-2-2
Cylinders:			
dia., in.	8	11	15
stroke, in.	16½	16	20
Driving wheel dia., ft in.	4-8½	5-0	6-0
Boiler pressure, p.s.i.	50	50	120
Total weight, tons	4¼	8	18
Nominal tractive effort, lb.	825	1,385	6,350

1851, when McConnell brought out the first of his 'Bloomers', the tractive effort, still on a 2-2-2 locomotive, had increased to no less than 8,500 lb. No fifteen years in the subsequent history of the British steam locomotive witnessed so remarkable an increase in tractive power. By 1874 one of the most powerful passenger locomotives of the day showed a tractive effort of 12,400 lb., and by 1903 the maximum had increased to 24,000. At the time of grouping in 1922 the figure had increased to no more than 29,500 lb., but while this was roughly 4½ times that of the Allan 2-2-2 the change had taken place over seventy-seven years, compared to the increase of 7¾ times between Rainhill and the first engine built at Crewe in 1845 – Allan's 2-2-2.

In very round terms the power required to haul one of the little trains of 1845–50 up the 1 in 75 gradients of the Shap and Beattock inclines at 15 mph was about the same as that needed to make 55 mph on level track. The speed requirements were not exacting, and Allan was on sure ground in standardizing his 2-2-2 and 2-4-0 designs for the Northern Division of the London and North Western Railway; and when he moved to Scotland at a somewhat later date, he perpetuated the same design there. The important point of principle to be noted at this stage is that for main lines with gradients of a maximum steepness of 1 in 75 no special mountain climbing engines were needed. The ordinary passenger engines used on the more level stretches of the line could cope adequately. This early concept, indeed, prevailed throughout the steam traction history of the West Coast main line from England into Scotland. At this stage it needs only to be emphasized that Allan was using a single pair of driving wheels, 6 ft in diameter.

It is interesting to compare the proportions of a contemporary 'maid-of-all-work' 4-4-0 built by Baldwin for the Pennsylvania Railroad. The cylinders were 14½ in. diameter

Climbing steep gradients   57

A typically ornamented 'American' 4-4-0 of 1863, showing an unusual form of the 'balloon' spark-arresting smokestack.

by 20 in. stroke; the coupled wheels were only 4 ft 6 in. diameter, and the steam pressure was 100 lb. per sq. in., and the tractive effort 6,600 lb. Its overall weight was 22½ tons, compared to the 18 tons of an Allan 2-2-2. By the late 1840s Norris had given up his famous 4-2-0 type, and was building 4-4-0s of much the same overall proportions, but all these American locomotives looked very different from their British contemporaries. Many of them were designed to burn wood, and had enormous smokestacks including a variety of devices for arresting the emission of sparks. The small British fireboxes designed to burn high-grade bituminous coal would have been useless in America. But the 4-4-0 increased in popularity for almost every kind of service, and was at one time reputed to represent nearly 80 per cent of all steam locomotives operating in the USA; those railroads that did not have the incubus of heavy gradients broke away from the more usual type, and developed 'high-speed' designs with much larger driving wheels.

This was particularly the case around 1850 when the Hudson River Railroad introduced at least one 4-4-0 with wheels as large as 7 ft diameter.

Reverting, however, to really steep gradients, while banks of 1 in 75 could be taken in the stride, as it were, it was another matter on the Semmering line in Austria, where for 17 miles south of Gloggnitz the gradient is little easier than 1 in 40, and for the most part on a constant succession of severe curves. It was only by means of the most skilful surveying that the great engineer, Karl Ghega, was able to keep the gradients down to this figure in a bewilderingly tumbled mountain country. Around the year 1850, when construction of the line was in full swing, it was evident that no ordinary locomotives of that era could cope with such an ascent, and those who had ridiculed the very idea of carrying a railway through such territory were loud in their views that even when the railway was built it would be impossible to work. There were faint hearts in the Austrian government, though the youthful Emperor Franz Joseph was full of enthusiasm. Then a German technical journal suggested a competition, following the precedent of Rainhill; this was advertised in 1850, and took place in the summer of 1851. The specified requirement was the haulage of a load of 140 tons up the 1 in 40 gradients at a speed of 8 mph. The maximum axle load of any locomotive entered for the competition was to be 14 tons, and a 10 chain radius curve had to be negotiated without difficulty. No existing locomotive on the continent of Europe could meet such a specification, and so the various entrants had to design special ones for the job.

While construction was proceeding the mere sight of the line struck a chill into the hearts of some who had hitherto been optimistic, including the Minister of State who had authorized the construction. If one stands on the station platform at Plympton, in Devonshire, and sees the abrupt

One of the earliest British examples of the 4-4-0 type, built 1860, for the westward extension of the Stockton and Darlington Railway over the 1,369 ft altitude of Stainmore Summit. The large cabs were quite exceptional in British practice at that time, and savoured more of the USA.

The 'American' type developed into the 4-6-0 (1865). This engine, the *John Conness* was the first freighter on the Central Pacific. It is shown here on its maiden trip out of Sacramento, 17 March 1865.

change from level track to Brunel's 1 in 42 gradient of Hemerdon Bank, one can realize something of what the Austrian onlookers felt, particularly when it is remembered that the incline that began near Gloggnitz continued for 17 miles! Even Ghega began to show signs of nerves, and when a sufficient stretch of line up the mountain was completed, he arranged for a trial of one of the existing locomotives of the Südbahn. There was no question of trying to fulfil the conditions laid down for the competition. A little engine, the *Save*, was given a load of no more than 56 tons, and with the Chief Mechanical Engineer of the Südbahn, Col. von Rosslerstamm, beside him on the footplate, Ghega signalled the right-away. There was no trouble, and when the engine was pedalling its way up the 1 in 40 gradient, Ghega's emotions gave way. He shed tears of joy, and seizing Rosslerstamm by the hand and shouting loudly he exclaimed: 'This is the greatest moment of my railway life.' It was indeed a pointer to the future, for what could be done with an older non-specialized locomotive could certainly be surpassed by one designed expressly for the job.

So it transpired, and when it came to the time of the competition in 1851, the judges were put in a very awkward position. Here was no repetition of Rainhill. The government offered four prizes, and as there were only four entrants, and all four fulfilled the stipulated conditions, what was to be done? Some details of the locomotives and their respective performances are given in Table 6.2. The line diagrams show that the locomotives were a queer-looking lot. Both the *Seraing* and the *Wiener Neustadt* were in effect double engines, and the *Seraing*, in its double boiler, was a definite prototype of Robert Fairlie's productions of a later date. The first prize was awarded to the *Bavaria*, which hauled the heaviest of all loads at the highest speed, and produced substantially the highest power output in the process. There was nevertheless one similarity with Rainhill, in the aftermath. There was not only dissatisfaction that the prize had gone to a non-Austrian competitor, but also that eventually not one of the competitors was adopted as the standard locomotive of the line. It was known that the railway would not be opened for traffic for another two years and, based on the experience of the trials, opportunity was taken to work out a new design altogether. This was done under the direction of Baron Wilhelm Engerth, a departmental chief in the

Table 6.2 Semmering Trial locomotives, 1851

Locomotive name	Bavaria	Seraing	Wiener Neustadt	Vindobona
Builder	Maffei	Cockerill	Gunther	Masch-Fabrik ol. Glogg Bahn-Vienna
Wheel arrangement	0-8-0 tender	0-4-0+0-4-0 tank	0-4-0+0-4-0	0-8-0
Wheel dia., ft in.	3–6½	3–5½	3–8¼	3–1½
Steam pressure, p.s.i.	120	99	120	120
Load hauled, tons	190	152	154	145
Max. speed, mph	12	10½	10½	9¾
Average performance, horsepower	395	302	277	259

Ministry of Industry. His first step was to take the prize-winning locomotive *Bavaria* and rebuild it as a tank engine. There were six coupled wheels under the leading end, and the tender portion had two axles only, one of which was in front of the firebox. The rearmost of the engine coupled wheels was connected to the leading tender wheels by gearing, while the two pairs of tender wheels were coupled, by outside flycranks. As thus rebuilt the engine was something of a freak, and the geared connection was soon discarded. Otherwise, however, the working was reasonably satisfactory, but in 1854 twenty-six new engines of the Engerth type were ordered, in which the gear connection between the six coupled front engine and the tender wheels was revived. These curious locomotives, designed especially for mountain climbing, remained the standard type on the Semmering line for a few years.

These Austrian developments were being watched very closely in Italy, where the Giovi Incline, on the main line from Genoa to Turin, included lengthy gradients of 1 in 29 and 1 in 36. The Italian engineers did not consider any of the four Semmering competitors would meet their needs, nor Engerth's rebuild of the *Bavaria*, and they made some consultations in England. T. R. Crampton made a suggestion totally unlike his famous rear-driver express passenger design, for having two tank engines placed back to back, arranged with the equivalent of a single footplate so that one driver could be responsible for the working. Crampton had patented this idea as long previously as 1846, but when the attention of the Italian engineers was drawn to it they consulted Robert Stephenson, and he commended it for use on the Giovi Incline. His firm built a pair of 0-4-0 saddle tank engines for the job in 1855, and they were operated by two drivers and a single fireman – an inversion of what might have been expected in manning. They were powerful little units, but their capacity was limited by bad rail conditions in a long tunnel, on the worst part of the incline. These 'twin' tank engines are interesting as the first practical application of the 'double-engine' idea, first

Climbing steep gradients

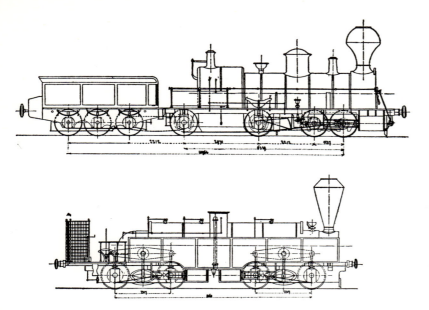
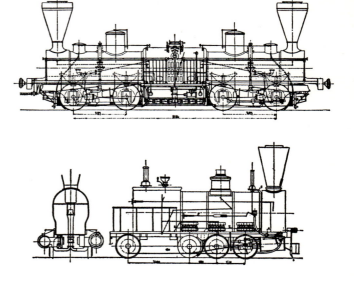

Competitors in the Semmering Trials of 1851. One of the trial engines, the *Seraing* (built by the Belgian firm of Cockerill, although not accepted afterwards), is interesting as a faint prototype of the Fairlie 'double engines'.

propounded in the *Seraing* in the Semmering Trials, and later developed into the 'Fairlie' articulated engine.

In the meantime a mountain climbing problem of a different kind was looming up in India. During Lord Dalhousie's administration as Governor General, the first schemes for the opening up of India by railway communication had been formulated in 1843; but although the Great Indian Peninsula Railway Company was being organized in London as early as 1845, the Act authorizing construction was not passed until four years later. James J. Berkley was appointed Chief Resident Engineer, and in building a line eastwards from Bombay, as the beginning of main routes to both Calcutta and Madras, he was faced with the tremendous obstacle of the Western Ghats which rise like a formidable wall of great near-vertical cliffs 2,000 ft above the wilderness of rock and jungle which runs parallel to the coast. The change in altitude is so abrupt that a straightforward approach was impossible. It was at first thought that nothing short of cable haulage would be practicable; but then Berkley conceived the idea of a zigzag. A gradient of 1 in 37 was already being worked by steam on the Lickey Incline in England, and Ghega was constructing the Semmering on 1 in 40, and so Berkley found a route up the Bhor Ghat, on 1 in 37, with the aid of a reversing station, where the trains in climbing are brought to a location where the direction of running is reversed, to continue up the mountain side still rapidly gaining height.

There are two separate zigzags, one on the Thul Ghat, which is the route towards Calcutta, and the second – considerably the longer – on the route to Madras. It was not until 1870 that through communication was established, and in the meantime special locomotives had been ordered. Except that they were confined to the Ghat sections there was nothing special about these locomotives, of which the first were built by Kitsons of Leeds in 1866. They were just a massive eight-coupled tank engine, with saddletanks and all the weight on the driving wheels. They had cylinders 18 in. diameter by 24 in. stroke, and wheels 4 ft diameter. Even these massive straight-forward engines had been preceded by a few experimental types; but these did not last and the Kitson 0-8-0 of 1866 became a standard type to such an extent that there were eventually no fewer than seventy-four of them, doing nothing but hauling and pushing trains over the Ghats. The later examples had larger cylinders with 26 in. stroke.

On the Anglo-Scottish West Coast Route in Great Britain arrangements were made at an early date to provide rear-end banking assistance on the Shap and Beattock inclines in cases of exceptional loading, with the ordinary train engine continuing at the head end; but on the Ghats ordinary locomotive working ceased at the foot of the inclines and the 0-8-0 tank engines took over the haulage of all trains. It is indeed a revelation of the extent to which these routes became used that as many as seventy-four of the special locomotives were needed. The development of steam haulage on railways in the foothills of the Himalayas is described in later chapters of this book, but at this point a word about rail gauges in India is needed. The fact of three separate gauges existing today might suggest a haphazard, unco-ordinated start, as in the USA and Australia, but in India it was not so. The gauges were part of an overall strategic plan, in which the main trunk routes were to be 5 ft 6 in. gauge, the principal feeder routes metre gauge, and the subsidiary lines 2 ft 6 in. The narrower gauges were chosen to minimize constructional costs.

In the Australian colony of New South Wales there was a closely parallel geographical situation to that of the Western Ghats in the range of the Blue Mountains, presenting just such another barrier to railway construction westwards from Sydney to the great plains beyond the mountains. In this case there was not a great distant city with which communication was desired, but a need to open up a rich agricultural and grazing area. The civil engineer surmounted the escarpments in just the same way as Berkley had done on the Ghats, by use of zigzags. The line included some fearsome gradients, of 1 in 33, and 1 in 42, but from its first opening, in 1869, it was not until 1874 that locomotives specially for it were introduced. From the inception of railways in New South Wales, J. E. McConnell of the London and North Western Railway was consulting engineer, and the first engines to run in the colony were a simple modification of his standard express goods locomotives in England. Like most things with which McConnell was associated they were exceptionally large and powerful and of the 0-6-0 type, but for Australia he recommended the 0-4-2 type, and four of them were built by Stephensons, and delivered in Australia early in 1855. They proved rather in advance of their time, both in power and in their weight on the track; and as this was some years before the line over the Blue Mountains was even contemplated, McConnell's big engines led a somewhat constrained existence on goods trains around Sydney.

LNWR. F. W. Webb's small-wheeled 2-4-0 *Precursor*, built in 1874 for the north main line over Shap. Although climbing well these locomotives could not run fast enough downhill, and were moved elsewhere.

One of the first locomotives in New South Wales, designed by J. E. McConnell, of LNWR fame, and adapted from his very successful 'Wolverton Goods' 0-6-0s, one of the most powerful freight engines of its day in England. Engine No. 1 in New South Wales, now preserved, was built by Robert Stephenson & Co. and ran first in 1855.

An American hill climber: a 4-8-0 of 1882 for the Central Pacific.

When the need for power on the mountain sections did come the New South Wales Government Railways turned to the Stephenson 'long-boiler' type. Some useful and successful experience with locomotives of this kind had already been obtained on goods 0-6-0s introduced from 1865 onwards. About the type generally it may be said that while they were not successful as fast passenger engines in England, because of their unsteady riding, they did excellent work on slow goods and mineral trains, particularly on the Stockton and Darlington Railway. The long boiler provided a valuable reservoir for building a good reserve of steam while the engine was standing, and the relatively small firebox ensured that a minimum of fuel was consumed when just standing by – 'simmering' as it were. The Australians were evidently so satisfied with the overall capacity of the long-boilered type that they ordered two varieties of a much enlarged version for the Blue Mountains section, both 0-6-0s. The goods version had coupled wheels of 4 ft diameter, and the passenger, 5 ft. They were large and impressive looking engines, that except for their canopied cabs would have looked entirely at home on the North Eastern Railway of England. They had the stove-pipe chimneys of Edward Fletcher, and Salter type safety valves mounted on the top of the steam dome. The tractive effort was very high, appropriate to the mountain road they had to negotiate, 16,200 lb. for the passenger engines and no less than 19,400 lb. for the goods. Whether those small fireboxes could burn coal rapidly enough to sustain such an effort continuously is another matter.

In England, following the failure of Brunel's atmospheric venture, the broad gauge line in South Devon was encumbered with some exceptionally steep gradients, while the continuation into Cornwall, though engineered afterwards, included many long and severe inclines. There was no question of attempting to use normal passenger engines on a through run from Bristol to Plymouth. Everything changed at Newton Abbot, and for west of that junction Daniel Gooch provided a stud of 4-4-0 saddle tank engines that, whatever their efficiency may have been, were among the most functional and ugly engines ever to run the rails – in England at any rate. They had domeless boilers, no cabs, and no splashers over the coupled wheels, while the setting back of the bogie, with its centre well aft of the chimney, gave them a crouching, hunched-up effect. Nevertheless, it must be admitted that they did the job, and held the fort in South Devon and Cornwall for upwards of forty years, until the time came for the abolition of the broad gauge. But the speeds were not heroic, and the crack passenger train, the up 'Zulu', took 3 hr. 56 min. to do the 112 miles from Penzance to Newton Abbot. On railways built in the latter part of the nineteenth century, in distant parts of the world, there were gradients far longer and steeper than Brunel's bequest to the Great Western; but by the time the Stephenson long-boilered 0-6-0s were struggling up the zigzags of the Blue Mountains it was abundantly clear that there, as on other steep gradients of the railway world, steam could do it.

In search of efficiency

By the 1860s the steam locomotive had well and truly arrived. It had passed through its experimental and formative years, and although there were still freaks being introduced, it was, taken all round, a good working proposition. In many ways its capacity for traction had drawn ahead of what the track would carry, or what its primitive brakes would stop, and there came a most fascinating period when engineers all over the world began to look for greater efficiency. In Great Britain particularly the early boom in railway business had been followed by severe depression, and everyone concerned with the running of the trains was under heavy pressure from management to reduce working expenses. One of the most immediate problems in Great Britain was with fuel consumption. To avoid the emission of black smoke, coke had been used from early days, but it was of course much more expensive than raw coal, and after the days of the gauge trials many engineers were experimenting with different forms of firebox.

The problem was to secure as complete combustion as possible, because the black smoke so beloved of photographers of trains at speed is a manifestation of unburnt fuel being carried over into the exhaust. Some of the forms of fireboxes were as weird and wonderful as locomotives themselves in the very early days, and the solution when it did come was, like most great inventions, extremely simple. One unsuccessful attempt is worth recalling because it formed the basis of a later development. On the London and North Western Railway J. E. McConnell tried a very large grate and firebox volume, obtaining the latter by extending the upper part of the firebox into the boiler barrel. This formed what later came to be known as a combustion chamber. By placing the firebox tube plate some distance inside the boiler, he sought to avoid getting the tubes choked up with cinders. In the meantime Matthew

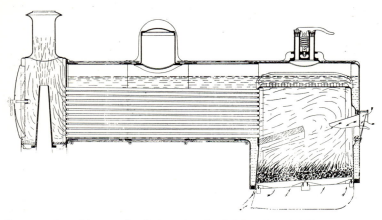

Cross-section of locomotive firebox showing brick arch and deflector plate inside the fire door, with directions taken by the gases of combustion.

Kirtley, on the Midland Railway, who with McConnell must be regarded as one of the most forward-looking locomotive men of the day, was supervising a series of experiments being made by one of his assistants, Charles Markham by name, and by the end of 1859 they had the answer that is likely to last for the rest of the life of the steam locomotive. This was the brick arch, combined with a downward deflecting plate from the firehole door.

It was an extremely simple and effective way of getting complete combustion. The brick arch was built transversely across the firebox, covering the forward part of the firebed, and so positioned that the air for combustion entering the firebox through the dampers had to pass backwards as it were over the fire, under the action of the draught, and then sweep round the rearward end of the arch in order eventually to pass forward to the tubes. The air was thus compelled to pass closely over the surface of the firebed, instead of going straight to the tubes as previously. Additionally, by means of the deflector plate, the secondary air entering through the firehole door was deflected downwards towards the fire, instead of being drawn straight through to the tubes. The resulting economy was remarkable. On two otherwise identical Midland 2-4-0 express engines, one burning coke in the old style, and the other burning coal in a firebox fitted with a brick arch, both evaporated the same amount of water per pound of fuel, but the coal burner used only 19 lb. per mile, against $23\frac{1}{2}$ lb. by the coke burner. This was not all. The abrasive action on the tubes was very severe with coke, and it was found that the brass tubes then in use lasted for 150,000 miles with coal, against only 100,000 miles with coke.

Another important factor was that of boiler pressure. Theoretically the efficiency of the steam engine cycle depends upon the range of expansion, and one method of improving this, and at the same time securing greater tractive power, is to use a higher boiler pressure. In the 1860s however engineers hesitated to do this. With constructional methods in vogue there were undoubted risks in venturing higher, with the increased costs in materials, and greater weight resulting from thicker boiler plates and more elaborate joints, and with some justification pressures generally had remained around 120 lb. per sq. in. Two British engineers, the enterprising J. E. McConnell of the LNWR and Archibald Sturrock of the Great Northern, were using 150 lb. per sq. in., though as it eventuated both their practices were short lived, for political rather than technical reasons. Both engineers built very fine 2-2-2 express locomotives in 1860–1, and Sturrock followed in 1866 with a large and powerful 2-4-0, just at the time when he was retiring to the leisured ease of a country gentleman, and was succeeded on the Great Northern by the cautious Scot, Patrick Stirling. Sturrock's giant 2-4-0s were not at all to the liking of his successor, who rebuilt them as 2-2-2s and reduced the boiler pressure to 130 lb. per sq. in., but those 2-4-0s had already blazed the trail in quite a different direction.

At the end of the 1860s the Northern Railway of France, dissatisfied with its own locomotive position, made some studies of English practice and decided to base a new design upon Sturrock's big 2-4-0. The basic dimensions adopted were almost exactly the same, with cylinders 17 in. diameter by 24 in. stroke, 7 ft diameter coupled wheels, and a boiler pressure of 150 lb. per sq. in. Apart from typically French boiler mountings and the contemporary French form of outside framing they were the same. A first batch of twelve was built by Koechlin, and they began to do very fine work. But then it was the old story all over again, and they proved unkind to the permanent way. It was not that they were too heavy. Their long rigid wheelbase, which had been remarked upon when Sturrock's engines were introduced on the Great Northern, was the main trouble, and later batches of them were provided with a leading bogie. As such they became very popular, hard working engines, to such an extent that they were nicknamed 'Outrance', because they could be worked *à l'outrance* – to the limit. In later years the severe treatment they received led not infrequently to broken crank axles, and this in turn was the beginning of another momentous development, to be described later in its chronological sequence.

On the Northern Railway of France the 'Outrance' locomotives were the direct successors of the Crampton rear-drivers, of which there had been some almost exact counterparts on the Paris, Lyons and Mediterranean Railway. It was in 1868 that the latter company began modernization of its locomotive power, but in a totally different way to the Nord. The new engines were lengthy 2-4-2s with outside cylinders, and taking into account the successive varieties there were eventually 400 of them. An interesting technical feature that was characteristic of many French locomotives of the period was the use of Stephenson's link motion outside the frames. The working of the eccentrics, in full view instead of being concealed, was an intriguing sight. Apart from this feature, in the cause of accessibility, they had no particular significance in the general line of locomotive development, and carried the relatively low pressure of 114 lb. per sq. in.

In England there was a temporary recession on the London and North Western Railway, as well as on the Great Northern. McConnell resigned in 1861 and the directors thereupon decided to amalgamate the Southern and Northern Divisions, with John Ramsbottom as Chief Mechanical Engineer of the entire railway. The new chief was under strict orders to economize, and although he built a number of locomotives that were excellent in their several ways he did not use a higher boiler pressure than 120 lb. per sq. in. His outstanding achievement was the reorganization of Crewe Works for what was virtually mass production of locomotives. The 'DX' 0-6-0 fast goods engine was an extremely successful and long-lived design. The first one was completed at Crewe in September 1858, and by the end of 1874 no fewer than 943 had been put into traffic – more than sixty a year. Ramsbottom discontinued the use of the Allan link motion, which had been traditional at Crewe since 1845, substituting the Stephenson; but when he in turn was succeeded in 1871 by Francis W. Webb the valve gear situation was, for a time, once again reversed.

With the mention of Webb I now come to one of the most important locomotive designs of the age. Ramsbottom had built two classes of 2-4-0 for the main line traffic, and the larger of these, the 'Newton', was developed by Webb. In the design of the later engines, known as the 'Precedent'

Northern Railway of France: one of the 'Outrance' 4-4-0s developed from the copy of Sturrock's Great Northern 2-4-0 of 1866.

class and introduced in 1874, Webb had most clearly in mind the keeping of running and maintenance costs to a minimum, and the layout of the machinery was designed so as to permit of large bearing surfaces for the driving axle boxes, so minimizing the risk of over heating. To do this the slide valves were moved from their conventional position between the cylinders, and the cylinders themselves brought closer together, with their centre lines only 24 in. apart. The valve faces were inclined; the steam chest in cross section was V-shaped, and the valve spindles were considerably above the centre line of the cylinders. Using the Allan valve gear a very neat and compact layout of the machinery was achieved, but quite apart from this Webb provided very short and direct steam passages, and a very large steam chest volume. This latter point was proved of great importance for an express engine. When running fast the pressure of the steam always has a tendency to drop during the time when the admission port of the valve is open. It has been shown that this effect can be greatly lessened by having a large reservoir of steam on the boiler side of the valve, and the larger this reservoir is the less will the pressure in it be reduced as each successive gulp of steam is taken by the cylinders. This large steam chest volume, together with the short, direct steam passages was a big contributory factor in the fast running of the 'Precedent' locomotives.

There was another factor also that was coming to play an increasing influence, and that was the use of steel, instead

A contrast in French styles: one of the celebrated 'Henry' 2-4-2s of the Paris, Lyons and Mediterranean Railway.

of wrought iron, in locomotive construction. The London and North Western Railway was a pioneer in this respect. In 1864 while Ramsbottom was still in office, the steel works was put into commission – the first plant anywhere in the world for the production of steel by the Bessemer process. At that plant the North Western rolled its own rails. Reverting to the 'Precedent' class locomotives, however, their performance on the road went some way towards disproving two cherished theories in locomotive design. To run fast and freely it had generally been accepted that one must have a single pair of driving wheels, and that those wheels must be large. During the thirty years he was Locomotive Superintendent of the Great Northern Railway, Patrick Stirling used none but single-drivers for express passenger work, most of them with wheels 7 ft 7 in. or larger. In his dry Scots way he likened a coupled engine to 'a laddie runnin' wi' his breeks doon'! But Webb's four coupled 'Precedents' with 6 ft 9 in. wheels could outpace any of Stirling's engines, because they had a much better valve and steam chest design.

Although till the end of the 1870s it was still Great Britain that was making all the running so far as fast express work was concerned, it is interesting to note the stage to which the popular 'American' 4-4-0 had attained by about the same period. In the early 1880s it still accounted for about 60 per cent of all new locomotives purchased from builders in the USA. They were still relatively light. A typical 4-4-0 of the late 1870s would have cylinders 17 in.

In search of efficiency 71

Ramsbottom's forerunner of the celebrated 'Precedent' 2-4-0 class on the LNWR photographed outside Crewe Works in 1866, in its original form, with the simplest of controls and no cab.

diameter by 24 in. stroke (as in the LNWR 'Precedents') 5 ft 8 in. coupled wheels, and a boiler pressure of around 140 lb. per sq. in. The boilers were fairly large with grates suitable for lower grade fuel than in Great Britain. Outside cylinders were universal, and mostly with inside Stephenson's link motion. But the major development to the mammoth American locomotives of the twentieth century had not begun at that time.

The idea of realizing the theoretical advantages of a longer range of expansion by carrying out that expansion in two stages, rather than one, dates back to 1834 when a Dutch engineer named Roentgen took out English patents for a multiple expansion two-cylinder locomotive. Nothing more was heard of it, and suggestions made in 1847 and 1866 did not progress beyond the design and experimental stage; but in 1875 a Frenchman, Anatole Mallet, designed and had built by Creusot a locomotive for the Bayonne and Biarritz Railway, later part of the Midi system, in which the steam was expanded in two stages, through two cylinders. After experiments lasting several years he had achieved sufficient success to show a six-coupled compound tank engine at the Paris Exhibition of 1878. This created a remarkable amount of interest, and inspired many engineers to devise compound systems of their own. In the twenty years that followed that exhibition in Paris a great variety of designs were prepared. Some of the earliest concerned were from F. W. Webb and T. W. Worsdell in England; from A. von Borries in Germany; from Karl

72   In search of efficiency

Great Northern Railway: Patrick Stirling's bogie 8 ft single-wheeler express locomotive, originated in 1870, and working the principal express services until 1898.

Gölsdorf in Austria, and from Vogt and Vauclain in the USA. The complications arose in providing for starting from rest. The earlier work of Mallet, Worsdell, von Borries, Gölsdorf and Vogt involved the use of no more than two cylinders: one high pressure and one low pressure; and because the low pressure cylinder could not get any steam until the high pressure had moved and exhausted it meant that the train had to be started with one cylinder. That meant a rather feeble start compared to that of an ordinary engine, unless the crank happened to be on dead centre, and then there would be no start at all. So much ingenuity and diversity was displayed, and complication involved, in devising methods of starting. In most cases admission of boiler steam to the low pressure cylinder was provided for.

The basic principle of compound working was to ensure that an equal amount of work was done in the high and low pressure cylinders. Quite apart from any thermodynamic considerations this was vital in a two-cylinder engine, otherwise the motion along the line could become unsteady to the point of danger. While many calculations could be made, the actual proportioning of the high and low pressure cylinders to secure the desired equalization of effort was usually a matter of trial and error. The cross-sectional drawing of Mallet's first compound locomotive shows the great difference in diameter between the high and low pressure cylinders, while the application to a relatively large inside cylinder passenger locomotive on the North Eastern Railway shows ingenuity in design needed to

In search of efficiency 73

Cross-section of Anatole Mallet's first compound locomotive: a tank engine of the Bayonne and Biarritz Railway built in 1875.

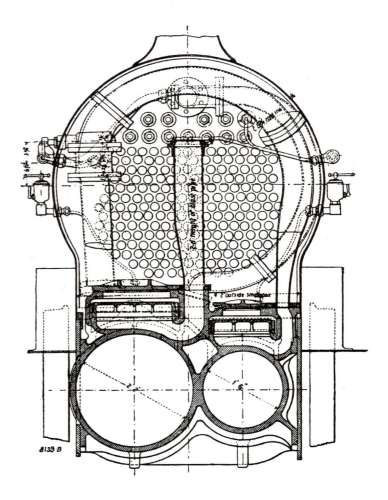

Cross-section of two-cylinder compound locomotive: Worsdell-von Borries system.

accommodate a low pressure cylinder as large as 26 in. diameter. This engine was equipped on the Worsdell-von Borries system. On the Austrian State Railway, for operating on the heavy gradients of the Arlberg route, through the Tyrol, Karl Gölsdorf at first used a two-cylinder system, with cylinders outside. Even before Mallet had built his first locomotive for trial, in 1875, an engineer of the Northern Railway of France had proposed a three-cylinder compound tank engine. In Morandière's locomotive a single high pressure cylinder drove the rearward group of four-coupled wheels, while two low pressure cylinders mounted outside drove the leading group. This proposal, made in 1866, did not go so far as to suggest any method of starting.

It was the famous Chief Mechanical Engineer of the London and North Western Railway, F. W. Webb, who was

74   In search of efficiency

Austrian State Railways: Gölsdorf two-cylinder compound 2-8-0 for the Arlberg route.

instantly attracted to the compound system, having seen Mallet's 0-6-0 tank engine in Paris, in 1878. He took one of the old 2-2-2 Allan 'singles' having cylinders 15 in. diameter by 20 in. stroke, and lined up one of the cylinders to 9 in. With the necessary rearrangement of the steam pipes within the smokebox this little engine worked light trains on the Ashby and Nuneaton branch, at first under close observation from Crewe, and then in 1882 Webb built the first of his three-cylinder compounds. The layout of the machinery was exactly the reverse of Morandière's proposal of 1866, and at first sight appears quite illogical, because Webb used two high pressure cylinders exhausting into a single low pressure cylinder. To obtain an approximate equality of work and correct volumetric proportions for the expansion of the steam the high pressure cylinders had to be made very small, and the one low pressure very large. With this arrangement, however, Webb got over the difficulty of having only one high pressure cylinder to start the train, but introduced another peculiarity. Despite the outstanding success of his 2-4-0 'Precedents' as high speed, free-running locomotives he seems to have been anxious to get rid of coupling rods and he arranged his compounds as 'double singles' in that the high pressure cylinders drove the rearward pair of wheels and the one low pressure cylinder the forward pair. There were no coupling rods.

Although Webb evaded the complications of special starting valves introduced by most of his contemporaries his three-cylinder compounds were generally very awkward engines to get under way. Without the extra adhesion to be derived from coupling rods the wheels driven by the high pressure cylinders would frequently slip and send such a volume of steam into the intermediate receiver that it was choked, if it did not cause slipping of the forward pair of driving wheels. Without coupling rods there was no co-ordination between the working of the high and low pressure cylinders, and resulting unevenness of motion was transmitted far down the train. But in successive designs of Webb three-cylinder compound there was a basic fault, in that the proportions of high and low pressure cylinders were incorrect. The low pressure cylinders were not large enough, and the valves were unable to exhaust the steam freely, so that although they were powerful engines up to a point and strong on a bank, they could not develop any good speed on the level, or downhill. It was only on the last batch of the six-wheeled express compounds, the 'Teutonic' class of 1889, that Webb solved this difficulty by actuating the valves of the low pressure cylinder by a loose eccentric, which involved no notching up at speed, and provided a maximum flow of steam to exhaust. So that while the original LNWR compound engines of 1882 rarely exceeded 60 mph, and their immediate successors 70 mph, the 'Teutonics' used to race into the high 'eighties' on favourable stretches of line.

All in all, however, Webb's three-cylinder compounds had no lasting influence on the locomotive practice of the LNWR, and the same was the case with the Worsdell-von Borries two-cylinder type on the North Eastern. The latter system nevertheless became a standard for many years on the Belfast and Northern Counties Railway in Ireland. In contrast to the enthusiasm with which the compound system was taken up by many inventors, Mallet's own work seems to have proceeded on a more modest scale, and his lasting and richly deserved fame became centred upon the articulated type of locomotive, which was developed to gigantic proportions in the twentieth century. His first design for a compound articulated locomotive, with four cylinders, came in 1885, and the first example was actually two years later. The Americans also were quick to take up compounding, and the famous manufacturing firms of

LNWR. Webb 'Teutonic' class three-cylinder compound *Jeanie Deans*, seen here working the Scotch corridor train between Euston and Crewe.

One of William Stroudley's 'Gladstone' class 0-4-2 passenger engines on the London Brighton and South Coast Railway; a classic two-cylinder simple.

Rogers, and Baldwin, were among those developing their own systems, which generally meant methods of starting. Mallet was also a pioneer, in suggestion if not in practice, of a form that became popular in the USA, and that was the so-called tandem system.

It was realized that short, direct steam passages and free-flow of steam through ports was one of the main desiderata of compound locomotives, and in 1889 Mallet, in collaboration with Herr A. Brunner, Chief Engineer of I. A. Maffei, of Munich, devised an arrangement in which the high and low pressure cylinders were arranged on the same axis, immediately adjacent to each other. The locomotive proposed was a 2-4-2, with the cylinder assembly arranged centrally, with the shortest connection from the steam dome, and the respective pistons driving to fore and aft. It was an ingenious proposal and, although not adopted in this precise form, the tandem idea was taken up on a considerable scale by American designers, though with four cylinders, all outside. The tandem assemblies were arranged so that both high and low pressure cylinders drove on to a common piston rod, and with one on each side of the engine a balance was obtained. In America also, Samuel Vauclain, the distinguished Chief Engineer of the Baldwin Locomotive Company, devised a system of compounding, with four cylinders, in which the high pressure cylinders were mounted directly above the low pressure, on each side of the engine; and although each cylinder had its own piston, the high and low pressure cylinders on each side each drove on to a common crosshead. This arrangement was also widely adopted in the USA.

In retrospect however it cannot be said that any of the compound systems so far described achieved their prime object, of increasing thermal efficiency. It was the system introduced in France by Alfred de Glehn in 1891 that began the development leading to one of the greatest success

A fine example of the Vauclain compound system: an 'Atlantic' of 1896, on the Chicago, Milwaukee and St Paul Railroad.

stories in steam locomotive history. But this is so very much a story of the twentieth century that reference to it is reserved for a later chapter. By the end of the 1880s no locomotive design for fast passenger work had appeared to surpass the achievements of the ultra-simple two-cylinder single expansion type, the performance of which in Great Britain and the USA is described in the next chapter.

8 The elements of speed

The last twenty years of the nineteenth century witnessed a marked increase in the speed of railway passenger travel. The growth of population, the quickening tempo of business and the emergence of tourism as a potential source of revenue were among the factors that lay behind this trend, and with the abolition of discriminatory fares the competing companies in Great Britain and the USA were led into the way of increasing speed over that of their rivals as a means of attracting patronage. In this chapter I am concerned with the way those responsible for traction met this increasingly exciting trend. Acceleration of service was of course not solely a matter of providing the necessary tractive power. Several times already in this book I have referred to periods when locomotive capacity has stepped rather ahead of the carrying capacity of the track; but with increasing weight of trains and speed of travel, together with increasing density and complication of traffic on the principal routes, the need to provide improved brake power became urgent. In the 1870s the Great Northern Railway of England could with full justification have claimed to be the fastest line in the world, and yet, incredible to recall, its express trains were dependent for their brake power on the manual efforts of three men, screwing on hand brakes on no more than three vehicles – the fireman on the tender, and guards at the front and rear of the train. There were no brakes at all on the wheels of the locomotive, nor on any of the passenger coaches; and the only co-ordination between the applications at the three points of the train was when the driver, using a recognized code, 'whistled for brakes'!

In the USA technical advance in brake design was considerably ahead of that in Great Britain, though the overall position was equally unsatisfactory. But the invention of the air brake by George Westinghouse in 1869 and the demonstration of its efficacy in a spectacular incident at a level crossing just outside Pittsburgh, began what became almost a stampede to get the brake fitted on all major American railroads. Heartened by this success Westinghouse visited Europe in 1871, but received a very mixed reception in Great Britain. It is a pity to have to record that the controversy that ensued and which was not resolved until 1889 was not waged entirely on the grounds of technical achievement. Shortsighted railway managements begrudged the expense of putting on improved brakes; engineers devised systems of their own, while many British railwaymen opposed the Westinghouse form of brake from a mistaken sense of principle – purely because its origin was American! The outcome was typically British. When, following the terrible accident at Armagh in 1889, Parliament made obligatory the fitting of continuous automatic brakes to all passenger trains, less than half the main line railways adopted the air brake; the rest used the automatic vacuum which was entirely British in its inception and development.

No less important among the factors contributing to the attainment of higher service speeds was signalling, and in this respect British practice, though still rudimentary in many ways, was considerably in advance of that in the USA and on the continent of Europe. Much reliance was placed on the sense of responsibility of individual engine drivers, and their knowledge of the routes over which they ran. There were inconsistencies in the indications displayed and variations on different routes. White was still the most generally accepted colour for 'all clear' at night, but perhaps the most remarkable feature when seen in retrospect was that no distinction was made at night between the danger indications displayed by distant signals and stop signals, which were uniformly red. Yet in the first case the message was: 'you can pass at speed, but expect to find the next signal at danger', and the other required a dead stop, short of the actual signal post. From his knowledge of the route the driver was expected to know, in the dark, which were distant and which were stop signals. Moreover this was an anomaly that persisted in Great Britain until the 1920s! There is no doubt however that the country through which the main lines run was a good deal darker at night than it is today, particularly in the neighbourhood of towns. Prominent street lighting had yet to come, and in the country districts houses were lit by gas and candlelight. Distractions away from the railway signal lights were few. Such were two of the important background features against which the acceleration of train services from 1880 onwards took place.

From the locomotive point of view one of the most important developments was in the 4-4-0 type, in quite a different context from that of its American counterpart. There had been some preliminary introductions of the type, above all on the Stockton and Darlington Railway, under the aegis of William Bouch, but in such a way as to provide no lasting pointer to the future. The true British development came at first from the work of three engineers – David Jones on the Highland, S. W. Johnson on the Midland, and Dugald Drummond, first on the North British and then on the Caledonian. Jones's engines were in process of direct evolution from the practice of Alexander Allan, with the same encasing of outside cylinders, between inside and outside frames, and use of the Allan straight link motion. But although Jones's engines could and *did* run very fast downhill they were primarily mountain climbers, and it was the work of Johnson and Dugald Drummond that had the greater significance towards future practice. Alone of his contemporaries who had to provide for fast express service, William Adams on the London and South Western Railway used outside cylinders, but in so doing produced

The elements of speed 81

Highland Railway: one of the very powerful Jones 4-4-0s of the type introduced in 1874. *Atholl* was one of the so-called 'Clyde bogies', with a higher boiler pressure of 160 lb. per sq. in.

a locomotive very far removed from the still popular 4-4-0 'American'.

The Drummond engines require a special mention. Their designer had been works manager at Brighton under the legendary William Stroudley. The Brighton railway of the nineteenth century was not the place to seek any exposition of the speedworthiness of British locomotives. Its booked speeds were slow, and the timekeeping execrable – due to the incompetence of the traffic control systems of the day. But at Brighton works Stroudley set up magnificent standards of locomotive maintenance, and Dugald Drummond took these with him to Scotland, where he was immediately faced with the provision of locomotives for hard and fast running over very difficult routes. His North British 4-4-0s of 1876 set the pattern, and when he transferred to the Caledonian Railway in 1882, he developed his basic 4-4-0 into one of the most remarkable locomotives of the nineteenth century. It had a superbly designed front end, with cylinders proportioned to make the most economical use of steam, a very efficient layout of the Stephenson link motion, and a good though not exceptionally large boiler. By later standards his Caledonian 4-4-0s of 1884 looked slender, but the proportions were perfect. Drummond was well enough aware of the theoretical advantages to be gained from a long range of expansion, and he built one or two of his standard 4-4-0s with a boiler pressure as high as 200 lb. per sq. in. But he himself confessed that he could never get the drivers to work these engines expansively. They persisted in running with a partly closed regulator, and against such ingrained methods of handling high boiler pressures were useless. These engines were nevertheless the first ever in Great

Caledonian Railway: one of Dugald Drummond's 4-4-0 class of 1884, an outstanding nineteenth-century express locomotive.

Britain to develop an indicated horsepower of 1,000 or more.

There was no comparable development in the USA or Canada of this British advance of a very simple inside-cylinder 4-4-0 designed for economical high-speed running. It is strange in a way that some of the earliest examples of this new trend came in Scotland, where there were severe gradients to be mounted, as well as many stretches where sustained high speed could be run. But some very beautiful examples of the inside-cylinder 4-4-0 were introduced by S. W. Johnson on the Midland Railway, which for elegance of line as well as in efficiency in performance were probably unequalled anywhere in the world at that time. The new found British standard express passenger design had some interesting counterparts in locomotives exported by British builders. Some of the most elegant were those built by Beyer, Peacock & Co. for the Netherlands State Railways, a development of an equally ornate 2-4-0, of which many had been supplied in earlier years. Rather more functional, but equally well designed and splendidly finished, were some 4-4-0s from Sharp, Stewart & Co. for the Dutch Rhenish Railway, wholly in the English tradition so far as their proportions and machinery were concerned.

Just when it seemed that the 4-4-0 was becoming firmly established almost everywhere in Great Britain as the standard type of express passenger locomotive, F. Holt, the Works Manager of the Midland Railway at Derby, invented an apparatus for applying sand on to the rails in front of the driving wheels by a jet of steam. Hitherto sanding had been by gravity, and not only was the sand necessarily dry to enable it to flow freely, but it did not readily adhere to the rails, and in a strong cross wind

The elements of speed

Midland Railway: one of the Johnson 'Spinners', 4-2-2 type; a later engine of this series attained a maximum speed of 90 mph in 1898.

right
A very swift Worsdell two-cylinder compound, 7 ft 7 in. driving wheels, and attainer of 90 mph in ordinary service. This class was introduced in 1890. The low pressure cylinder was no less than 28 in. diameter, and the valve chests had to be accommodated outside the frames, as clearly shown in this illustration.

could be blown clear altogether. Wet sanding made such a difference that all the old affection of steam locomotive men for the single-wheeler rose up again, and first on the Midland, and then elsewhere, there came a new generation of modern 4-2-2 engines. The Midland development from 1887 until as late as 1901 produced a range of splendid engines that proved some of the swiftest yet to run on British rails, but which with the aid of wet sanding could pull surprisingly heavy loads. One of the largest Midland 'singles' of the '115' class introduced in 1896 reached the record maximum speed for the nineteenth century of 90 mph. On the North Eastern Railway T. W. Worsdell, building two-cylinder compounds on the system that he owned jointly with Herr von Borries, applied the system to a class of very fine 4-2-2s with 7 ft 7 in. driving wheels, and one of these equalled the Midland record with a maximum speed of 90 mph. Ever since the days of Daniel Gooch the Great Western had never been deflected from its policy of using nothing but single-wheelers for its express trains; but at the time of which I am now writing the Great Western had fallen well below the standards of speed that had become characteristic of the northern lines. Its great resurgence lay, as yet, some years ahead.

Although the 4-2-2 was enjoying a second youth, as it were, and the 4-4-0 in the British style was coming into prominence, a high proportion of British express traffic of the period was still in the hands of 2-4-0 engines, and two classes in particular must be mentioned, both North

The elements of speed 85

North Eastern Railway: one of the Fletcher '901' class 2-4-0s of 1872.

Eastern. Since the amalgamations of 1854 which brought the great pioneer railways of the north-east together in the newly formed North Eastern Railway the locomotive department had been ruled in a kind of benevolent autocracy by Edward Fletcher, a veritable patriarch whose railway career had begun as a fireman on the Stockton and Darlington Railway. By perception and experience, and a profound understanding of the men who served him, he had become one of the greatest locomotive designers of the day. His highly distinctive '901' class 2-4-0 of 1872 embodied a wealth of positive 'horse sense' in practical features and superb workmanship. When the 'Old Mon' did eventually retire, and his successor, from Ireland, produced an allegedly improved design – a 4-4-0 – there was almost a revolution among the enginemen on Tyneside. That successor was virtually dismissed by the men, for having dared to alter Fletcher's practice, and a modernized version of the '901' was produced by an interim committee assembled under the chairmanship of the General Manager, Henry Tennant. The new engines, which included all the cherished Fletcher features, were immensely popular, and went by the name of the 'Tennants'. They put in more than fifty years of service in passenger traffic.

It was in 1888 that the first of the great British railway races took place, between London and Edinburgh. The trains concerned were the day expresses leaving Euston and King's Cross respectively at 10 a.m., and before the race taking 10 and 9 hours respectively for the journey. How these overall times were gradually brought down to about 7½ hours by each route is a matter of statistics, but some of the greatest feats of engine performance are shown in Table 8.1. On the West Coast route the work of the 'Precedent' class 2-4-0s between Preston and Carlisle, over Shap, will be noted, while in Scotland only one engine was used throughout the race. The Caledonian 4-2-2 No. 123 was the only one of its class, and was a 'single' engine equivalent of the standard Drummond 4-4-0. The Great Northern used both the 8 ft 4-2-2s and the 7 ft 7 in. 2-2-2s, and it was one of the latter that made the fastest run; while on the continuation to Edinburgh by the North Eastern the working was shared between the 'Tennant' 2-4-0s and certain new Worsdell two-cylinder compound 4-4-0s,

Table 8.1 **The race to the north, 1888**

Railway	Engine no.	Engine type	Trailing load, tons	Section	Distance, miles	Time, min.	Av. speed, mph	Engine wt, tons	Load* in relation to engine wt
GNR	233	Stirling 2-2-2	105	Kings Cross–Grantham	105·5	105	60·3	39¾	3·61
GNR	95	Stirling 4-2-2	105	Grantham–York	82·7	85	58·3	45·1	3·06
LNWR	275	Precedent 2-4-0	80	Preston–Carlisle	90·1	90	60·1	33	3·24
NER	1475	Tennant 2-4-0	105	York–Newcastle	80·6	80	60·5	42·1	3·24
Caledonian	123	4-2-2	80	Carlisle–Edinburgh	100·6	102½	58·8	41¾	2·77

* Ratio includes the weight of the tender as part of the load.

New York Central Lines: the much publicized '999' reputed once to have attained 112 mph with the Empire State Express. This speed is, however, not nowadays accepted as authentic.

Chicago and North Western Railway: one of the final developments of the 'American' 4-4-0 type, used on the 'Fast Mail' between Chicago and Omaha.

which proved very fast runners like the 4-2-2s that followed them in 1889.

The news of the race did not fall upon deaf ears in the USA. In the year 1893 there was a great international exhibition in Chicago and some very fast running was claimed for the Empire State Express. This train had been put on in 1891 by the New York Central and its associates, and it was being run by one of the largest examples of the 'American' type 4-4-0 yet built. There was surprise and no little consternation among British locomotive men when it was reported that on 9 May 1893 the train had attained a maximum speed of 102·8 mph, and still more so when two days later a still more sensational speed of 112·5 mph was claimed. But careful enquiry revealed that the methods used in recording did not include the kind of corroborative detail that was, even then, considered necessary in England before such a claim could be accepted; and it later transpired that two very experienced European observers were actually travelling on the day of the alleged record. They obtained no higher speed than 81 mph, but even this was enough to show that the Americans were stepping it out, if not fast enough to justify their claim that the Empire State Express was the 'Fastest Train on Earth'. These runs together with those of the rival 'Pennsylvania Limited' and the 'Fast Mail' of the Chicago and North Western represented the swan song of the 'American' 4-4-0. Before the century was out much larger locomotives were being built.

The elements of speed

So far as maximum speed was concerned, the records actually set up in Great Britain, and claimed in their watered-down form for the USA, could not be equalled on the continent of Europe. In France maximum speed was limited by law to 120 km. per hour (74½ mph), but the booked start-to-stop speeds were mounting steadily, and the quality of individual engine performance was becoming very fine indeed. A major factor in this development was the introduction, first on the Northern Railway, of the de Glehn four-cylinder compound locomotives. All de Glehn's earlier work was done in close collaboration with M. du Bousquet, the Chief Mechanical Engineer of the Northern Railway. One basic feature of de Glehn's system of compounding was to divide the drive between two axles, with the outside cylinders outside, and driving the rearward axle, and low pressure cylinders inside, driving the forward axle. This idea of dividing the drive, and thus reducing the strain imposed on any one axle, appealed strongly to M. du Bousquet, because with increasing age and continued hard driving *à l'outrance* the single expansion 4-4-0s, based

90 The elements of speed

left
The first de Glehn compound: engine No. 701 of the Northern Railway, with uncoupled driving wheels.

Paris, Lyons and Mediterranean Railway: a striking example of a de Glehn compound 4-4-0, with streamlined fairings to counteract the effects of the Mistral in the Rhone delta.

originally on Sturrock's Great Northern 2-4-0s of 1866, were suffering from broken crank axles. The first de Glehn four-cylinder compound was little more than a compound version of the 'Outrance', but with the unusual feature that the two axles were uncoupled, as in F. W. Webb's three-cylinder compounds on the London and North Western Railway. The Nord locomotive evidently had the elements of success in it, because it was followed by successively larger 4-4-0 compounds. All the later engines had their wheels coupled, though the pioneer, No. 701, was never altered. She has been preserved for posterity, and is now in the French railway museum at Mulhouse in Alsace, in the original bright green livery instead of the more familiar chocolate brown by which locomotives of the Nord became so familiar to British travellers to the continent.

In the ordinary daily scheduled runs both France and the USA were striding ahead and robbing Great Britain of her one-time supremacy in speed; but then, in 1895, came the dangerously exciting 'race' to Aberdeen, between the east and west coast Anglo-Scottish routes. In contrast to

The elements of speed

the previous contest of 1888 this time the night trains were involved, and the contest was from the outset all the more exciting in that the routes converged at Kinnaber Junction, about three miles to the north of Montrose. The first train to be 'belled' to that signal box, either the West Coast, from Bridge of Dun or the East Coast from Montrose itself, was the winner. At the climax of the race, when over most parts of both routes the competitors were going all out, the only stopping stations were Crewe, Carlisle, Stirling and Perth on the one hand, and Grantham, York, Newcastle, Edinburgh and Dundee on the other. The locomotives used were as shown in Table 8.2. The best individual engine performances are summarized in Table 8.3.

Among the competitors the Great Northern disappointed its most ardent supporters, but there is evidence to show that alone of the railways concerned its enginemen were inclined to hold their locomotives in, and the performances were not representative of the best that could have been done. Their allies on the other hand, and particularly over the Newcastle–Edinburgh section, turned in some hair-raisingly exciting runs. Wilson Worsdell's 'M' class were among the heaviest and most powerful in the country at the time. On the West Coast route the sensation, of course, was the tremendous run of the little 'Precedent' 2-4-0 from Crewe to Carlisle, with an average speed of 67·2 mph including the ascent of Shap. The Caledonian runs were both very good, especially that of the Drummond No. 78 from Carlisle to Stirling, including the ascent of the Beattock Bank.

While the overall average speeds on the two fastest runs had been 60·4 mph over the 523 miles of the East Coast route, and 63·3 mph over the 540 miles of the West Coast – appreciably faster than anything that had been achieved anywhere else in the world over so long a distance – the more significant points so far as the present theme is concerned were centred upon individual engine performance, and its relation to future practice. The immediate consideration on two of the railways concerned was to provide still greater motive power against the possibility of racing being resumed in 1896. On the Caledonian, John F. McIntosh, the new Locomotive Superintendent, took the very efficient Drummond engine, and put on a much larger boiler, while on the North Eastern, Wilson Worsdell built two new 4-4-0s specially for racing, a development of his large and speedy 'M' class, but with coupled wheels no less than 7 ft 7 in. diameter. These latter were never called upon to 'race', although they were certainly swift runners in ordinary traffic, but the Caledonian 4-4-0s had an influence far outside their own railway and indeed of Great Britain itself.

In the summer of 1896 they were put on to the Tourist express, the train concerned in the racing of the previous

Table 8.2

Railway	Section	Locomotive class
LNWR	Euston–Crewe	3 cylinder compound 'Teutonic' class
LNWR	Crewe–Carlisle	2-4-0 'Precedent'
Caledonian	Carlisle–Perth	Drummond 4-4-0
Caledonian	Perth–Aberdeen	Lambie 4-4-0 *
GNR	King's Cross–York	Stirling 8 ft 4-2-2 †
NER	York–Edinburgh	Worsdell 'M' class † 4-4-0
NBR	Edinburgh–Aberdeen	Holmes 4-4-0 †

*A development of the Drummond type.
†Engines changed intermediately, at Grantham, Newcastle and Dundee.

Table 8.3   The race to the north, 1895

Railway	Engine no.	Trailing load, tons	Section	Distance miles	Time, min.	Av. speed, mph	Engine wt, tons	Load* in relation to engine wt
GNR	775	101	Grantham–York	82.7	76	65.3	45.1	2.98
NER	1620	101	Newcastle–Edinburgh	124.4	113	66.1	50.7	2.8
LNWR	1309	72½	Euston–Crewe	158.1	148	64.1	45.5	2.18
LNWR	790	72½	Crewe–Carlisle	141.0	126	67.2	32.7	2.98
Caledonian	78	95	Carlisle–Stirling	117.8	114	61.8	45.0	3.0
Caledonian	17	72½	Perth–Aberdeen	89.7	80½	66.8	45.2	2.46

*Ratio includes the weight of the tender as part of the load.

year; and with normal as distinct from racing loads, 170 to 200 tons against 75 to 100 tons, they were climbing the 49¾ miles from Carlisle to Beattock summit, 1,015 ft above sea level, in as short time as the Drummond engines had made a year earlier, but hauling double the loads. Writers of international repute such as Charles Rous-Marten published the most laudatory accounts of their work. The first of them was named after the Perthshire residence of the Caledonian chairman, *Dunalastair*, and for a time their name became synonymous with all that was best in British locomotive practice. Their fame attracted the attention of the Belgian government at a time when the engineers of the State Railway were considering some radical departures in their own locomotive practice. Until that time Belgian locomotives had been among the most unconventional in Europe, and although two features that were eventually to have the widest application – the Belpaire firebox and the Walschaerts valve gear – both originated in Belgium, the most recent passenger engines of the 2-4-2 with many quaint-looking details, did not offer much ground for development.

The Belgian engineers studied contemporary French, German and British practice, and eventually an invitation was given to the Caledonian Railway to supply some locomotives of the enlarged 'Dunalastair' class introduced in 1897. This, of course, the railway company itself could not do, being authorized only to build locomotives for its own use. But the directors were able to authorize McIntosh to act as consultant to the Belgian government and to supply drawings to the Glasgow firm of Neilson, Reid & Co. to enable them to build the required locomotives. They were finished in the splendid Prussian blue livery of the

Caledonian Railway: one of the 'Dunalastair' type 4-4-0s of 1896, which was not only the originator of a notable series of Scottish locomotives, but which markedly influenced Belgian practice.

Netherlands State Railways: a handsome British-built 2-4-0 for fast express traffic introduced in 1881.

Caledonian Railway, and made such an impression in Belgium that they were adopted as a standard type, and many more were built afterwards by various Belgian firms. Although British train services did not show any appreciable accelerations as a result of the racing of 1895, the prestige of its locomotive practice had much increased. On the major companies the design features that contributed to a fast passenger locomotive were all the better appreciated.

9 Problem of the commuters

The rapid growth of urban populations stimulated by the Industrial Revolution was further encouraged by the success of steam railways to such an extent that by the 1860s and 1870s a major problem of congestion was arising in the environs of many large cities. The streets themselves which were often narrow and relics of a less hurried age became crowded with slow horse-drawn vehicles, while large congregations of steam locomotives at running-sheds adjacent to the new railway stations added their quota of atmospheric pollution to the smoke from factories and closely packed, overcrowded dwellings. In London particularly the enterprising building of new railways from the south and south-east, crossing the Thames and making their way to terminal stations in the heart of the City, resulted in the destruction of old houses on a vast scale, and brought transportation problems to the railways of their own making. The many thousands who had lived on the very threshold of their places of work now had to be brought in daily from hurriedly built suburbs. The London Chatham and Dover Railway was perhaps the most heavily affected of all, and in ever probing for new connections, and possible new traffics, it became entangled, as it were, in its own web, and its trains became notorious for their slowness and subjection to chronic delays.

North of the Thames some relief had been obtained by the construction of the first underground railways, though these had connections at many points to the main lines, and provided at least one through route from north to south of the river that was extensively used by transfer freight trains. Towards the end of the century similar situations were building up in Glasgow, Paris and elsewhere, and the problem so far as traction was concerned was to provide locomotives that were capable of rapid acceleration, but yet created the minimum of discomfort through emission

Stroudley's light 0-6-0 suburban tank engine, London Brighton and South Coast Railway.

The Metropolitan 4-4-0 tank type as adapted to service on London and South Western suburban trains.

of smoke and exhaust steam. The difficulty of traffic regulation was always present, but so far as the present theme is concerned, the concept was to minimize line occupation by having locomotives that could accelerate to maximum running speed as quickly as possible. It soon became evident that on many counts steam was not the ideal form of traction for the job; but before beginning to consider the alternatives, two notable instances of densely trafficked urban railways must be noticed, one in London and one in New York.

From a somewhat shaky start, after its opening in 1863, the Metropolitan Railway got some excellent 4-4-0 tank engines from Beyer, Peacock & Co. These were designed specially for the job, and embodied all the expertise and

Early Great Northern Railway, London suburban 0-4-2 tank engine by Archibald Sturrock.

constructional excellence for which that firm was already famous. Even so they were not quite an original design, for the firm had built some similar engines for the Tudela and Bilbao Railway in Northern Spain two years previously. But the Metropolitan tank engines were important in having apparatus for condensing the exhaust steam when they were working in the tunnels. They had very large side tanks and an excellent steaming boiler – as was vitally necessary when for so much of their running they could not exhaust through the chimney, and thus create the normal draught through the tubes for combustion. They had no cabs, and one inevitably thinks of the tough enginemen who drove and fired them through the underground tunnels. Their success may be assessed from there being no other

Problem of the commuters

type of steam locomotive on the intense Inner Circle service from their first introduction, in 1864, till the line was electrified in 1905. The type was adopted not only by the Metropolitan District Railway, which owned the southern part of the Inner Circle and some extension lines into the western suburbs, but by the London and South Western, by the Midland, and by the London and North Western, for working services of their own that penetrated on to the central underground lines. One of the LNWR varieties was converted experimentally to a three-cylinder compound on F. W. Webb's system.

In New York the problem of urban transport was tackled quite differently. There appears to have been originally a great reluctance to travel underground. The city was built on a rectangular plan with straight wide streets; there were few if any buildings of architectural or historical importance in the central area, and it was therefore no affront to the amenities to build a railway on overhead galleries running down the main streets. So was conceived the once famous 'Elevated'. The first section was opened in 1872, and by the year 1897 when there were 36 miles of track in operation, no fewer than 326 locomotives and 1,116 cars were in use. All day long the trains followed each other at about one-minute intervals. There was no signalling; drivers followed the train in front, on sight. The rumble and rattle of the traffic was incessant, punctuated by the staccato exhausts of hard working locomotives. It was not pleasant for those who lived and worked in the streets concerned, accentuated by the noise and dirt. The locomotives nevertheless did their job smartly. They were all of the same type – handy little 0-4-4 tank engines, with outside cylinders, convenient for rounding the sharp curves, where one of the lines suddenly turned through a right-angle into an intersecting street. By the turn of the century the New Yorkers felt that the Elevated had gone far enough. Even if it were electrified the noise would remain, and so it became generally agreed that any further development in urban transport must be underground.

Before that, however, there had been a sharp difference of opinion elsewhere as to what the form of traction for future underground railways should be. While it was generally agreed that steam must go, it was not taken for granted that its successor would be electricity. Despite the pioneer work of George Westinghouse in the USA, and of Ganz in Budapest, electric railway traction had barely passed through the experimental stage, and when the deep level City of London and Southwark Subway was first projected, the line that eventually became the City and South London Railway, cable traction was proposed. While this line was under discussion, the Glasgow District Subway, authorized in 1890, was being pushed ahead to completion as an all-cable railway. It was a continuous circuit of $6\frac{1}{2}$ miles, with two independent tracks, one for each direction of running. The cable also was continuous, and it was kept running all the time at the running speed of the trains. Each train was equipped with a clamping device, and when ready to start from a station the driver set the clamp, which gripped the cable. On entering the next station the clamp was ungripped, and the train brought to rest at the platform. Although the service was not very rapid compared to that of later underground railways the system gave reliable service for thirty-eight years. Fortunately for the future expansion of the London tube railway network the idea of cable haulage on the City and South London was dropped and it became Britain's first electric railway.

Before passing on to consider some of the earliest projects using electric traction, honour is due to those who operated services of remarkable density with steam in the suburban areas of main line railways. It must be admitted that the traction problem was made easier in most British instances by the smallness and spartan internals of the standard suburban carriages. Not for nothing were some of them nicknamed 'dog-boxes'! The majority of travellers were either third-class season ticket holders, or those travelling earlier in the mornings at the still cheaper workmen's rates; and for these, small four-wheeled boxes, with back rests little more than waist high, bare boards to sit upon, and accommodating six a side, were a joy to the locomotive department. On the heaviest worked suburban lines of the London, Brighton and South Coast, and of the Great Eastern Railway, very small 0-6-0 tank engines ran these packed cavalcades smartly enough. Some of the trains made circuits of the most populous districts in South London, beginning at Victoria, venturing no further from the heart of the city than Peckham Rye, and terminating at London Bridge. The corresponding service of the London Chatham and Dover Railway began also at Victoria and worked its way round to Ludgate Hill, operated by picturesque little 0-4-2 tank engines named, oddly enough, after Scottish rivers. To the few railway enthusiasts of seventy years ago, these trains and their gaily painted locomotives were a delight – to behold from the lineside, that is! The Brighton engines, painted in Stroudley's famous yellow livery, were immaculately kept and all bore names, sometimes highly incongruous; but to a railway operating man they were rapidly becoming an anachronism.

A similar situation was developing in Melbourne, Australia, where the Victorian Railways were depending upon small very English-looking 2-4-2 tank engines to work over some radiating lines that included severe gradients. There the situation was temporarily relieved by the introduction of much larger steam locomotives of the 4-6-2 type, based upon the standard main line power of the day; but the traffic intensity in that Australian city was not long in overtaking the tractive power of the larger locomotives. In England the main line companies most beset by acute problems in their suburban areas were for the most part least favourably placed to launch into heavy capital investment to improve the entire situation. Large and wealthy English companies such as the London and North Western, the Midland, and the Great Western had no suburban problems to speak of. But around the turn of the century the advocates of electric traction presented it as the panacea for all ills; the only disadvantage to a struggling company was then, as now, its high capital cost. As with the diesels some forty years later there were plenty of critics ready to point out how Great Britain was falling behind in the development of newer forms of railway traction and to extol the merits of overseas practice to the disparagement of the 'home railways'.

What can probably be set down as the first electrification project undertaken anywhere in the world by a main line railway company was in the city of Baltimore, which the Baltimore and Ohio Railroad crossed by a succession of overhead and underground lines totalling seven miles. It was no more than a short section of a main line, but the local council had become insistent that steam working should be eliminated by 1895. The solution to the problem was provided by the General Electric Company of the USA, in a system using 675 volts direct current, from an overhead contact wire. It was a curious arrangement of current collection, in its details, and trains were hauled by powerful electric locomotives of 1,440 horsepower each weighing 96 tons. The four traction motors on each locomotive were gearless, and transmitted the power to the wheel spokes by rubber blocks. Through the alternation of tunnel and overhead sections there were some stiff intermediate gradients, and to obviate any difficulty of starting, the locomotives

Victorian Railways: 2-4-2 tank engine for Melbourne commuter traffic, now preserved.

were specified as being able to handle trains of 1,870 tons in any of the prevailing conditions. In Europe the use of the relatively low voltage of 675 was criticized, but the American pioneers were playing safe; in the event of failure of the supply, relief could be conveyed to sections of the line from accumulators.

Before the nineteenth century was out European engineers were pioneering the three-phase alternating current system, having the immediate advantage of needing no commutators on the motors, and having a lower weight of equipment both on the locomotives and in the generating plant. An experimental line was put into service between

Burgdorf and Thun, Switzerland, in 1899, using a pressure of 750 volts. But apart from the difficulty that prevailed at that early period in providing a stand-by supply, in case of emergency, those concerned with the commuter problem saw a major disadvantage, in that the three-phase alternating current system provided running at constant speed, instead of the flexibility that was essential in traffic that needed frequent starting and stopping. The three-phase system, it was thought, could have its points in main line express service where a maximum speed, for example, of 60 mph could be laid down, and adhered to regardless of any manipulations of the controls by the driver, but for suburban working the flexibility of the direct current system seemed to be essential. Nevertheless, when the decision was taken by the Metropolitan Railway to electrify the Inner Circle in London, a tremendous fight developed between the rival proposals put forward by the Westinghouse Electric Company of the USA, with relatively low voltage direct current, and those of Ganz of Budapest, which advocated 3,000 volts, three-phase alternating current. One difficulty lay in the division of the ownership of the Inner Circle tracks between the Metropolitan and the District Railways. The latter company had no doubts that the direct current system was the best, whereas the Metropolitan had been persuaded, chiefly on promises of more economical operation, in favour of the Ganz. The power politics that decided the issue in favour of Westinghouse form no part of the present theme; but on technical grounds, and its provision of high starting torque and power while accelerating, the direct current system was unquestionably the better.

From the moment the decision to electrify the Inner Circle on the direct current system was taken, in 1901, other interests began to urge the electrification of further London suburban areas. Rapid acceleration from rest was proclaimed to be the trump card of the new system, with the slogan '30 mph in 30 seconds from rest'. One of the companies most beset with pro-electrification propaganda was the Great Eastern, a line in no way prepared to face the capital cost involved. At that time James Holden was Locomotive Superintendent, and he had a very able and enterprising assistant in F. V. Russell; and against the repeated claims that steam traction could not produce the 'target' acceleration they received authority to build an experimental locomotive. The result was the famous 'Decapod', an enormous 0-10-0 tank engine, with three cylinders, and working at a pressure of 200 lb. per sq. in., with a weight of $78\frac{1}{4}$ tons. As a piece of locomotive designing it was a masterpiece, vastly ahead of its time, and handsomely surpassing the target of attaining 30 mph in 30 seconds from rest, with a train of about 250 tons. This, for the year 1903, was an outstanding achievement. But although the weight of the locomotive was spread over five axles, its concentration in a wheelbase of only 19 ft 8 in. was too much for the track, and this great locomotive never went into regular service. But so far as the Great Eastern Railway was concerned it silenced the cries of those who said that steam could not do it, and electrification of the suburban lines was indefinitely postponed.

While the controversy over electrification systems, with their rival international sponsors, was in progress in London, the traction problems of another busy commuter service were simply and swiftly solved in a very English way. The train service of the Lancashire and Yorkshire Railway between Liverpool and Southport was in part suburban, and when improvement was decided upon, no one thought of looking further than Lancashire to find the technical expertise and the manufacturing capacity. The great General Manager, John A. F. Aspinall, went to Dick, Kerr & Co. of Preston, later to become one of the

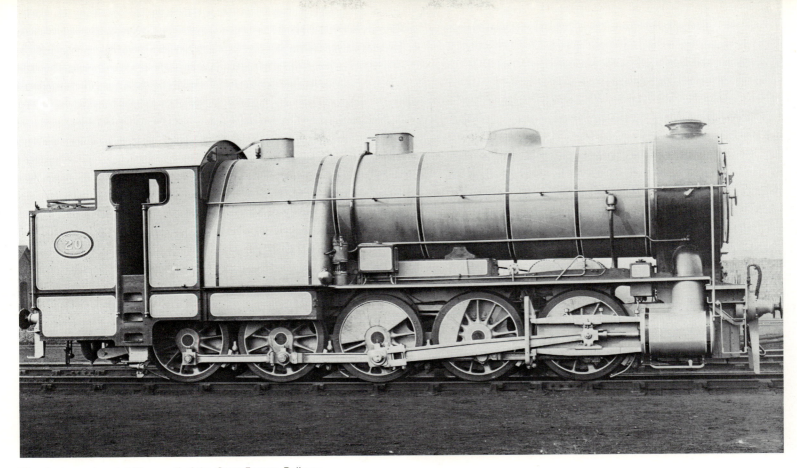

The giant experimental 'Decapod' of the Great Eastern Railway.

left
The Great Eastern standard suburban 0-6-0 tank engine: a contrast to the 'Decapod'.

London Tilbury and Southend Railway express 4-4-2 tank engine for the Southend residential service.

major constituents of the English Electric Company, and the scheme was decided upon and installed so quickly that it actually preceded the completion of the Inner Circle electrification by more than a year. The system was virtually identical, 625 volts direct current, using a positive conductor rail outside the track and a centre rail for the traction return. The rolling stock was all arranged on the multiple-unit system as propounded by F. J. Sprague, and other than the local underground line in London between Waterloo and the City it was the first example of its use in heavy commuter traffic. The original trains consisted of four-car formations and were remarkable in providing for nearly as many first-class as third-class passengers. Each train had two motor and two trailer cars, with the third-class passengers in the motor cars and the firsts in the trailers, totals of 138 and 132 passengers respectively in a four-car train. The total number of trains run daily was nearly doubled, and while there was no improvement in the steam times with the non-stop express trains between Liverpool and Southport, 25 minutes for the run of $18\frac{1}{2}$ miles, the time of the stopping trains was reduced from 54 to 37 minutes. This, in 1904, was a striking foretaste of what was to be achieved later in other areas with multiple-unit electric trains.

A classic example of a commuter service over a rather longer distance was provided by the steam operated London Tilbury and Southend line, an independent company until 1912, and then taken over by the Midland Railway. This was essentially an express route serving the group of dormitory towns ranged along the north coast of the Thames estuary, from Leigh-on-Sea eastwards to Shoeburyness. The trains which were composed of commodious bogie non-corridor stock were all worked by 4-4-2 tank engines having the large-sized coupled wheels, for such a service, of 6 ft 6 in. diameter. But with the residential trains no stops were made in the inner London area, where the route lay alongside that of the electrified District Railway, to Barking. The service, which was sharply timed, was run with regularity and success, due in the first place to the locomotives having been designed specially for the job, and no less to their being maintained in first-class condition. Trains were loaded up to the maximum formation that could be accommodated in the platforms at Fenchurch Street station, thirteen bogie coaches and one six-wheeler, and fully loaded totalled up to about 370 tons. It needed hard work to cover the 35 miles from Fenchurch Street to Westcliff-on-Sea in 45 minutes.

While the Great Eastern Railway, with the 'Decapod' gesture, brushed off the suggestions that it should electrify, the London Brighton and South Coast had a more serious problem on their hands, and called into consultation the eminent engineer, Philip Dawson. He was presented with a rather different problem from that of the Metropolitan and District lines, or that of the Liverpool and Southport section of the Lancashire and Yorkshire Railway. In South London the railway was losing some of its traffic to electric street cars, but the Brighton railway position was rather more extensive than that of an intense commuter traffic. Season ticket holders travelled to London from as far afield as Brighton, Worthing and Eastbourne, and the terms of reference given to Philip Dawson were to draw up plans that could eventually be extended to a high proportion of the total route mileage of the railway. As it was expected that the system of traction adopted would be extended to rural areas it was at the outset considered that a pick-up from live rails was undesirable, and that on the grounds of economy a higher voltage than the 600–625 of existing British lines was necessary. Dawson recommended a single-phase alternating current system at the relatively high tension, for that period, of 6,600 volts, with an overhead conductor line, as being a system that permitted the use of low voltage direct current traction motors with characteristics ideal for rapid acceleration in suburban service, but also a minimum of transmission losses, when the network came to be extended to the country sections of the railway. It was the beginning of what could have been a national system of electrification, but amid the rather parochial attitudes that prevailed between some of the British railways of pre-grouping days, it was not adopted by any other company when the time came for further electrification south of the Thames.

The first stage of the Brighton installation covered the South London line, between Victoria, Peckham Rye and London Bridge. It was known colloquially as the 'Elevated Electric' from the current collection being from overhead wires instead of a live rail. It was brought into service in 1909, and was an immediate success. The smart new trains, with their brisk running, provided such a contrast to the earlier steam days, and they attracted passengers from their very novelty; and those who sampled them came again, often. At the time of their introduction the Brighton railway was still using an attractive two-tone colour scheme for its coaching stock, of sepia-brown and cream;

Netherlands State Railways; a powerful British-built 4-6-4 tank engine of 1913 for inter-urban traffic.

108 Problem of the commuters

and the new electric stock was painted similarly. Fifteen years after its first introduction, when I was a postgraduate engineering student at Imperial College, Sir Philip Dawson, as he had then become, was the special lecturer in railway electrification, and I have vivid memories of his enthusiasm for the single-phase system. He had a fight on his hands at that time, because after the grouping of the railways in 1923, when electrification of the former South Eastern and Chatham lines was under consideration, it was a question of whether the Brighton single-phase alternating current system, or the third rail direct current of the London and South Western should be adopted as the future Southern Railway standard. But by mention of the LSWR electrification I have drawn rather ahead of the period covered by this chapter, and I must retrace steps.

In recommending and installing the single-phase alternating current system in 1909, Dawson was distinctly ahead of his times, though he was not the first to suggest it. The great Swiss engineer E. Huber-Stockar, in association with the firm of Oerlikon, had equipped, at the firm's expense, a 14 mile section of the Swiss Federal Railways between Seebach and Wettingen in 1905, at the high voltage of 15,000. This had worked very well, and was indeed a pace-setter for the future. But at that time the Swiss Federal Railways were not ready for electrification and it was dismantled after $1\frac{1}{2}$ years of running. But in that time Dawson had seen it, and referred to it frequently in his lectures, and it was a variation of it that he had installed on the Brighton railway.

In the period up to the year 1910 the commuter problem on main-line railways was mainly British. In Paris there had been a most peculiar situation when the first proposals for an electrified underground network were made. The civic authorities were insistent that it should be entirely separate and unconnected with any of the main-line railways, and made doubly sure by settling upon a different rail gauge. Throughout the nineteenth century strategic considerations governed most transport problems in Paris. The siege during the winter of 1870–1 was fresh in memory and the only steam railway that could be called metropolitan made a circuit within the walled fortifications of the city. This line, the Petite-Ceinture, was however more of an exchange line between the great trunk routes, for mail and through carriages, than a local passenger service. There were a number of trains, but they were slow and relatively infrequent, and could not be placed in the commuter category.

The world of the narrower gauges

At the opening of this chapter one might well put the question: 'What is a narrow gauge?' In England of the nineteenth century, in the territory of the Great Western Railway, it would doubtless have been understood as that used in the rest of the country. Nor could one become very 4 ft 8½ in. minded and refer to 'sub-standard' gauges when great systems like those of South Africa and parts of India are laid on the 3 ft 6 in. and metre gauges. But as most of this book so far has been concerned with the 4 ft 8½ in. gauge, and upwards, I feel that 'narrower' meets the case for the theme I now wish to develop. By the latter half of the nineteenth century railways were being projected in many parts of the world primarily for opening up remote territories, or for colonizing. There was little prospect of immediate profitability and the lines had to be constructed as cheaply as possible. The use of a rail gauge less than the standard 4 ft 8½ in. of Great Britain, most of Europe and of North America offered an immediate reduction in first costs, though from the viewpoint of traction there were eminent engineers who considered it impossible to build a satisfactory locomotive on a narrower gauge.

In contrast, the narrower gauges had no more enthusiastic nor more forthright protagonist than Robert F. Fairlie. He came into prominence in the provision of traction for the 1 ft 11½ in. gauge Festiniog Railway, in North Wales. This had been built to convey slates from the quarries at Blaenau Festiniog to Portmadoc for shipment, and had been very skilfully engineered so that the loaded trains could descend the entire way by gravity. The empties were drawn uphill by horses. When the traffic increased to such an extent as to demand heavier trains and faster uphill speeds, small steam locomotives were introduced; but in 1869 the whole situation was revolutionized by the putting into traffic of Robert Fairlie's articulated double engine

Little Wonder. It was actually a development of the idea first adopted on the Semmering line in having two engines back to back, with their boilers fed from a composite firebox in the centre. Fairlie's double engine was mounted on two steam bogies, which provided a means of articulation that readily adapted itself to the curves and gradients of the track, and which provided two engines that could readily be controlled by a single crew. As originally built the *Little Wonder* had no cab and although the driver and fireman were thus exposed to all the vagaries of the Welsh mountain weather, they were probably much cooler in the summer than on later engines of the type, which with semi-enclosed cabs could be very hot at times. Fairlie claimed that the *Little Wonder* could haul a load of three passenger carriages (first, second and third class), a guard's brake van, six goods wagons and 112 empty slate wagons, a total weight, excluding the engine, of 108 tons.

The enthusiastic reception given to the engine when a gathering of railway officers and engineers attended a demonstration run on the line seems rather to have gone to Fairlie's head, especially when one distinguished onlooker said afterwards that with engines like the *Little Wonder* he would work the entire traffic of the London and North Western Railway – on the 1 ft 11½ in. gauge! Fairlie was no modest man. In 1872 he published a book entitled *Railways or No Railways*, with the sub-title, 'Narrow Gauge, *economy with efficiency*' versus '*Broad Gauge, costliness with extravagance*'. One feels that he lost a great deal of the goodwill his double engine gained for him on the Festiniog by his own flamboyance. In Colorado he had a great opportunity of pressing his claims for the narrower gauge by the construction of the original main line of the Denver and Rio Grande on the 3 ft gauge, whereas all the other railways radiating from that city were 4 ft 8½ in. This line was originally intended to be a trunk route from north to south extending eventually to Mexico City, and its constructional costs in comparatively easy country south of Denver were compared on very favourable terms with those of the standard gauge Kansas and Pacific which came into Denver from the east. But the railway never got as far south even as the Rio Grande river. The discovery of rich metals in the Colorado Rockies led the promoters of the railway to send out branches westward into the mountains, and one of these over the tremendous gradients of the Tennessee Pass to reach Salt Lake City, Utah.

As a major east–west link the traffic built up to such an extent that an entirely new link, on standard gauge, had to be built with an improved alignment though not greatly easier gradients. The old narrow gauge route over the Marshall Pass may have been cheaper to construct in the first place, but the inclusion of such an incline as that leading to the Cerro summit, on 1 in 25, left an operational bugbear that was not removed until the new standard gauge line was built. The stories that persist of railroading on the Colorado narrow gauge are legion. Loads were not unduly heavy, but neither were the locomotives large, and if speed could not be made uphill then the intrepid engineers ran at breakneck pace downhill. The locomotives themselves were of no particular design or engineering significance except that they were built for tough conditions. When cargo was in a hurry, livestock for example, it was no unusual thing for a driver to be definitely instructed to ignore all speed restrictions and get through as quickly as he could. But the reader should not imagine that the result was a Coloradian equivalent of the British race to Aberdeen. A record run of 1894 on the Rio Grande from Ridgeway to Gunnison, 80 miles, gave an average speed of 18 mph. This was a factor to which Robert Fairlie seemed completely blind. From his voluminous writings it would appear that speed, either at the time or in the future, meant

Denver and Rio Grande Western: one of the narrow gauge 2-8-0 locomotives at Durango, Colorado.

left
Festiniog Railway, North Wales: one of the Fairlie 'double engines' crossing the causeway near Portmadoc.

South Australian Railways: a vintage 2-6-0 from the 3 ft 6 in. gauge section, now in the Railway Museum at North Williamstown, Adelaide.

nothing to him, and it became a critical item in the development of many railways that were constructed on one or another of the narrower gauges.

Initial cost was a major consideration for many of the early railway projects in Australia and New Zealand, yet when the various states of Australia were crown colonies in the very dawn of their settlement, the home government was very anxious to secure uniformity of gauge, after all the controversy and difficulties in England at the time of the Battle of the Gauges. But both Queensland and Western Australia, remote from the larger areas of colonization and not expecting to be linked up in the foreseeable future, stood out against adoption either of the 4 ft 8½ in. gauge, or of the still larger 5 ft 3 in. of Victoria and South Australia. Both the remoter colonies adopted the 3 ft 6 in. gauge. In Queensland the gradients on the earlier lines radiating from Brisbane were not difficult, and it was not until the extensions to the system made in the late 1920s that the motive power practice began to attain some degree of significance; but in Western Australia there were many difficulties. The earliest railways were little more than lumbering bush tracks in the tumbled hill country of the Darling Range; but the discovery of gold in the neighbourhood of Kalgoorlie made railway communication with Perth urgent, and the bush tracks became part of a 3 ft 6 in. gauge main line. One of the great difficulties in Western Australia has always been with water, which often had to be pumped over great distances to the locomotive water stations. Furthermore, although there was an abundance of coal in the south-west of the state, at Collie, it was not an ideal fuel for steam locomotives and called for specialized firebox design, even with the early low-powered locomotives of the nineteenth century. Some of the finest Western Australian locomotives were exported from Great Britain in the 1950s.

In both the north and south islands of New Zealand railway construction started on the 4 ft 8½ in. gauge; but in 1870 a great scheme of railway construction was launched, and for this the 3 ft 6 in. gauge was specified, under the auspices of the Public Works Department of the colonial government. Although the scheme was grandiose to a point the standard of performance was not high. Average speeds of 15 mph were to be considered adequate. One of the earliest orders for locomotives, however, came from the privately owned Dunedin and Port Chalmers Railway, for two double-ended Fairlie engines, from the Vulcan Foundry. The two engines, *Rose* and *Josephine*, began work in 1872. On the 3 ft 6 in. gauge they were larger and more powerful than their Festiniog counterparts. The second of them has been preserved in Dunedin, but it has been said of her: 'As a

New Zealand Railways: a powerful 2-6-2 shunting engine of 1930, now preserved and working on the Ferrymead line, near Christchurch.

The world of the narrower gauges

revered relic of pioneer days this flighty old lady has achieved fame to which she is scarcely entitled, for "Old Joss", as she was known, never was a good locomotive.'

Two more Fairlies were exported by the Avonside Engine Company in 1874, but despite their originators' claims these two engines were poor tools on a steep gradient. By the drivers and firemen it was regarded as 'punishment drill' to be assigned to these engines. Nevertheless six more, of a larger design, were ordered from Avonmouth in 1875. They were big and handsome engines, but it was felt that they were too powerful, there rarely being full-load trains worthy of their capacity. Apart from the Fairlies, New Zealand locomotives of the late nineteenth century were incredibly small, as indeed they could be, seeing that average speeds of no more than 15 mph were expected of them.

The incident – one might almost refer to it as the 'accident' – by which the standard rail gauge in South Africa was determined at 3 ft 6 in. was unfortunate, yet no country has gone further in overcoming its restrictions. For whatever the oratory or verbiage of Robert Fairlie may try to claim, a railway running on the 3 ft 6 in. cannot compete on level terms with one on the 4 ft $8\frac{1}{2}$ in. – all other things being equal. At the time railways were first projected in the Cape of Good Hope, and in Natal, there was certainly need for economy, for those areas were being colonized from primitive beginnings as much as those in Queensland and Western Australia. But from a very early date in South Africa the vision of railway development was infinitely broader, and by the time Cecil Rhodes was propounding his concept of the 'Cape to Cairo Railway' it would not have been too late to have changed to 4 ft $8\frac{1}{2}$ in. As in Australia the development in the Cape and Natal was at first quite independent and unconnected. Both had to cope with very steep gradients; the former in climbing the Hex River Pass to the Great Karoo Desert, and the latter, from Durban up to Cato Ridge.

The locomotives of the Cape Government Railway were certainly not designed for speed. The earliest standard engines were of the 4-6-0 and 4-8-0 types, and even the former, used on the long distance passenger trains, had coupled wheels no larger than 4 ft 6 in. diameter. The 4-8-0s had driving wheels of 3 ft 6 in. diameter. They were all British built, by Neilson & Co. of Glasgow, and later batches by the North British Locomotive Company. They were sturdy solid jobs, and many of them have put in more than seventy years of hard work. As the main line of the Cape Government Railway was extended northwards, to Kimberley and eventually to Mafeking, blazing the trail of the projected 'Cape to Cairo' line, these engines in ever-increasing numbers bore the brunt of the work. When the line was continued through the Bechuanaland Protectorate, and reached Bulawayo, the Rhodesia Railways, or the Beira and Mashonaland Railway as it was originally known, adopted the same two types of locomotive, and one of the 4-8-0s is preserved in the Railway Museum at Bulawayo.

In Natal the original development was quite different. The climb up to Cato Ridge, on the alignment first followed, included no less than 38 miles, inclined almost continuously at 1 in 66. In 1880, in collaboration with Dübs & Co. of Glasgow, a design for a powerful 4-8-2 tank engine was worked out, again with wheels of no more than 3 ft 9 in. diameter, and these remained the standard locomotives of the line for nearly twenty years. There were eventually 120 of them, and they worked all trains, passenger, mail and goods alike. Some of them, dating from the 1880s, are still in service today – not on the South African Railways but in the Grootvlei Proprietary Mines, near Johannesburg. A still larger tank engine design was put into service in 1901, of the 4-10-2 type, having the tremendous tractive

One of the former Natal Government Railways' 4-8-2 tank engines of the 1880 design now working for the Grootvlei Proprietary Mines, near Johannesburg.

effort for that period of 29,500 lb. – far greater than that of any contemporary British goods engine. The inherent restrictions of the 3 ft 6 in. gauge were being handsomely overcome in South Africa, even by the turn of the century.

In India the term 'narrower gauge' needs some qualification. When the 5 ft 6 in. gauge was chosen for the principal main lines, a network of main feeder lines was also envisaged, and to reduce the costs of construction these were planned on the metre gauge. While it would be an oversimplification to suggest that the motive power on the metre gauge lines was a scaled down version of that on the broad gauge, there was in general not a great distinction in design. In addition to these two gauges, however, India possesses a considerable mileage operated on the still narrower gauge of 2 ft 6 in., much of it built in the present century, by private companies under government incentive schemes. A very special Indian narrow gauge line, one of the most remarkable and picturesque anywhere in the world, is the Darjeeling Himalayan Railway, opened in 1880. It was built as far as possible adjacent to the existing road, with all its sharp twists and turns, not to mention the very steep gradients, and a gauge of 2 ft was chosen. The first locomotives were scarcely powerful enough, but in 1899 a design of 0-4-0 saddle tanks from Sharp, Stewart & Co. was introduced, and was so successful that the class has remained on the job ever since. They are powerful engines for the 2 ft gauge, having cylinders 11 in. diameter by 14 in. stroke, coupled wheels 2 ft 2 in. diameter and carrying a boiler pressure of 140 lb. per sq. in. The rate of ascent, when these locomotives were first introduced, was 1,000 ft vertical rise per hour.

The construction of narrow gauge lines, on the 2 ft 6 in. gauge, proceeded steadily in India during the first decade of the twentieth century. Some of these were strategic lines,

The world of the narrower gauges

others were privately sponsored, and between them they collected a great variety of small locomotives. The largest were of the 4-8-0 tender, and 2-8-2 tender types. The great majority of these came from British manufacturers. One of the most specialized in design was the 2-6-2 side tank built for the Kalka–Simla mountain railway, which climbed through scenery second only in its magnificence to that of the Darjeeling line. The special 2-6-2 tank engines were considerably larger and more powerful than those for the former line, and had cylinders 14 in. diameter by 16 in. stroke, coupled wheels 2 ft 6 in. diameter, and carried a boiler pressure of 180 lb. per sq. in. They have only recently been replaced by diesels.

The development of the narrow gauge in Ireland, from 1872 onwards, on the 3 ft gauge was encouraged by a series of Light Railway Acts in which government assistance was provided to ensure the establishment of some kind of transport in rural areas. In the Regulation of Railways Act of 1878 there was the nearest approach to the definition of a 'light railway', in which the maximum axle loading was laid down as 8 tons, and maximum speed specified as 25 mph. Many of the lines constructed up to the year 1905 were of an exceedingly 'light' character, and exhibited many of the vagaries traditionally associated with Irish country life. They became of far greater interest to the lovers of the quaint and unusual in railways than to students of locomotive practice in its more serious and technical forms. In this chapter the locomotives of only two of these picturesque little railways may be specially noticed. These were the narrow gauge sections of the Belfast and Northern Counties, and the Londonderry and Lough Swilly.

It was in 1876 that Bowman Malcolm, then no more than 22 years of age, was appointed Locomotive Superintendent of the Belfast and Northern Counties Railway. Two years later the narrow gauge Ballymena and Larne Railway was opened, providing a potential short cut from the packet station of the Scottish steamers to the north-west of Ulster. Ordinarily one would not associate Irish narrow gauge railways with time-saving projects, but from its very inception it put on a 'boat express' between Larne and Ballymena, and ran it at a brisk pace. In 1889 the Belfast and Northern Counties Railway took over this enterprising narrow gauge line, and with increasing traffic Bowman Malcolm was required to supply some increased engine power. He had become very impressed with the Worsdell-von Borries two-cylinder compounds operating on the North Eastern Railway in England, and in 1890 built two 2-4-0 broad gauge passenger engines on this system, for comparison with his earlier single expansion engines. The results were such that he built nothing except two-cylinder compounds for the broad gauge lines for the next twenty years. But what could be done on a large engine running on the Irish broad gauge of 5 ft 3 in. was not possible when it came to narrow gauge power, and his solution of the Larne boat train problem was one of the neatest and most successful anywhere in Ireland on the narrow gauge.

In 1892 he designed, and Beyer, Peacock & Co. built, two remarkable two-cylinder compound 2-4-2 tank engines. The cylinders had necessarily to be outside, but they were very neatly arranged, immediately below the smokebox and ahead of the leading pair of coupled wheels. When viewed head-on they looked rather unbalanced, with different sized cylinders, but in service they proved steady and fast running machines. The actual cylinder dimensions were $14\frac{3}{4}$ in. high pressure, and 21 in. low pressure, both with a stroke of 20 in. They were interesting in having the Walschaerts valve gear – one of the earliest designs in the British Isles to be so equipped. The two engines built in 1892 ran the boat trains very successfully; two further

One of Bowman Malcolm's two-cylinder compound 2-4-2 tank engines (1892), working on the Ballycastle Railway in 1935.

identical engines were built at the Belfast works of the company in 1908–9, and yet another two in 1919–20. Two of them were later transferred to work the Ballycastle Railway, where I saw them doing good work in the late 1930s. On that line some stiff hill climbing was involved from the coastal terminus up to Capecastle, but with trains of two or three of the long bogie coaches originally built for the Larne boat train no difficulty was experienced.

The Londonderry and Lough Swilly Railway had one difficult line to operate. In 1898 by an order under the Light Railway Act of 1896, the Letterkenny and Burtonport Extension Railway had been authorized, wandering for nearly 50 miles in the wildest and most desolate country in the Highlands of Donegal. The main part of the capital for building this line had been provided as a free grant by the government. It was one thing to get this 3 ft gauge line built however, and another to operate it; the 'traffic' developed into one heavy mixed train a day in each direction, over the full 74 miles between Londonderry and Burtonport, and in 1905 the company obtained from Hudswell, Clark & Co. of Leeds two relatively large tender engines of the 4-8-0 type. A tender engine was chosen in preference to a tank, to provide the necessary coal and water for the long through run. With numerous intermediate stops, and slow running, the journey took the best part of a day to perform. They were the only 4-8-0 tender engines to operate in the British Isles, though on account of weight restrictions they were small compared to some of the 4-8-0s on 3 ft 6 in. gauge lines in Africa.

Early railway development in Japan was entirely on the 3 ft 6 in. gauge, and for many years operation was in a leisurely and somewhat haphazard style that gave little suggestion of the tremendous high-speed electric lines that were to be introduced in the 1960s. The main routes along the eastern shores of the main island of Honshu followed the indented coast line, and no rapid services were called for. The first two locomotive superintendents were British, and of these W. M. Smith, after setting up workshops and getting the traffic into motion, returned to England to a notable career in engine designing on the North Eastern Railway, and it was R. F. Trevithick, a grandson of the great Cornish pioneer, who carried the locomotive department of the Japanese railways into the twentieth century. Most of the early locomotives were imported from Great Britain, and were small 4-4-0s; but Trevithick also built the first locomotive in Japan. It was not however until the 1920s that steam power on the Japanese 3 ft 6 in. gauge began to attain any degree of significance.

It was in South Africa in the early years of the twentieth century that a strong line of development on the 3 ft 6 in.

The world of the narrower gauges 119

preceding page
Rhodesia Railways: the 12th class 4-8-2 locomotive of 1926, built by North British Locomotive Company, and developed from the original South African designs of 1904.

The only narrow gauge section now operated by British Railways. The 2 ft gauge line from Aberystwyth to the Devil's Bridge, Central Wales, here seen as in Great Western Railway days.

gauge began to emerge. At the conclusion of the Boer War the railways in the two former republics of the Orange Free State and the Transvaal were grouped in the newly formed Central South African Railways, and two notable new designs were introduced immediately. In contrast to the practice of the Cape and Natal railways the new CSAR types both had carrying wheels under the firebox: 4-6-2 for passenger, and 2-8-2 for freight. The contract for the first fifteen of the 'Pacifics' was awarded to the North British Locomotive Company, and their production was considered a great event in Glasgow. This was not until after this new company had been formed by amalgamation of Neilson Reids, Dübs, and Sharp, Stewart & Co., and the directors of the new company were photographed in front of the first 'Pacific'. In Great Britain it was considered that the supply of these two classes would set the motive power situation in South Africa so much in advance of day-to-day requirements that nothing larger would be needed for many years to come. So, indeed, it turned out. The new 4-6-2s and 4-8-2s were exported in 1904, and it was not until 1910 that anything larger, on any of the lines in South Africa, was introduced.

The CSAR engines of 1904 require a special mention, not only because of their significance in South Africa itself, but because they represented one of the earliest moves to eliminate the disadvantages of the 3 ft 6 in. gauge. Certainly there were no restrictions over height and width, and with steady improvements to the track heavier locomotives could be accepted. The main problem so far as an express passenger locomotive was concerned was stability at speed. The increase in the coupled wheel diameter from the 4 ft 6 in. of the Cape 4-6-0s to 5 ft 2 in. suggested that faster running was contemplated and the large fireboxes were designed to promote a continuously high rate of steaming. The main lines in the Transvaal and in the Orange Free State did not include any gradients of the severity met with in the Cape, or Natal, and the adoption of the 'Pacific' as an express locomotive was in keeping with the growing trend on 4 ft 8½ in. gauge lines in the USA. Both classes, 4-6-2 and 2-8-2, put in many years of sterling work, and I was able to photograph a number of them still in active service in 1968.

Worldwide technical advances: 1900–14

One of the most important developments in the entire history of the steam locomotive was due to a German engineer, Herr Wilhelm Schmidt, a man primarily concerned with stationary engines and boilers, but who was responsible for the first successful application of superheating to locomotives. Two of its fundamental advantages may be set down at the outset:
(a) to provide 'dry' steam at a higher temperature than that corresponding to its pressure, thus to minimize cylinder cooling and condensation, and enable extended expansive working to be used,
(b) to increase the volume of the boiler steam before it is used in the cylinders.

It was Herr Müller of the Prussian Ministry of Public Works, and Herr Garbe, member of the Berlin Board of Directors of the Prussian State Railways, who recognized the value of Schmidt's original proposal, and who facilitated the building of the first superheater locomotives in 1898. In the first Prussian locomotives the superheater was in the smokebox, and it was due to the interest and co-operation of Messrs R. Bertrand and B. Flamme of the Belgian State Railways that the familiar later form, the smoketube type, was adopted, and immediately afterwards standardized. The first locomotives with this type of superheater were put into service in Belgium in 1901. By the year 1907 the Schmidt superheater was employed on the railways of Austria, Belgium, the Cape of Good Hope, Canada, France, Hungary, Poland, Russia, Sweden and Switzerland, in addition to several German states, in a total of several hundreds of locomotives; but at that same time only one British locomotive had been experimentally fitted – a 4-6-0 on the Great Western Railway. Yet even within the period of this chapter no country was using superheating to greater advantage than Great Britain.

Northern Railway of France: de Glehn four-cylinder compound 4-4-0.

While its merits for increasing thermal efficiency were, in a general sense, recognized, the inclination at first was to regard it as an alternative to compounding, and in the early 1900s attention to the latter was strongly focused on the work of Alfred de Glehn, in France. The 4-4-0 locomotives introduced in collaboration with M. du Bousquet of the Northern Railway of France had been followed by some large and powerful 'Atlantics', and the use of these on the English boat trains between Paris and Calais had attracted notice that was worldwide. It was enough to lead G. J. Churchward, the distinguished Locomotive, Carriage and Wagon Superintendent of the Great Western

Great Western Railway: the first of the de Glehn compound 'Atlantics' purchased from France, in 1903.

Railway, of England, to arrange for the purchase of one of these engines for trial purposes. This was an interesting development when, with one exception, British railways were turning from the compounding phase that had been so popular from the 1880s. The British exception was the Midland, which had adopted the three-cylinder system of W. M. Smith on its largest 4-4-0 express passenger locomotives. These locomotives however numbered only 45, out of a stud of some 3,000 on the Midland Railway, and their influence towards contemporary practice in Great Britain was negligible. It might have been much stronger if the later engines of the class had been equipped with the same controls as those of the original two; but these were considered too complicated for the average Midland engineman to manage, and in consequence they were simplified, and the capacity of the locomotives unfortunately reduced. In Europe, in addition to the work of M. de Glehn, that of Herr Karl von Gölsdorf must also be noticed, who from 1900 onwards was developing his successful two-cylinder system into four cylinders, and built a range of hand-

Worldwide technical advances: 1900–14

One of the Midland three-cylinder compound 4-4-0s leaving Carlisle, with an express for London (St Pancras).

some and successful locomotives for a great variety of duties on the Austrian State Railways.

While European engineers were developing the technical features of their locomotives, in the USA a strong movement had begun towards much larger and heavier engines. The popular 'American' 4-4-0, which was reaching its climax in designs like that of the New York, New Haven and Hartford of 1900, with 20 in. by 26 in. cylinders, 6 ft 6 in. coupled wheels, a large boiler, with firebox grate area of 30·3 sq. ft and a pressure of 200 lb. per sq. in., began to give place to the 'Atlantic' on which a still larger grate could be accommodated over the pair of trailing wheels. The problems connected with the efficient burning of American coal will be apparent from the New York Central, in some 'Atlantics' built by ALCO in 1905 having to use a grate area of no less than 50·3 sq. ft on a two-cylinder engine with cylinders $21\frac{1}{2}$ in. diameter by 26 in. stroke. Furthermore, while the British and European development from the 4-4-0 lay generally towards the 4-6-0, the 'tenwheeler', as the type was popularly known in the USA,

New York Central four-cylinder compound 'Atlantic' of 1905. The cylinders were $15\frac{1}{2}$ in. diameter high pressure, and 26 in. low pressure. There were some similar single expansion 'Atlantics' with $21\frac{1}{2}$ in. cylinders. Both types had boilers with a grate area of 50·3 sq. ft.

never found much favour as an express passenger type in North America, chiefly through the difficulty of accommodating a wide firebox, so necessary for burning the indigenous fuel. The tendency was to progress directly from the 'Atlantic' to the 'Pacific'. During the first years of the twentieth century a considerable number of American locomotives continued to be built as four-cylinder compounds, either on the tandem or the Vauclain systems; but gradually the trend began to set in favour of two-cylinder simples, particularly as the Walschaerts valve gear, mounted outside, was generally superseding the inside Stephenson link motion that had been almost universal at the turn of the century.

Contemporary British practice was to strive for the greatest simplicity in design, while taking advantage of the small fireboxes that the high grade coals available made possible. It might have seemed a reactionary policy; but superheaters added expense to the first cost, and compounding had not so far shown any of the technical advantages that were claimed for it. Except in a few cases reliance continued to be placed on the traditional inside cylinder 4-4-0, and of this type the LNWR 'Precursor' of

Table 11.1 A British and American comparison

Railway	Type	Cylinders (2) Dia. (in.)	Stroke (in.)	Coupled wheel dia., ft	in.	Valve gear	Position	Total heating surface, sq. ft	Grate area, sq. ft	Boiler pressure, p.s.i.	Nominal TE, lb.
London & North Western	4-4-0	19	26	6	9	Joy	Inside	2,009·7	22·4	175	17,250
North Eastern	4-4-2	20	28	6	10	Stephenson	Inside	2,455	27	200	23,300
Caledonian	4-6-0	21	26	6	6	Stephenson	Inside	2,323	26	200	24,990
Great Western	4-6-0	18	30	6	8½	Stephenson	Inside	2,143	27	225	23,150
New York, New Haven & Hartford	4-4-0	20	26	6	6	Stephenson	Inside	2,109	30·3	200	22,650
Pennsylvania	4-4-2	20½	26	6	8	Stephenson	Inside	2,640	55·5	205	23,750
New York Central	4-6-2	21	28	6	1	Stephenson	Inside	3,457	50·2	200	28,750
Baltimore & Ohio	4-6-2	22	28	6	2	Stephenson	Inside	3,418	56·5	200	31,000

1904, proportions of which are shown in Table 11.1, was an outstandingly successful example. Apart from good all-round design, two features in particular contributed to its reputation. The proportion of free gas area through the boiler tubes in relation to the grate area is always considered the yardstick of steaming efficiency, and whereas eight contemporary British locomotives of good repute had ratios varying between 14·4 and 17·4, that of the 'Precursor' was 20·2. Similarly the area of the exhaust ports in relation to piston area was one of the highest then to be found in British practice. Though having the lowest nominal tractive effort of the British locomotives quoted in Table 11.1, the 'Precursor' was called upon for the most consistently hard work of any in the years 1904–9. The American locomotives of which details are quoted reflect upon the huge fireboxes that were by that time considered necessary.

The 'Caledonian' 4-6-0, which at that time had the highest tractive effort of any British passenger locomotive, was of entirely conventional design, but while doing much good work was perhaps *too* conventional to admit of subsequent development. It was on the Great Western Railway that the most significant work for the future was then in progress. But while the drawing office at Swindon was intensely engaged upon detail features of the new 4-6-0s, the 4-4-0 'City' class, G. J. Churchward (1903) was doing very fine work with the traffic then offered, and attaining exceptional maximum speed on occasions. These locomotives, like the LNWR 'Precursor', had good valve and boiler proportions, and the maximum speed of 100 mph, or

The most powerful British locomotive of the early 1900s. J. F. McIntosh's 'Caledonian' 4-6-0 of 1903.

right The stationary locomotive testing plant at Swindon, Great Western Railway with one of Churchward's new 'Atlantic' engines *in situ*.

slightly over, attained by the *City of Truro* when hauling an Ocean Mail on 9 May 1904, remained a British record for thirty years. At this point it should be added that on the Great Western and on the Midland Railway at that time a considerable proportion of first class express mileage was still handled by 4-2-2 'single-driver' locomotives. On a typical day in July 1904 no fewer than nineteen expresses leaving Paddington between 9 a.m. and 6.30 p.m. were hauled by Dean 7 ft 8 in. 4-2-2s.

The purchase by the GWR of a de Glehn four-cylinder compound 'Atlantic' in 1903 has already been mentioned. This was one step in Churchward's highly significant development programme. For having obtained this engine, and examined its performance comprehensively, he then set out to produce a single expansion locomotive of equal, or greater, efficiency. The boiler, with a working pressure of 225 lb. per sq. in., was a development of its own, but the design of the cylinders and valves to permit of a range of expansion equal to that of the French compound was epoch-marking to a degree. The stroke of the pistons,

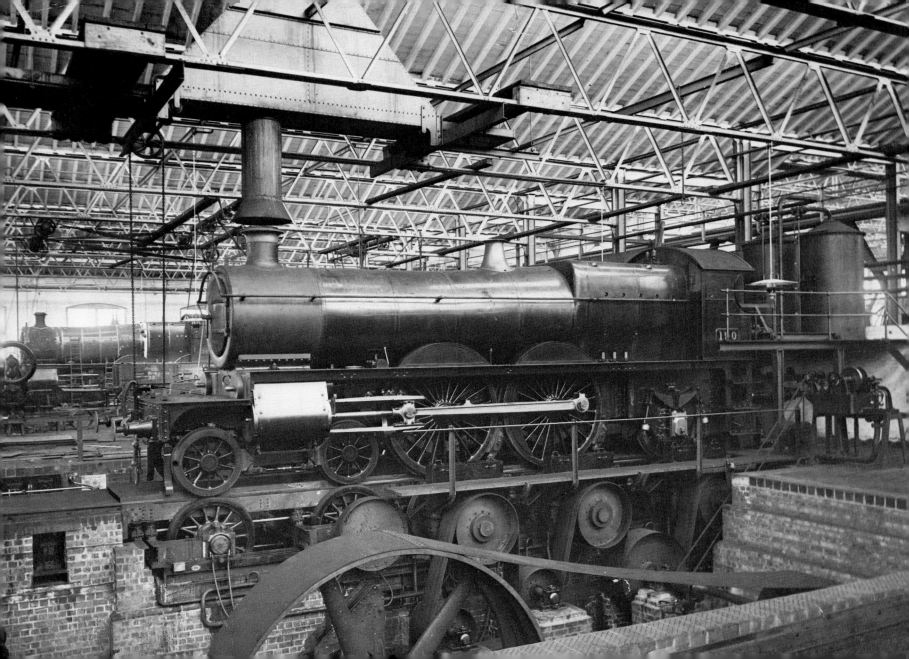

Chicago, Milwaukee and St Paul four-cylinder 'balanced' compound 'Atlantic', with all four cylinders driving on to the leading pair of coupled wheels.

30 in., was made long in relation to the bore, 18 in., and by a then novel setting of the Stephenson link motion a large port opening to exhaust was obtained even when the engine was linked up to less than 20 per cent cut-off. This not only permitted of a long range of expansion, from the initial boiler pressure of 225 lb. per sq. in., but a free exhaust that resulted in a fast running locomotive. In the course of the trial runs the speed-worthiness of the de Glehn compound engine was demonstrated to an extent not possible in France where the maximum speed was everywhere limited by law to 120 km. (74·5 mph). On the Great Western the French engine ran freely up to 85 mph.

It was shortly after Churchward's appointment as Locomotive Carriage and Wagon Superintendent of the Great Western Railway that the first steps towards the more precise testing of locomotives were taken in England. Prior to the year 1903 stationary testing had taken place at Purdue University, Lafayette, Indiana, and at the University of Illinois, Urbana, Illinois. But in setting up the new stationary plant at Swindon, Wiltshire, in 1903, Churchward had primarily in mind not so much the analytical testing of performance as the avoidance of 'running in' trials on the road of new and repaired locomotives. Consequently the plant was made of no more than limited capacity. In the following year, however, the Pennsylvania Railroad set up and operated at the St Louis Exposition a stationary testing plant on which high power output could be sustained. After the exposition closed down the testing plant was re-erected at Altoona Works, and became extensively used afterwards. If the Great Western plant was not, until some forty years later, used for high power testing, Churchward's new dynamometer car certainly was, and the records taken provided the data on which the effectiveness of the new locomotives was judged. Not for the first time in its history the Great Western was proving a pace-setter, and the North Eastern, the Lancashire and Yorkshire, and the London and North Western Railways built dynamometer cars of similar capacity.

There were some interesting pointers to future practice in the larger locomotives currently being introduced in Europe in the 1900–10 period. It must nevertheless be borne in mind that except in France booked speeds were considerably less than those in Great Britain and the USA, and that technical developments, such as those with compound locomotives in Germany and Austria-Hungary, were progressing against a background of less severe service requirements. About the years 1906–7 an interesting situation was arising in Holland. The international traffic across the country from both Flushing and the Hook of Holland was increasing to such an extent that the existing locomotives of the State Railway could scarcely cope. It is true that the beautiful Beyer, Peacock 4-4-0s had been reinforced by some inside-cylinder 'Atlantics', built by the same English company for the Flushing mail trains; but there was clearly a need for more powerful engines, preferably six-coupled. A difficulty on Dutch railways generally had always been the soft nature of the ground, which precluded the use of heavy axle loadings; but a co-operative

Difficulty of sighting signals past large American boilers led to cabs being mounted astride the boiler, as in this Lehigh and New England 2-8-0 of 1911. Note the enormous firebox.

study by locomotive and permanent way engineers produced a solution of vital importance, the significance of which was not immediately appreciated outside the continent of Europe.

It concerned the dynamic balance of the revolving and reciprocating parts of a locomotive. The Bavarian firm of Maffei had, for some little time, been building four-cylinder compound locomotives in which the layout of the machinery differed from those of Gölsdorf, and of de Glehn, both of whom divided the drive between two axles. This in itself had advantages in that the thrust from the cylinders was divided between two axles and the loads on the bearings were reduced. But Maffei arranged for all four cylinders to drive on to the leading coupled axle. By so doing he obtained an almost complete dynamic balance, with no hammer blow developing at speed to augment the dead weight on each of the coupled axles. In a compound engine there was bound to be some disturbing effect, because of the different sizes of the high and low pressure pistons; but it was very small compared with that arising in a locomotive with divided drive, like a de Glehn. The result of the Dutch investigation was that the civil engineers were prepared to accept the heavier locomotives, providing they had four cylinders, all driving on to the leading coupled axle. Two notable designs resulted from this, both four-cylinder simple 4-6-0s, in which the dynamic balance was perfect. Those for the Netherlands Central Railway were built by Maffei, while those for the State Railway were built by Beyer, Peacock & Co. The latter became the forerunners of a very numerous class, of which one is now preserved in operating condition, and used for special trains. At the time of their introduction they were the most powerful passenger engines in Holland and this, it should be emphasized, was possible only by the arrangement of the cylinders.

In 1907 the first 'Pacific' for a European railway was completed, a de Glehn compound for the Paris-Orléans Railway. It was a large and powerful engine with coupled wheels 6 ft 0¾ in. diameter, for use on the heavily graded line south of Limoges, where the main route to Toulouse passes through the country of the Massif Central. It was followed in 1908 by two further 'Pacific' designs, one built by the Western Railway of France at the Sotteville Works near Rouen, and the other by G. J. Churchward, for the Great Western Railway. The second French 4-6-2 had a cylinder arrangement that was the reverse of de Glehn's practice, and had the low pressure cylinders outside. It was a huge engine distinguished externally by an enormous extended smokebox. The Great Western engine, *The Great Bear*, was really an exercise in boiler design. Churchward had been so impressed with the smooth riding and easy action of the four-cylinder de Glehn compound 'Atlantics' that he had decided upon four cylinders, with divided drive, for his own high speed express engines; and half anticipa-

Netherlands State Railways: one of the 'Atlantic' type express locomotives used on the Flushing mail trains.

ting that a 4-6-0 would not be enough for the traffic of the future built an experimental 'Pacific' with the same engine layout as his standard four-cylinder 4-6-0s. The need for such a large engine did not however eventuate.

In the meantime American development at about the same time is typified by the K2 class 'Pacific' of the Pennsylvania, introduced in 1911, with 24 in. by 26 in. cylinders, and a total heating surface of 4,620 sq. ft. This class represented the climax of the non-superheater passenger locomotive in the USA, and only four years later the very famous K4 'Pacific', superheated, had cylinders no less than 27 in. diameter by 28 in. stroke, and a tractive effort of 44,400 lb. On the continent of Europe many new 'Pacific' designs were introduced between 1909 and 1912, in Belgium, the various French railways, Germany, Italy and Spain, while in Austria Herr Gölsdorf produced his very handsome 2-6-4s. Most of these were compounds; but one of the most distinctive, and undoubtedly the ugliest, was that of M. J. B. Flamme, for the Belgian State Railways, due to all four cylinders being located ahead of the smokebox and covered by an extensive flat platform. But the most remarkable European locomotives of the period were two experimental 4-6-4 four-cylinder compounds designed by M. du Bousquet, for the Northern Railway of France, but not completed until he had retired and had been succeeded by M. Georges Asselin. They were introduced in 1911, but like the Churchward 'Pacific' were somewhat in advance of their time, and were not developed.

The introduction of superheating in Great Britain had originally been slow, but it received a tremendous fillip in 1910, following some interchange running between the London Brighton and South Coast, and London and North Western Railways, between Rugby and Brighton. A 4-4-2 tank engine of the LB & SCR fitted with the Schmidt superheater had shown remarkable economy in working,

Netherlands State Railways: four-cylinder 4-6-0 express locomotive (British built) with all four cylinders driving on to the leading coupled axle.

The first British 'Pacific': *The Great Bear* built at Swindon (GWR) in 1908, by G. J. Churchward.

albeit with relatively light trains, and C. J. Bowen-Cooke, who had become Chief Mechanical Engineer of the LNWR in 1909, built for trial a new 4-4-0, generally of the 'Precursor' type but with an improved front end, piston valves, and a Schmidt superheater. The improvement over the 'Precursor' both in economy and increased performance was little short of sensational. The new engine, named *George the Fifth* after the new monarch on the throne of the United Kingdom in 1910, ran a fast test trip from Euston to Crewe on 24 July of that year with a 357 ton train, at an average speed of more than 60 mph, but later engines of the class consistently improved upon this standard of running with still heavier trains, while showing an economy of about 25 per cent on the coal consumption standards of the 'Precursor' type. Moreover, while there had been a wave of larger engine building, with 4-4-2 and 4-6-0 types in the period 1906–9, the success of the 'George the Fifth' class brought a revival in building of 4-4-0s, now of course superheated. In relation to the modest size of the engines concerned, weighing no more than 64 tons without tenders, the performance daily between Euston and Crewe in the period 1910–15 was some of the finest and most economical in the world.

James Holden's 'Decapod', shortlived though it was, with its three-cylinder engine layout and cranks at 120 degrees, proved the starting point of an important line of British practice. The even turning movement and six exhausts per revolution were very effective in starting heavy loads from rest, and on the Great Central Railway J. G. Robinson adopted it for some very large 0-8-4 tank engines built for propelling coal trains over the humps in the large freight concentration yard at Wath near Barnsley, Yorkshire. Wilson Worsdell followed in 1909, with some three-cylinder 4-8-0 tanks for similar work in the Erimus Yard,

Pennsylvania Railroad: one of the earliest 'Pacifics'; two-cylinder simple with a tractive effort of 33,400 lb. The huge firegrate had an area of 61·8 sq. ft.

near Middlesbrough. Vincent Raven, who succeeded Worsdell as Chief Mechanical Engineer of the North Eastern Railway in 1910, applied the three-cylinder principle to express passenger 4-4-2s, and to 4-4-4 and 4-6-2 tank engines, all within the period of this chapter; but it was H. N. Gresley, then on the Great Northern, and later the very celebrated Chief Mechanical Engineer of the London and North Eastern Railway, who developed the principle to its most successful extent, as will be related in further chapters of this book.

It is interesting to reflect upon the changing trends of world practice towards the close of this present period, for which British engineers seemed to be veering towards multi-cylindered single-expansion locomotives. In the USA the complications of compounding were being abandoned and the fashion was setting definitely towards the simplest of all engine layouts – two cylinders only, with outside Walschaerts valve gear. Furthermore, in England the outstanding success of the superheater 'George the Fifth' class 4-4-0s on the LNWR was in many quarters regarded as giving the final *coup de grâce* to the compound, which was inclined to be regarded as an alternative rather than an allied method of securing higher thermal efficiency. In this atmosphere, despite what was currently happening in France, the fitting of one of the Midland three-cylinder compounds with a superheater in July 1913 passed almost unnoticed. Yet it was the first step towards a remarkable phase in later British locomotive history. Another method of increasing thermal efficiency is by heating the feed water to the boiler, and some very interesting work towards this end was done on the Egyptian State Railways by Frederick Harvey Trevithick, another grandson of the great Cornish pioneer. One of the standard 4-4-0 express locomotives fitted with Schmidt superheater and Trevi-

Imperial Royal Austrian State Railways: a Gölsdorf four-cylinder compound 2-6-4 express locomotive.

thick's high degree feed water heater not only showed a considerable advantage in consumption of coal per ton mile as compared with a superheater engine without heater, but a still more pronounced advantage over a de Glehn compound 'Atlantic' several of which had been purchased from France in the early 1900s. Taking the coal per ton mile of Trevithick's latest engine as unity, the following was the proportionate order of merit:

1	4-4-0	Schmidt superheater and the Trevithick's heaters	1·0
2	4-4-0	Schmidt superheater without heaters	1·28
3	4-4-2	De Glehn compound	1·58
4	4-4-0	Standard non-superheater without heaters	1·82

Of course the fitting of the high degree feed water heaters increased the cost, but as will be seen from the above comparison the reduction in fuel consumption in equal work was striking.

Reverting to British practice, the application of superheating to the standard LNWR 4-4-0 had a success far beyond what had been anticipated at Crewe and the power developed was somewhat in excess of what the chassis would sustain. From the moment of his appointment as Chief Mechanical Engineer in 1909, C. J. Bowen-Cooke was indeed thinking in terms of much larger express passenger locomotives. Unlike many of his colleagues he was very much aware of, and interested in, European continental practice, and he had noted the circumstances in which relatively large four-cylinder 4-6-0s had been introduced on two of the Dutch railways, with the full approbation of the civil engineers; and he began planning an engine with a similar layout of machinery. Unfortunately the civil engineer of the LNWR was not receptive to the proposal of considerably heavier axle loads, even though the effect on the track at high speed, with perfect dynamic balance, would have been very much less than that of the 'George the Fifth' class 4-4-0, which had a substantial hammer blow effect. So the design of the new LNWR 4-6-0s had to be modified, by use of a smaller boiler than was originally intended.

Nevertheless the locomotives of the 'Sir Gilbert Claughton' class, the first of which took the road in 1913, were capable of a high output of power, and very fast running, and in some tests carried out in November 1913, the indicated horsepower recorded was the highest of any British locomotive up to that time, namely 1,669, at a speed of 70 mph. This was no isolated effort, but made during a 35 minute spell of hard steaming in which successive indicator cards showed outputs of 1,504, 1,407, 1,494, 1,526, 1,669, 1,606, 1,593 and 1,496 horsepower. Towards the conclusion of this strenuous effort the steaming continued to be very free, with the boiler pressure at 170 lb. per sq. in. and the steam chest pressure 156 lb. per sq. in. The basic dimensions of

LNWR. One of the 'George the Fifth' class superheater 4-4-0s of 1910. The engine illustrated is named *Coronation*, in honour of the crowning of King George V in 1911.

One of the earliest British three-cylinder simple locomotives: North Eastern 4-8-0 tank, for hump shunting at Erimus Yard, Middlesbrough.

LNWR. One of the first four-cylinder 4-6-0s of the 'Claughton' class, working a 460 ton express near Harrow, part of a daily round trip of 387 miles, in 1913.

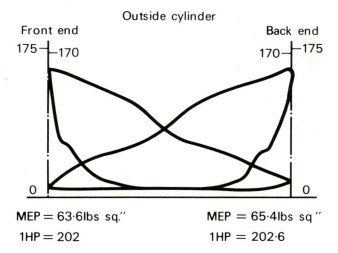
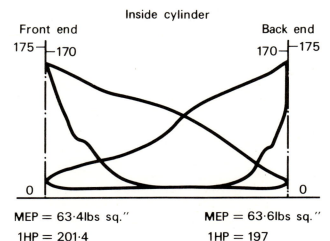

LNWR. Indicator diagrams taken from LNWR 4-6-0 engine No. 1159, at 58 mph on Shap Incline.

these locomotives were, cylinders 15¾ in. diameter, by 26 in. stroke; coupled wheels 6 ft 9 in. diameter; total heating surface 2,232 sq. ft, including 413·6 sq. ft in the superheater; grate area 30·5 sq. ft and boiler pressure 175 lb. per sq. in. How much better they might have been with the boiler originally designed for them must remain a matter for conjecture; but up to the outbreak of war in August 1914, they held the British record for maximum power output.

Articulated locomotive development

Little has so far been said in this book about freight locomotives. In the nineteenth century on railways in most parts of the world passenger working made the most severe demands upon both men and machines, and a high proportion of the attention of designers and manufacturers was concentrated upon locomotives for such duties. But by the turn of the century circumstances were changing, particularly in North America. The fitting of all vehicles with the Westinghouse automatic air brake enabled very much longer and heavier trains to be operated, and freight locomotive development began to partake of a practice of its own, rather than production of smaller wheeled, multi-coupled versions of the contemporary express passenger designs. It was a change all the more significant because for many years in North America the 4-4-0 with outside cylinders and compensated suspension had been the veritable maid of all work. But early in the present century, while passenger locomotives were passing from the 4-4-0 to the 'Atlantic', and then to the 'Pacific' type, freight engines were increasing in size from the 2-8-0 to the 2-8-2. This latter, beginning from a design created in 1905 by ALCO for the Northern Pacific Railway, became extremely popular in the USA, with cylinders increasing from the 24 in. by 30 in.

When however a move was made to enlarge the basic freight locomotive from the 2-8-2 to the 2-10-2 type, it did not meet with the same success. The first of the latter type did actually precede the first 2-8-2 by three years, and was embodied in a large tandem compound built by the Baldwin Locomotive Works in 1903, for the Atchison, Topeka and Santa Fe Railway. It was first shown to the public and tested on the stationary plant at the St Louis Exposition in 1904. But the tracking qualities of this large engine were not good, and few were built other than for the Santa Fe.

Canadian Pacific Railway: 0-6-6-0 compound Mallet articulated locomotive, one of five built at Angus shops, Montreal, in 1909–11, for rear-end banking on the Field Hill and in Rogers Pass, British Columbia.

In 1915, however, the development of lateral control devices for the leading and trailing trucks led to a revival of the type and some impressive examples were built in 1918 for the New York, New Haven and Hartford. Nevertheless the 'Santa Fe', as the type became known, large though it could be built, did not provide the entire answer to the kind of freight traffic that was developing on such railways as the Chesapeake and Ohio, the Norfolk and Western, and on the Chicago, Milwaukee, St Paul and Pacific; and attention turned to the Mallet compound articulated type.

The development was one of the many that had their origin from the St Louis Exposition of 1904. The first locomotive of the 0-6-6-0 type to be built in the USA was to the order of the Baltimore and Ohio Railroad. It created much interest at St Louis but, because of the short wheelbase of each engine unit, proved to be unstable on the road, and unsuited to anything but rear-end banking and hump shunting work, in which the speeds were low. Like all true Mallets it was a compound, designed on similar lines to the many that were then operating on the continent of Europe. It had nevertheless a very high tractive effort of 71,500 lb. and clearly demonstrated what could be done with an articulated locomotive once the principle was successfully adapted to running, as distinct from yard conditions. The B. & O. No. 2400, non-superheated, with a boiler pressure of 235 lb. per sq. in., had a large boiler with a total heating surface of 5,586 sq. ft and a grate area of 72·2 sq. ft. The cylinder diameters were 20 in. high pressure, and 32 in. low pressure, with a common stroke of 32 in. Apart from the absence of any leading or trailing trucks the instability was also due to top-heaviness, because the large boiler was pitched very high to accommodate the firebox above the rear (high pressure) engine. Despite these disadvantages in a prototype unit, the locomotive did undoubtedly point

Articulated locomotive development

the way to a new conception of power for heavy freight operation.

The articulated steam locomotive began its real advance towards successful main line running service in the USA in 1906, with the production by the Baldwin Locomotive Works of the first 2-6-6-2 Mallet compound, for the Great Northern Railway. This epoch-marking locomotive did not have so high a tractive effort as the B. & O. 0-6-6-0 through using a lower boiler pressure of 200 lb. per sq. in. Again the firebox was placed above the 4 ft 9 in. driving wheels of the high pressure engine; but the locomotive as a whole was vastly superior as a vehicle and, when developed from 1910 onwards to have the firebox entirely in rear of the driving wheels, the 2-6-6-2 became the most popular and widely produced articulated type in the USA. The Great Northern engines of 1906 were not superheated. The cylinders were $21\frac{1}{2}$ in. diameter high pressure and 33 in. low pressure; the stroke of both was 32 in., and the boiler had 5,658 sq. ft of heating surface, and a grate area of 78 sq. ft. The valve gear was Walschaerts operating flat slide valves on top of the cylinders. The tractive effort when working compound was 64,400 lb.

These compound Mallets were no greyhounds. They were at their best in heavy slogging freight haulage at about 20 to 25 mph. They rode well on curving stretches of line, and had good starting characteristics, because provision was made to admit live steam directly into the low pressure cylinders in such circumstances. While this method could not be used for more than a few minutes without denuding the boiler, it was generally considered to provide about 20 per cent extra tractive effort for the immediate start from rest. Although having different detail features the various designs of 2-6-6-2 built in large numbers for American railroads up to about 1920 were generally similar in their basic proportions. A comparison in dimensions may be made as in Table 12.1.

From 1909 articulated locomotives of the 2-8-8-2 type began to be built in the USA. The first was supplied to the

Table 12.1

Date	1906	1915
Railroad	Great Northern	Chesapeake and Ohio
Cylinders H.P. dia., in.	$21\frac{1}{2}$	22
L.P. dia., in.	33	35
stroke, in.	32	32
Coupled wheel dia., ft in.	4–7	4–8
Total heating surface, sq. ft	5,658	5,875*
Grate area, sq. ft	78	72·2
Boiler pressure, p.s.i.	200	210
Tractive effort, lb.	64,400	76,100

*Including superheater, 975 sq. ft.

Chicago, Burlington and Quincy Railroad, a powerful compound Mallet of 1909, of the 2-6-6-2 type.

Southern Pacific, and afterwards it became quite generally adopted on the majority of railroads having mountain divisions. Again it was a slow speed type, rarely being required to exceed 25 mph. The driving wheels rarely exceeded 4 ft 9 in. diameter, and even at medium road speed the piston speed, particularly in the large low pressure cylinders, resulted in high maintenance charges. Nevertheless, for many years the American railroads, while strongly inclining to the two-cylinder simple in non-articulated types, remained faithful to the compound in the heavy freight Mallets.

Comparative dimensions in Table 12.2 of the pioneer 2-8-8-2 of 1909, and a Rio Grande development of 1923 show the manner in which the type was enlarged, while still retaining the compound principle.

Table 12.2

Date	1909	1923
Railroad	Southern Pacific	Denver & Rio Grande Western
Cylinders H.P. dia., in.	26	25
L.P. dia., in.	40	39
stroke, in.	30	32
Coupled wheel dia., ft in.	4–9	4–9
Total heating surface, sq. ft	5,173	7,701 *
Grate area, sq. ft	68·4	96·5
Boiler pressure, p.s.i.	200	240
Tractive effort, lb.	85,400	106,600

*Including superheater, 1,582 sq. ft.

Baltimore and Ohio, a large 2-8-8-0 non-compound Mallet of 1918. The size of the cylinders driving the rear group of wheels will be particularly noted.

An isolated but interesting articulated locomotive of 1911 that was not compound was No. 3396 of the Pennsylvania Railroad; also a 2-8-8-2 but with four cylinders 27 in. diameter by 28 in. stroke all taking live steam. The driving wheel diameter was 4 ft 8 in., and the boiler provided a combined total heating surface of 7,382 sq. ft, with a grate area of 96·5 sq. ft. The boiler pressure of 160 lb. per sq. in. was relatively low, and the tractive effort 99,200 lb. Although it was quite successful in running, the American railway world was apparently not ready for large non-compound articulateds, and it was not until many years later that current practice changed to the non-compound rather than the compound type.

American-built compound articulated locomotives were exported to a number of countries. Among the most interesting was a large 2-6-6-2 built by the Baldwin Locomotive Works for the North Western Railway of India operating on the 5 ft 6 in. gauge. It was intended for experimental running on the 1 in 25 gradients of the Bolan Pass in the Quetta division where it was worked in competition with

Union Pacific Railroad: a typical example of the great proportions attained by the American compound Mallets. Note the enormous low pressure cylinder, in front, the intermediate receiver pipe, and the Westinghouse cross-compound air brake pump in duplicate.

an English-built articulated locomotive of the Beyer-Garratt type. The Mallet was of somewhat smaller proportions than the American examples of the 2-6-6-2 type previously referred to, having cylinder 19 in. diameter high pressure, and 29½ in. low pressure, each with a stroke of 30 in., and the nominal tractive effort was 52,587 lb. Although inclined to slip on a bad rail, this large engine worked on the Bolan Pass section for eight years, and was then transferred to the Rawalpindi division, where it took freight trains of double the tonnage worked by the ordinary 2-8-0 freight engines of the North Western Railway.

Mallet compound articulated locomotives were also built by British manufacturers for service overseas, including some very large units for the 3 ft 6 in. gauge South African Railways. The Mallet principle was popular on this latter line, so much so that when the proposals to operate the rival form of articulated locomotive of the Beyer-Garratt type were made the protagonists of the latter found themselves up against much prejudiced thinking. This was surprising, because although steep gradients involving lengthy spells of hard collar work are ideal ground for a compound Mallet, the curvature experienced on some of the metre gauge lines in South Africa and elsewhere is certainly not ideal when the overall length of the locomotive, without its tender, exceeds 60 ft. Furthermore, while the compound principle offers much in the way of theoretical advantages, the distance between the high pressure and low pressure cylinders, often more than 20 ft, involves pressure drop and loss of temperature. The ideal situation in the working of a compound engine is for an equal amount of work to be done in the high and low pressure cylinders; but knowing how difficult it is to attain that ideal, even with such compact and well designed an engine as a de Glehn compound, one can only guess at what was happening in the low pressure cylinders of a large compound Mallet. Interesting examples of the type were built by the North British Locomotive Company for Burma, Uganda and China, in addition to the very large locomotives for South Africa, the performance of which latter is referred to later.

Ever since the day of the Semmering Trials locomotive engineers have been contriving different methods of articulation, to get round sharp curves. Engines of the double-boiler Fairlie type continued to be built in small numbers down to the year 1910, while the project of John Haswell of Weiner Neustadt, having two motor bogies supporting a single boiler, continued, albeit spasmodically, into the twentieth century in the form of the Kitson-Meyer articulated locomotive. It was left to a British engineer, H. W. Garratt, to put that touch of genius, that is combined with utter simplicity in all great inventions, to the problem of the articulated locomotive, and achieve a solution that was very near to the ultimate ideal for steam operation in mountainous and difficult terrain. He took the double bogie idea of the Kitson-Meyer, but instead of having a single frame mounted across the two bogies he carried the boiler

A 3 ft. 6 in. gauge British-built Mallet, 0-6-6-0 type, for the Kenya and Uganda Railway where the gradient is 1 in 50. In the 1920s the rail gauge was changed to metres.

on a separate cradle slung between. The boiler could be enlarged in size independently of what was underneath, because in Garratt's proposal there was not anything. His original patent dates from June 1908, and the manufacturing rights were taken up by Beyer, Peacock & Co. a year later. Whether Garratt himself foresaw the use to which his type of locomotive would be so happily applied is doubtful, because his original drawing shows large diameter driving wheels such as would be fitted to a fast running express passenger engine.

The first Beyer-Garratt locomotive was a tiny little thing, for the 2 ft gauge sections of the Tasmanian Railways. It was a compound with high pressure cylinders no more than 11 in. diameter and 16 in. stroke, and a total weight in working order of only $33\frac{1}{2}$ tons. It was of the 0-4-0+0-4-0 type. It was not long however before larger and more powerful Beyer-Garratt locomotives were supplied for 3 ft 6 in. gauge lines in Australia. In 1912 two interesting designs were prepared for the Tasmanian Government Railways. The goods engine was of the 2-6-2+2-6-2 type, each unit being driven by two cylinders 15 in. diameter by 22 in. stroke; but the passenger engines, of which two were initially built, were unusual in that the power units each had four cylinders. The wheel arrangement was 4-4-2+2-4-4, with coupled wheels 5 ft in diameter, and the eight cylinders 12 in. diameter by 20 in. stroke. These locomotives were expressly designed for the attainment of speeds of 50 mph on the straight parts of the line. They rode so smoothly and ran so freely that the crews were sometimes misled as to the speed at which they travelled, and on one occasion in 1916 this led to a serious accident. But they certainly demonstrated in no uncertain manner the effectiveness

South African Railways: 2-6-6-0 Mallet compound, built by North British Locomotive Company, for rear-end banking service on the Hex River Pass, Cape Province.

of the Beyer-Garratt type, though the process of evolution lay in heavy haulage of freight on steep gradients rather than express passenger service.

In the meantime the development of the Mallet type of locomotive was approaching its climax in South Africa, in two fine examples built by the North British Locomotive Company. The first, which was of the 2-6-6-0 type, was designed for rear-end banking of heavy trains in the Hex River Pass, Cape Province. They were essentially slow-speed engines, but having no trailing truck the firebox had to be accommodated above the wheels of the hind engine. It was skilfully designed, of the Belpaire type, and as will be seen from Table 12.3, had a grate area of 40 sq. ft. The South African Railways are fortunate in having ample supplies of good quality locomotive coal in the Transvaal. The second type was a veritable giant for the 3 ft 6 in. gauge, designed for working heavy freight trains over the severely graded section of the Natal main line between Durban and Cato Ridge. They were the largest tender locomotives ever to run on the 3 ft 6 in. gauge.

Table 12.3 gives a rather modest estimate of the tractive capacity, which the builders quote at no more than 50 per cent boiler pressure. With single expansion superheater engines it is usually calculated at 85 per cent of boiler pressure. At 75 per cent the tractive effort of the 'MH' was 65,000 lb.

In 1921 a large engine of the Beyer-Garratt type, with the wheel arrangement 2-6-0+0-6-2, was purchased for trial, and tested against one of the 'MH' Mallets in Natal. While the extent of the severe climbing out of Durban is usually considered to extend to Cato Ridge, it is in the 27 miles from South Coast Junction to Botha's Hill that the ascent averages 1 in 58 throughout. It includes gradients 1 in 30, on a 300 ft radius curve. The Garratt engine, although having a tractive effort at 75 per cent boiler pressure of 47,385 lb. had very much the best of it in the first set of trials, and the report of the engineer-observer in charge was so enthusiastic as to cause displeasure to the Chief Mechanical Engineer. At the beginning, 'top level' sentiment was very much on the side of the Mallet. Despite the fact that the Garratt pulled a heavier load up the bank in less time than the Mallet, the Chief Mechanical Engineer defended the latter as being vastly superior to the Garratt in the design of its wheelbase. Nevertheless, far from dismissing the Garratt he proposed a spell of three months continuous working, under close observation, between Durban and Cato Ridge. By December 1921, in the light of this experience, the atmosphere was clearly changing, and the report of the Acting Superintendent (Mechanical) to

Table 12.3 South African Railway Mallets

Class	'MJ'	'MH'
Type	2-6-6-0	2-6-6-2
Cylinders H.P. dia., in.	$16\frac{1}{2}$	20
L.P. dia., in.	26	$31\frac{1}{2}$
stroke, in.	24	26
Coupled wheel dia., ft in.	$3-6\frac{1}{2}$	4–0
Total evaporative heating surface, sq. ft	1,913	3,211
Superheater, sq. ft	398	616
Grate area, sq. ft	40	53
Boiler pressure, p.s.i.	200	200
Tractive effort at 50% boiler pressure, lb.	30,740	43,330

South African Railways: the 'GA' class Beyer-Garratt 2-6-0+0-6-2 of 1921. The successful contender in the 1922 trials against the 'MH' 2-6-6-2 Mallet.

the Assistant General Manager (Durban) was definitely favourable. While only local interests were immediately involved, these tests ultimately proved of the utmost importance, both for the Beyer-Garratt type and for the future development of the Mallet on a worldwide basis.

The result was a great triumph for the Garratt. The three-month trial was carried out in February, March and April 1922 between Ladysmith and Glencoe Junction, a distance of 44 miles, and each engine made 59 round trips, an aggregate of 5,104 miles. The average loads hauled were approximately the same, 830 tons with the Garratt and 820 with the Mallet, but despite its smaller size and lower nominal tractive effort, the Garratt burned 125 lb. of coal per mile against 143 lb. by the Mallet. Even if the performance had been equal in actual haulage of the loads, this economy in coal consumption of some 12 per cent, equal to a saving of roughly three-quarters of a ton on each round trip, would have been a most convincing demonstration; but this was not all. Detailed timings were taken of the work done on the three worst banks. There were two of these on the up journey, and one on the down, and the total time taken on these difficult sections – aggregate for 58 trips – was 5,358 minutes by the Mallet, yet only 4,130 minutes with the Garratt. This was an astonishing result, especially considering that it was achieved on a coal consumption 12 per cent in favour of the Garratt. It sounded the death knell of the Mallet type in South Africa, and indeed in all countries of the British Empire.

Apart from its superior tracking qualities the outstanding advantage of the Garratt was that the central cradle, unencumbered by any machinery below, enabled a boiler of ideal proportions to be used. The requisite heating surface could be obtained by a very large diameter barrel, and a relatively short distance between the tube plates. The firebox could be made large and wide, yet compact, and in consequence large locomotives of the Beyer-Garratt type were free in steaming. The immense length of the Mallet boiler was partly offset by a long combustion chamber at the firebox end, but even so the distance between the tube plates was 22 ft, against 11 ft $8\frac{1}{4}$ in. on the Garratt. The total heating surfaces of the two boilers was roughly the same, though in defence of the Mallet it must be added that it was not superheated, and therefore that the comparison was not entirely 'like for like'. In addition to a great difference in the form of articulation, it was a case of a non-superheated compound against a superheated simple, and the answer, in all round terms, was entirely convincing. Furthermore, the Garratt rode more steadily on the 3 ft 6 in. gauge track, and on favourable stretches of line attained as much as 40 mph. Those responsible would not have dared to try and run the immensely long Mallet at such speeds.

There is of course no doubt that the exigencies of the 3 ft 6 in. gauge hampered the basic design of the Mallet as much as they favoured the Garratt, when it came to the production of very large locomotives. There was no diminution in the production of even larger examples of the Mallet type in the USA, where the combination of 4 ft $8\frac{1}{2}$ in. gauge, and a generous loading gauge, enabled large boilers of good proportions to be fitted. For some time however there was a significant difference between the use of articulated locomotives in the USA and elsewhere. In the former it continued to be applied to slow, heavy slogging freight service, whereas the Garratt was gradually developed as an all-purpose locomotive, for passenger and freight alike. Reference has already been made to the eight-cylinder 4-4-2+2-4-4 locomotives on the 3 ft 6 in. gauge of the Tasmanian Government Railways; another early Garratt, designed purely for express passenger service, was a very handsome 2-4-0+0-4-2 built for the 5 ft 3 in. gauge

San Paulo Railway: the express passenger Garratt built in 1915, for the 5 ft 3 in. gauge system.

San Paulo (Brazilian) Railway in 1915. This was most successful and led to the introduction later of much larger Garratts on that railway, especially for express running. The development in parallel, as it were, of the Mallet in the USA, and of the Beyer-Garratt, reaching eventually to colossal proportions, embodied some of the highest skills in locomotive designing in the entire steam era, as will be told later in this book.

13 Rack railways

This chapter can well come as a holiday interlude: a pause in the tale of incessant demands for greater and more efficient main line power and the constant frustrations of commuter service. It takes us into wide open spaces, and great heights; yet strangely enough in its beginnings it poses once again the age old question as to which came first, the chicken or the egg! At the root of it lies the fundamental reality of adhesion, which can be as big a headache to the designers of modern high powered electric locomotives as it was to Richard Trevithick, floundering along the Penydaren plateway with his ponderous 'tram-wagon'. It was to secure more reliable adhesion that Blenkinsop adapted the rack and pinion to railway traction, but as I have told earlier in this book his first essay proved cumbersome, expensive and slow, on a railway that did not involve any very difficult gradients; and apart from an experiment at the Dowlais Iron Works in South Wales in 1832, the idea of rack and pinion working progressed no further in Great Britain. But in the USA an experimental line had been laid down in 1847, though no other practical application came until twenty years later.

An American engineer, Sylvester Marsh by name, took the Blenkinsop principle and made a much simpler application by having a 'ladder' in the middle of the running track with circular rungs, and anchoring it securely to the sleepers on which the running rails were mounted. His experiments with this were so successful that in 1869 a so-called cogwheel railway was opened climbing to the summit of Mount Washington, 6,293 ft above sea level, and the highest point in the White Mountains, in New England. It was an extraordinarily venturesome project at that period in railway history, but although its rack and pinion arrangement has long been superseded elsewhere by more sophisticated forms this pioneer rack railway has with-

The Mount Washington cog railway: one of the curious little steam locomotives in action, photographed in 1971, near the base station.

Mount Washington cog railway: complicated trackwork at Marshfield base station.

stood the test of time and apart from one year during the First World War, and three years during the Second World War, it has been in continuous operation ever since – and still with steam locomotives. Whether the idea of a railway up Mount Washington came first and Marsh invented his cogwheel track to meet the need, or whether the railway was conceived as a means of demonstrating his invention, seems obscure; but from whatever reason it originated, the Mount Washington railway remains a world pioneer.

In the meantime the locomotive engineer of the Central Railway of Switzerland, Nicklaus Riggenbach, had, in 1863, taken out a patent for railway traction by rack and pinion. This was a little surprising, for his own line had fairly flat gradients, although running through valleys that were flanked by some high mountains. Having taken out the patent however he took no further steps to follow it up, even to the extent of making a trial layout, until 1869, when he heard of the opening of the Mount Washington railway. Then he went to the USA, as quickly as transatlantic transport of those days could take him, to see Marsh's enterprise for himself. His own patent covered a

Rack railways 155

rack with more particularly shaped rungs in the ladder than Marsh's round bars; these were trapezoidal in shape, and on his return to Switzerland Riggenbach built a short section of rack and pinion railway in some quarries near Bern. The results were so encouraging that a full scale experiment was next considered.

Whatever may have been the origin of the Mount Washington line, there is no doubt about Riggenbach's development. The idea, and its patenting, came well before any actual application, and after the small quarry experiment, he and his friends began looking round Switzerland for a suitable mountain to climb. Whether they realized what a superb tourist attraction they were initiating is doubtful. Europe was in a very troubled state at the time, from the shattering upheaval of the Franco-Prussian War of 1870–1; but financial prospects or not Riggenbach and his friends decided upon the Rigi, the magnificent and conveniently isolated peak overlooking the Lake of Lucerne, and with its base skirted by a main line of railway. A concession was readily granted by the Canton of Lucerne, and work was pushed ahead with such vigour that a section of the line was opened to the public in May 1871. This line up the Rigi had a fairly constant gradient, not exceeding 1 in 5, whereas the Mount Washington line, most of which was built on timber trestle viaducts, had an average steepness of 1 in 4, and a maximum on the spectacular Jacob's Ladder trestle, of 1 in 2·7.

This considerable variation in the steepness of ascent led to a remarkable design of steam locomotive for the Mount Washington. In order to compensate for the changes in inclination the boiler was not only made vertical but mounted on a horizontal axis, so that it remained vertical no matter what the gradient of the track might be. Steam was taken from connections at the top, and passed to fixed pipes through revolving glands on the line of the boiler

One of the original locomotives of the Vitznau–Rigi, the first cogwheel rack railway in Europe.

pivots. Fortunately this remarkable locomotive, the *Peppersass*, has been preserved, and is on permanent display at the base station, Marshfield. On his visit to America in 1869 Riggenbach saw old *Peppersass* in action, but although he decided on a similar locomotive for the Rigi the greater uniformity of gradient enabled him to avoid the complication of the pivoted boiler. One of the original Rigi locomotives is preserved in the Swiss Museum of Transport by the lakeside near Lucerne.

The great success of both the American and the Swiss rack railways as tourist attractions led to the promoting of more, both in Europe and elsewhere, while engineers, mindful of the terrible results that might follow a derailment, sought greater means of safety in the connection

The Pilatus rack railway, Switzerland: the steepest in the world. A model of one of the original locomotives with boiler athwartships.

Later type of steam locomotive on the Vitznau–Rigi Railway, with boiler inclined to the line of the track.

between the locomotives and the track. One of these was invented by Edouard Locher, and used on the most breathtaking mountain railway yet constructed, up Mount Pilatus, on the opposite side of Lake Lucerne from the Rigi. In Locher's system there is a double-sided rack, with teeth extending horizontally instead of vertically and engaging with pinions on each side. The central support, on which the rack was mounted, also served as a guide for the locomotive, which had smooth rollers mounted on the same vertical axle as the driving pinions. The carrying wheels of the locomotive were flangeless, and had no other function. The boilers of the original locomotives were mounted athwart the frames – yet another method of dealing with the exceptional inclination of the track. The Pilatus railway climbed 5,344 ft in $2\frac{5}{8}$ miles, involving an average gradient of 1 in 2·6, and a maximum of 1 in 2. On such gradients the ladder form of track used by Marsh and Riggenbach would not have been safe.

It was not long before a simpler type of steam locomotive was devised for the less steeply graded rack railways, with the boiler in line with the track as in a conventional steam locomotive but with its centre line inclined downwards from the cab, so that when climbing the mountains it was roughly horizontal. Locomotives of this type superseded those with vertical boilers on the Rigi, while a most unusual variety was introduced and became standard on the Mount Washington line. As on the Rigi they were required to propel only a single coach, but the American design provided for an individual drive on to two axles. The four cylinders were placed back to back, roughly in line with the steam dome, one pair driving forwards and the other to the rear. They drive on to jackshafts each carrying

Rack railways

Snowdon Mountain Railway, North Wales: one of the Swiss-built locomotives. The drive, through the pivoted lever at the front end, varied. On some locomotives the pivot was at the base and the drive taken intermediately through a connecting rod to the rear pair of coupled wheels.

a central pinion; these, through a 5 to 1 gear reduction, drive larger gear wheels that engage in the central ladder-rack in the middle of the track. I have been a fascinated spectator of these little engines in action, which are amazing to behold in that the piston rods are 'whizzing' backwards and forwards at a speed five times as fast as that of the actual speed of the locomotive. All braking is done by steam compression in the main engine cylinders. At the busiest times there are often four and five locomotives with their cars on the mountain at the same time. The cylinders are 8 in. diameter by 12 in. stroke, with a boiler pressure of 130 lb. per sq. in.

The locomotives of the Mount Washington cog railway are very small, with a total weight in working order of only 12 tons. The later Swiss locomotives, with inclined-forward boilers, were much larger and more powerful. Some interesting examples were built for the opening of the Snowdon Mountain Railway, North Wales, in 1895. These, to outward appearances, were of the 0-4-2 type, though actually it is the pinions for the rack rails, and not the road wheels that are driven. One of these locomotives was involved in a sensational accident on the day of the official opening of the railway in 1896. The pinions over-rode the rack on a high and very exposed ridge and the engine plunged down into the valley, 2,000 ft below. To guard against any repetition of such a disaster safety rails almost enclosing the rack were laid in. These rails interlock with grippers on the underside of the locomotives, and prevent it from riding up if the driving pinions should become disengaged from the rack. The line was opened to regular traffic in April 1897 and has operated successfully ever since.

Because of the need to keep the overall length of these mountain rack locomotives as short as possible, the arrangement of cylinders and running gear is unusual. The cylinders are placed rearward and drive forward to a rocking lever to which is attached a connection transmitting the power to a crank on the rear-coupled axle. The reverse arrangement was adopted in some interesting locomotives built for the Manitou and Pikes Peak Railway, Colorado, by the Baldwin Locomotive Works in 1890. These were Vauclain four-cylinder compounds, working at 200 lb. per sq. in. The cylinders were in line with the smokebox, and drove on to a rocking lever at the cab end. These were powerful little engines. The cylinders were 10 in. diameter high pressure, and 15 in. low pressure, with a stroke of 22 in., and the weight in working order was 28 tons.

Two very picturesque mountain railways in Austria are still operated by powerful little 0-4-2 tank engines of generally similar design to those of the Snowdon railway. The Scharfberg line, in the Salzkammergut district, climbs from St Wolfgang to the summit of the Scharfberg, providing magnificent views over the Wolfgangsee, and other lakes in the neighbourhood, while the Schneeberg has its base station at Puchberg in the most easterly ranges of the Alps, south of Vienna. The locomotives working on the latter line, which is part of the Austrian Federal Railways, are interesting in having been recently modernized by fitting Giesl ejectors, to which reference is made in their main line application, in a later chapter of this book.

In Switzerland application of the rack principle has not been confined to purely mountain climbing railways. Development of secondary lines, often passing through highly scenic and popular tourist areas, yet not having a sufficiently heavy traffic to justify construction of first class main lines, such as the Gotthard route, had neces-

Schneeberg Railway, Austria: one of the smart 0-4-2 tank locomotives (with Giesl ejector) at the summit station.

sarily to include severe gradients. By limited application of the rack principle constructional costs were greatly reduced, carrying the railways over high mountain passes without the need for long tunnels, or other expensive works. Gradients as steep as 1 in $8\frac{1}{2}$ or 1 in 9 have been included in through routes, worked by locomotives capable of operating by ordinary adhesion, or by rack and pinion. The metre-gauge Brünig Railway, which provides the important link between Lucerne and Interlaken, is of this kind, and with electric traction and well designed modern equipment the climbing speed on a gradient of 1 in $8\frac{1}{2}$ is about 20 mph. This is no 'one engine and car' operation. The trains are genuinely express, on the non-rack sections, and consist of fine, modern coaches, with refreshment cars included – for working over 1 in $8\frac{1}{2}$ gradients! With electric haulage the 46 miles between Lucerne and Interlaken are covered in about two hours.

Perhaps the most remarkable example of the combination of rack and adhesion working is provided by the route of the 'Glacier Express' running between St Moritz and Zermatt, a distance of 167½ miles, on the metre gauge. The changes in altitude alone give some idea of the extraordinarily switchback nature of the route. St Moritz station is 5,833 ft above sea level, and after the Albula Tunnel, at 5,982 ft, the line falls to 1,994 ft at Chur in the Rhine valley. Then it climbs to the Oberalp Pass, at 6,670 ft; descends to 4,710 ft at Andermatt, before climbing to the Furka Tunnel at 7,088 ft. Then comes a steep descent to Visp, in the Rhone valley, where the altitude is only 2,133 ft, followed by the final ascent to Zermatt, to finish 5,266 ft up. The electric locomotives of three different companies are involved in this run – the Rhaetian, as far as Disentis; next the Furka–Oberalp, and finally the Visp–Zermatt. Powerful locomotives were needed, although the coaches working over this route have been designed to special lightweight proportions. Elsewhere in Switzerland electrification of the purely all-rack railways has made a vast difference to the operation; for while the elimination of steam has removed some of the romance of these venturesome projects of the nineteenth century it has also greatly speeded up the operation.

An interesting if brief use of a rack railway was made on the North West Frontier of India during the 1880s. For urgent strategic reasons it was necessary to establish railway connection with Quetta, in Baluchistan, but the physical difficulties encountered were quite exceptionally severe. The chosen route lay up the desolate Bolan Pass, which could be dry and insufferably hot in the summer, and then subject to tremendous flooding in the rainy season. Bridges could be washed away, embankments scoured out, but in order to secure some form of communication, it was decided to lay a temporary metre gauge section through the worst area of the pass, in the stony bed of the river. Fairlie double-ended locomotives provided the power for this line with its maximum gradients of 1 in 23. From its completion in 1886 traffic flowed without hindrance, save for the inevitable delays through the break of gauge at each end of the metre gauge section. Matters were then sufficiently consolidated for a permanent 5 ft 6 in. gauge line to be constructed, on an improved alignment, higher up the hillside in the Dozan Gorge, the most treacherous part of the metre gauge line. It was this new section on 5 ft 6 in. gauge that was equipped on the rack principle.

The Abt type of rack was adopted, the same as that used for the Snowdon Mountain Railway and elsewhere, which differed from the Riggenbach in having a double set of rack teeth, with their projections staggered. On this Indian mountain stretch it was intended to operate it as a section in itself, not like the Brünig Railway, and the route eventually completed and used by the Swiss 'Glacier Express'. Special rack locomotives were obtained from Germany and on the through trains engines were changed at the beginning and end of the rack section. How long operation in this style would have continued we are not to know because in 1889, barely a year after its opening, the Bolan Pass was scourged by heavy flooding, and some of the bridges washed away. The damage was repaired and trains ran again, but in the following year conditions were infinitely worse, and the bridges were so completely smashed up that no trace of the girders remained after the floods had subsided. There was nothing for it but to survey and build a line on a different alignment altogether, and this latter did not include any rack section.

The two famous Indian mountain railways climbing to Darjeeling and Simla, although very steeply graded, are neither of them severe enough to require any rack sections, but in the south there is the narrow gauge Nilgiri Railway,

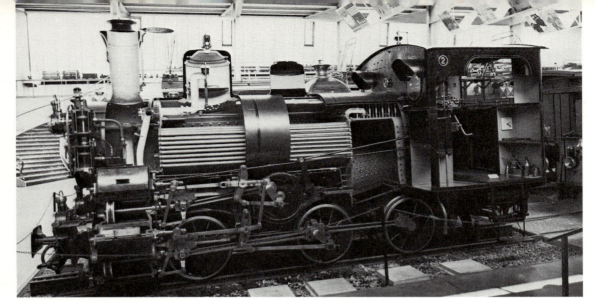

The four-cylinder compound type of rack locomotive developed by the Swiss Locomotive Works of Winterthur, for use on lines with both normal and rack working. It was first introduced on the Brünig Railway in 1909.

climbing to Ootacamund with many stretches of 1 in 12½ gradients. It begins with a junction with the broad gauge line from Madras at Mettupalaiyam, at an altitude of 1,071 ft, and ascends to its terminus, colloquially known as 'Ooty', 7,228 ft above sea level, in 28¾ miles. The rack section begins about 4¼ miles from the start and continues without a break for 12¼ miles. In that distance the line rises 4,363 ft, on continuous and severe curvature. The remaining 12 miles of the line, although including gradients as severe as 1 in 25, are worked by adhesion with the same locomotive running throughout. Unlike the Swiss, American and Welsh mountain rack railways, normal trains are operated, usually consisting of six coaches, and they are propelled on the upward journey by powerful steam locomotives.

Provision of motive power became the responsibility of the former South Indian Railway, and in 1911 consultations were held with the Swiss Locomotive Works, at Winterthur, and orders were placed for some very powerful 0-8-2 tank engines of special design, quite unlike the steam rack locomotives used elsewhere. They are four-cylinder compounds, but only work compound on the rack sections. The high pressure cylinders drive the road wheels, and on the non-rack sections the locomotives operate as two-cylinder simples, with 17¾ in. by 16¼ in. cylinders. With the change-over to compound working the low pressure cylinders, which are also outside, drive the rack pinions, and provide a boosting effect. This novel arrangement has proved very successful. The original engines of this type were delivered in 1920, but a further four of identical design were purchased as recently as 1952, and the line is still being operated by steam. The maximum load taken on the 1 in 12½ graded section is 100 tons. The locomotives themselves are massively constructed and weigh 48 tons in working order.

 Main line electrification

The growth of railway traffic in the early years of the twentieth century, particularly in freight, was becoming something of an embarrassment on certain lines. This embarrassment took two forms, one being the sheer haulage effort needed and the other that of line capacity. The situation was tending to become acute on routes where the gradients were severe and speeds were slow. Signalling was in many cases not so comprehensive or so complete as required by law in Great Britain, and the only way to increase the tonnage of freight passing was to run heavier trains. To particularize, the case of the Norfolk and Western Railway in the USA may be studied. In West Virginia, about 105 miles west of Roanoke, there is the severe Elkhorn Grade section, between Bluefield and Vivian, about 30 miles. There are long gradients of 1 in 75 and 1 in 50, and the problem of line occupation was complicated by the existence of a single-track section through the tunnel at the summit, which is 3,000 ft long. Traffic required the working of coal trains weighing 3,250 tons, and to operate these over the section *three* large Mallet compound steam locomotives were needed – two at the head end, and a pusher in rear up the steepest gradient, which extended for nearly 10 miles. Even with this powerful provision the speed of ascent was only about 7 or 8 mph.

Electrification of this difficult section was undertaken, and completed in 1915. The system adopted was 11,000 volts single-phase alternating current at 25 cycles per second; but the locomotives were then claimed to be unique in being equipped with phase converters, transforming the single-phase power from the overhead line to three-phase power for use in the induction type traction motors. Thus in this installation were retained the advantages of high voltage single-phase distribution and current collection; the advantages of three-phase induction motors

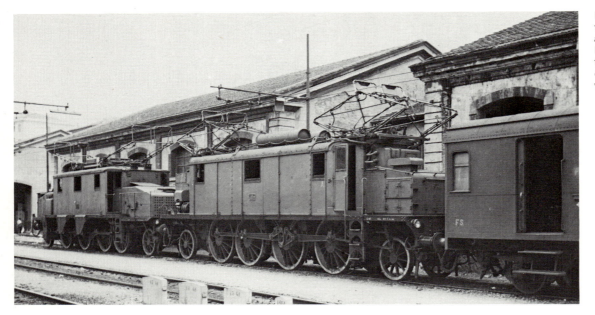

Italian State Railways: two 1-D-1 three-phase passenger locomotives at Ventimiglia, on the coastal main line between Genoa and the French frontier. These locomotives, introduced in 1925, operated on 3,300 volts.

for the mountain grade conditions were also obtained. Another important feature of such locomotives was that it was possible without the use of additional or complicated apparatus to utilize the locomotives themselves for electrically holding or braking the trains at constant speed while descending the steep gradients. It was one of the earliest examples of what is now called 'regenerative braking', utilizing the energy of the moving train to drive the traction motors as generators, and thus return electrical power to the overhead line.

The locomotives were arranged for operation in pairs. The diagram opposite shows one half, weighing 135 tons; the length of the complete twin unit was 105 ft. The speed of operation with the three-phase system being constant, provision was made for two speeds, 14 and 28 mph. To haul the maximum tonnage coal trains, one 270 ton twin combination was needed, instead of two Mallet steam locomotives, and on the steepest gradient a second electric locomotive was attached in rear. The rate of ascent, 14 mph, was however double that previously sustained with two Mallets at the head end and a third assisting in rear. The power plant and stud of new locomotives were designed to provide for an increase in the number of full load freight trains from 12 to 20 a day in the eastbound direction, in which the going was heaviest. At the same time power was available for providing assistance on the worst gradient for through passenger trains.

There was considerable difference of opinion between

164   Main line electrification

American railways as to what system was the best for main line electrification, and while the Norfolk and Western was installing 11,000 volts single-phase alternating current on its Elkhorn Grade division, the Chicago, Milwaukee, St Paul and Pacific chose 3,000 volts direct current, and by 1918 a total of 647 miles was electrified and operating in the severe climatic and grading conditions of the Rocky and Bitter Root Mountains. The original locomotives, weighing 265 tons, had fourteen axles, of which twelve were driven. They were used for hauling trains of 1,000 tons on gradients of 1 in 50 at a speed of 25 mph, and because of the very bad rail conditions often encountered, they were provided with a high factor of adhesion. The tractive effort required for this specified duty was 56,500 lb. – a drawbar pull of 25·2 tons, against an adhesion weight of 229 tons. This high adhesion factor of 9 per cent must be borne in mind against discussion of the performance of later electric locomotives. The 3,000 volt direct system was later adopted in Europe by both Belgium and Italy – interesting in the last mentioned case because the original installations used the three-phase alternating current system.

It is significant that nearly all the earliest installations of main line electrification were made on heavily graded routes, where the steam locomotive is at its most laborious, and least efficient. In chapter 12 of this book, I have described how the Mallet compound articulated locomotive was being developed to colossal proportions in the USA; but conditions that needed three and sometimes four of them on a single train, each with its own individual crew, were clearly approaching the limit. At a lower level of train loading the Swiss Federal Railway had a problem in the Gotthard line, but the most important pioneer work towards main line electrification in Europe came on the relatively small and independent Bern–Lötschberg–Simplon Railway. Reference has already been made to the pioneer work of Herr Huber-Stockar towards the introduction of single-phase alternating current, and as a preliminary to the equipment of the mountain section of the line, opened in 1913, the Lötschberg line converted the steam operated section between Spiez and Frutigen to electric traction, at 15,000 volts a.c. at a frequency of $16\tfrac{2}{3}$ cycles per second. The important difference between this experimental installation and that on the Norfolk and Western was that the traction motors were of the alternating current com-

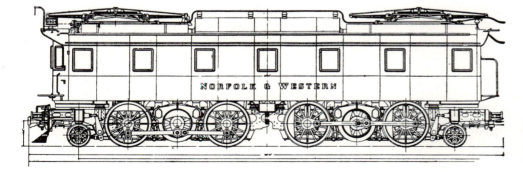

Norfolk and Western Railway: diagram of electric locomotive, taking power at 11,000 volts single phase from the overhead and through phase converters using three-phase traction motors.

Main line electrification

mutator type. This made use of a control circuit devised by another Swiss engineer, Herr Behn-Eschenburg in 1903, who found he could reduce to acceptable limits the commutation difficulties previously thought to be insuperable, providing that a current of low frequency was adopted. This offered immediate advantages for general railway electrification work.

The three-phase traction motor, with its constant speed characteristics, had its points where a closely defined duty was involved, such as the Elkhorn Grade section on the Norfolk and Western, with speeds of 14 mph uphill and 28 mph descending. But I also recall its limitations on the Mediterranean coast section of the Italian State Railways between Genoa and the border station of Ventimiglia, where speeds were limited by the traction system to 60 mph. The alternating current commutator motor on the other hand adjusts its speed to the load and is thus much more readily adaptable to the conditions of ordinary railway operation. On the Lötschberg line, for example, fast running would be required between Bern and the foot of the mountain ramp at Frutigen, and also through the lengthy Lötschberg Tunnel, while the gradients themselves would largely define the speeds when climbing the long adverse approaches to the great tunnel.

left
Chicago, Milwaukee, St Paul and Pacific: one of the earliest 3,000-volts direct current electric locomotives, built in 1920, and used between Harlowton, Montana, and Avery, Idaho.

Bern–Lötschberg–Simplon Railway: one of the original electric locomotives of 1913, here seen hauling an international express train.

The system of traction adopted by the Lötschberg for its opening of the mountain line between Frutigen and Brigue, in 1913, 15,000 volts a.c. at $16\frac{2}{3}$ cycles per second, became eventually the standard for main line electrification not only in Switzerland, but also in Germany and Austria. The original Lötschberg locomotives were of the 1-E-1 type, ten-coupled, with rod drive, as can be seen in the accompanying illustration. There were two motors driving through a beam connection to the centre point of a coupling rod, connected to all the remaining driving wheels in the fashion of a steam locomotive. They were powerful locomotives for the day, of 2,500 horsepower, built by the Oerlikon Locomotive Works, and the specified performance was the haulage of a load of 310 tons at 26 mph on a gradient of 1 in 37. At the time of their construction in 1912 comparison was made with contemporary steam operation on the Gotthard line, where the gradients leading to the summit tunnel were similar. On the Lötschberg, whereas one electric locomotive could haul the load at 26 mph, it would take two of the four-cylinder compound Maffei 4-6-0s of the Gotthard, weighing between them 230 tons, to maintain 22 mph with a similar load. Against modern standards of electric locomotive performance this may not sound very wonderful; but in 1913 it was an impressive beginning.

Main line electrification

Moreover, it pointed the way towards the first major electrification on the Swiss Federal Railways. From its first opening in 1902 the lengthy Simplon Tunnel had been electrified on the three-phase system, but from subsequent developments, and particularly that on the Lötschberg line, this was not considered to be the best system for standardization in Switzerland. After carefully weighing up the alternative of replacing the existing locomotive stock with modern steam power, it was decided in 1913 to electrify the whole route between Erstfeld and Bellinzona. This included the long ascents from north and south to the Gotthard Tunnel, with continuous gradients of 1 in $38\frac{1}{2}$ through spiral tunnels. Then before the project was fairly under way came the outbreak of the European War, in August 1914. Although work was at first suspended, the lack of indigenous supplies of coal, and the difficulty of importing from neighbour countries, all of which were deeply involved in the war, made it all the more clear how advantageous electrification would be to Switzerland, with ample hydro-electric potentialities for generating the necessary power. So, with much reduced traffic over the Gotthard line and steam locomotives having to be fired with wood, a restart was made on electrification, in 1916.

The single-phase a.c. system was chosen, with low frequency current to enable a.c. commutator motors to be used. This decision, to need power on the nationwide plan for electrification decided upon in 1918, necessitated the building of special railway power stations, because most of the existing Swiss hydro-electric power plants generated three-phase a.c. at 50 cycles per second. The construction of converter stations would have been very costly, but nevertheless the choice of a frequency of $16\frac{2}{3}$ cycles per second, an exact one-third of the normal three-phase frequency, facilitated the conversion where in certain special cases it had to be made. So was confirmed by the decision of the Swiss Federal Railways the choice of system that the Lötschberg line had made earlier. The first locomotives for the Gotthard line were of relatively moderate size and capacity, and with a one hour horsepower rating of 2,040 were designed to haul a trailing load of 225 tons up the major inclines at 37 mph. They were essentially mountain climbing units, with a rated maximum speed of only 46 mph, but they represented a very big advance upon the best that could be achieved with the steam power formerly in use. Nevertheless, 105 tons was a heavy weight of locomotive power for trains of 225 tons.

The increasing traffic over this line, consequent upon electrification, led to the introduction of a much larger type, for freight working, in 1926, the 'Ce 6/8 III' type illustrated. It consists of two inside framed main trucks connected by a short coupling. Each truck carries two rigidly mounted motors, which drive an intermediate shaft through reduction gears, and this intermediate shaft transmits the driving torque to the oblique connecting rods. The central locomotive body which contains the driver's cab, does not transfer tractive or buffing forces from one main truck to the other. This long locomotive, which had a rated horsepower of 2,620 and a maximum speed of 40 mph, has had a very satisfactory record of service on the Gotthard line, though in no more than five years the increase in traffic was such that considerably more powerful locomotives were needed. The heaviest trains on the line were by that time loading up to about 700 tons, so requiring a pair of the long 'Ce 6/8 III' type locomotives. In this connection it should be added that with continuous brakes on all trains there was little difference in the scheduled speeds of passenger and freight trains.

The 'Ae 8/14' locomotive, introduced in 1931, needs special mention, and emphasis upon its remarkable features.

Swiss Federal Railways: the IC-CI type 'Ce 6/8 III' electric locomotive, introduced in 1926 for working heavy freight trains on the steeply graded Gotthard line (2,620 horsepower).

Main line electrification

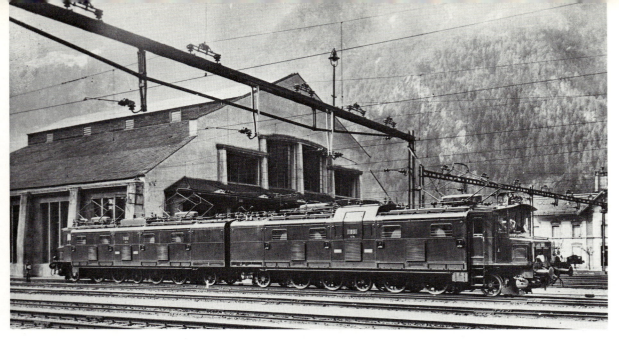

Swiss Federal Railways: the giant Gotthard freight and passenger locomotive type 'Ae 8/14' with the 1-Bo-1-Bo-1 +1-Bo-1-Bo-1 wheel arrangement, first introduced in 1931.

It was virtually a combination of two of the standard 'Ae 4/7' locomotives used in general service over the less hilly sections of the Swiss Federal Railways. The special double locomotive for the Gotthard line had the wheel arrangement 1-Bo-1-Bo-1+1-Bo-1-Bo-1, twenty-eight wheels in all, with eight driven axles. Its rated horsepower was 11,250, and its overall weight 235 tons. These proportions should be borne in mind when considering the later electric locomotives introduced in many parts of the world in a later chapter in this book. But the fact that in 1931 an electric locomotive had been built on which a single man could control more than 11,000 horsepower was a striking demonstration of the potentialities of electric traction on railways. Like many locomotives of a pioneer kind their utilization was limited. At that time the number of trains requiring such power was not great and no more than three of them were built. But they had certainly pointed the way.

The successful operation of electric locomotives on severe mountain gradients in the USA and in Switzerland no doubt prompted the first electrification work on the Great Indian Peninsula Railway, including the notorious Ghat sections. The system chosen for this installation was different from any of the major schemes that had preceded it; the power line was energized at 1,500 volts, direct current, with d.c. traction motors at 750 volts. This Indian scheme included not only the Ghat sections, but the relatively flat and fast running main lines leading to the foot of the mountains from Bombay, and provision had to be made for express passenger locomotives, in addition to powerful freight units for ascending the Ghats. Moreover,

Pennsylvania Railroad: one of the 'P5' class 2-Co-2 passenger and express locomotives introduced in 1933, when the main line between New York and Philadelphia was electrified at 11,000 volts single-phase a.c. at 25 cycles per second. The locomotive is here shown hauling a fast over-night freight train.

by the winter of 1929 the electrification had been extended beyond the Ghats to Poona, a distance from Bombay of 119 miles.

This important work, carried out mostly by British firms and entirely under the surveillance of British consulting engineers, was of great interest to all who were then concerned with railway electrification projects, because of the diversity of the service requirements. The first stages extending the electrified area from the Bombay suburban area to Kalyan, 33 miles, was mainly concerned with heavy commuter traffic. In fact the main line and the freight services continued at first to be operated by steam and all electric trains were composed of multiple unit stock. Particular interest centred on this account upon the system of traction chosen, which would be suitable also for the main line extension and operation over the Ghats. It is important thus at this stage to take a brief look at the systems of electrification currently being installed elsewhere in the world: the high tension single-phase a.c. with low frequency current, and a.c. commutator motors, in Switzerland and Germany; the high tension single-phase a.c. with three-phase induction motors, on the Norfolk and Western, and the 3,000 volts d.c. system of the Chicago, Milwaukee and St Paul. In addition to this there was the 6,600 volt single-phase a.c. of the London, Brighton and South Coast Railway, destined originally to extend from the London suburban area to the entire main line network, exactly as was programmed for the Great Indian Peninsula, and lastly the so-called 'Riverside Electric' of the London and South Western Railway.

Pennsylvania Railroad: class L6A freight locomotive of 1932, operating from 11,000 volts single-phase a.c. at 25 cycles per second. Continuous horsepower rating 2,500.

The choice of 1,500 volts d.c. for the GIPR anticipated the findings of two successive committees on railway electrification in Great Britain. The first was set up in 1927 under the chairmanship of Col. Sir John Pringle, then Chief Inspecting Officer of Railways, Ministry of Transport, to consider the most suitable system for main line electrification; and then in 1929, the Minister of Transport set up a further committee under the chairmanship of Lord Weir to enquire into the economic and other aspects of general railway electrification in Great Britain. The other members of this second committee were Sir Ralph Wedgewood, the Chief General Manager of the LNER, and Sir William McLintock. The recommendation of the Pringle committee for 1,500 volts d.c. with overhead current collection was endorsed by the report of the Weir committee, which was published in 1931. This, of course, cut clean across the policies that had been developed independently and in strong rivalry by the two constituents of the newly-formed Southern Railway, which had already electrified parts of their respective suburban areas.

Reverting to the Great Indian Peninsula Railway, by a major re-alignment on the Bhore Ghat section, the reversing station was eliminated, and a continuous ascent of 15 miles with a maximum gradient of 1 in 38 substituted. The plan of operation was that passenger locomotives would work through between Bombay and Poona, and rear-end banking assistance would be provided by freight locomotives on the Ghat section. The first contracts provided for the supply of 41 freight locomotives of the C-C type, and one express passenger locomotive for trial. The

Austrian Federal Railway: local train on the line from Innsbruck to the Brenner Pass, leaving Steinach.

Main line electrification

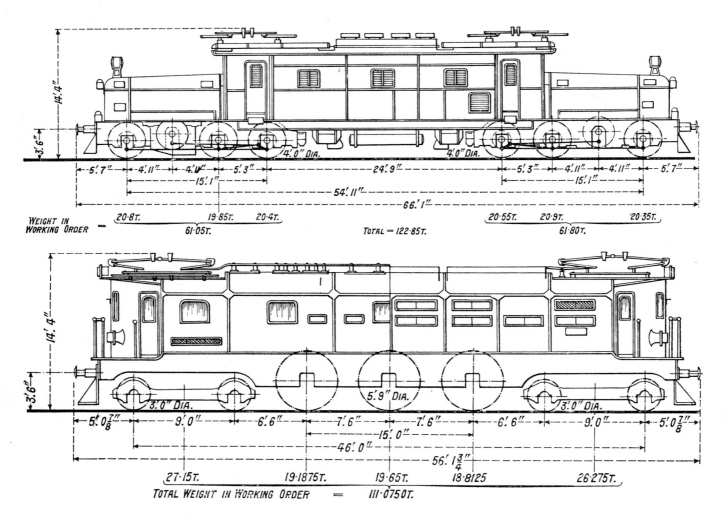

Great Indian Peninsula Railway: diagrams of C-C type freight and 2-6-2 electric passenger locomotives.

freight locomotives, known as Class EF/1, were extremely powerful units, with motors totalling 2,500 horsepower and weighing 122·8 tons. The Metropolitan Vickers Electrical Co. Ltd were the main contractors, with the mechanical parts for thirty-one of the locomotives built by the Vulcan Foundry and for ten by the Swiss Locomotive Company. Swiss experience in electric locomotive design could be detected in the articulated form of construction adopted, similar to that of the Ce 6/8 III locomotives of the Gotthard line previously referred to.

In the GIPR locomotives, which had the somewhat exceptional length of 66 ft 1 in. over buffers, the body was carried on two trucks which were coupled by a flexible joint. The rigid wheelbase was thus reduced to that of a single truck, 15 ft, which enabled sharp curves to be negotiated. Regenerating braking was employed to enable heavy trains to be handled safely on the steep descending gradients. The locomotives had four box type motors, two on each 'truck' driving on to a jackshaft, and applying power to the six-coupled wheels through a connecting rod mechanism. Each of the motors had a one hour rating of 650 horsepower. The line diagram of this class of locomotive makes an interesting comparison with that of one of the first GIPR express passenger electric locomotives supplied by Brown-Boveri, of Baden, Switzerland. This had six motors, each of 370 horsepower, and was geared for a maximum speed of 85 mph.

When the London and South Western Railway decided, in 1913, to electrify the 'Riverside' group of outer suburban lines there can have been few who saw in it the nucleus of a project of 'main line' electrification on a very wide scale. Perhaps even its originators did not visualize such a development, because in 1913 the grouping of the railways of Great Britain that took place in 1923 was hardly foreseen, and the neighbouring Brighton railway had embarked on its own system. The LSWR chose a system that was new in British practice, except for the rather specialized instance of the Central London deep-level tube railway. It was the third rail system at low voltage direct current, with traction return through the running rails. It was very simple and cheap to install, so far as the electrical pick-up was concerned, in strong contrast to the elaborate overhead arrangements necessary on the Brighton railway. It could be installed with very little interference to ordinary traffic, and on almost any existing line. Indeed once the decision was taken work went rapidly ahead, and continued through the early years of the First World War to the first openings at the end of 1915.

How this sytem, with its many incidental disadvantages, as well as its simplicity, came to be chosen as the future standard for the Southern Railway is no part of the present theme, for its extension to main line operation came many years later; but some of the problems may here be mentioned. One thing not becoming apparent until the line spread into more countrified areas was the frequency of level crossings, necessitating both a break in the conductor rails and careful provision to ensure that children or animals did not stray beyond the confines of the crossings themselves. There was also the difficulty of icing on the conductor rails, though this of course can develop on overhead wire systems in particularly severe winter conditions when freezing fog occurs. Technically, of course, the main disadvantage of the 650 volt d.c. system is the relatively high cost of transmission, and the need for sub-stations relatively close together. Be that as it may, however, this LSWR system of 1913 has now been extended to cover practically the entire main line network of the Southern Region of British Railways. The traction equipment introduced for the Dover services is discussed in a later chapter, in its chronological sequence.

 Steam: moving towards the climax

The decade from 1920 was a critical one for the steam locomotive throughout the world. It was not only in commuter traffic that its one-time omnipotence was being heavily assailed. The previous chapter of this book has contained only a few examples of how immeasurably superior electric traction could be in severe operating conditions. It was principally a question of economic justification, and in the meantime it was a period of much heart searching even amongst the most devoted of steam locomotive engineers. On the continent of Europe the ravages of war delayed the immediate plans for development while in the USA it was at first size and weight rather than thermal efficiency that was increasing. In Great Britain on the other hand the grouping of the former independent companies into the four large groups initiated a period of general re-appraisal of design practice from which some highly beneficial results were obtained.

At the time of the grouping the Great Western, alone of the four new companies, had a settled locomotive policy. No other main line railways were involved in this amalgamation, and Churchward's successor was content to continue the established precepts, while greatly improving the quality and precision of constructional methods. At the same time the continuance, with no greater development than enlargement of Churchward's principles, was eventually to lead the Great Western into something of a blind alley, and its theoretical design practice gradually passed from something that was unquestionably pre-eminent into a secondary place among the railways of Great Britain. That a situation was not however to occur in the decade now under consideration, and the first design practice that came to be contrasted unfavourably with that of the Great Western was that of the newly formed London and North Eastern Railway. H. N. Gresley who was appointed Chief

Mechanical Engineer shortly after the amalgamation had achieved outstanding success on the former Great Northern Railway by the application of high degree superheating and piston valves to the large boilered 'Atlantic' engines introduced by H. A. Ivatt in 1902. Although of relatively small tractive power the modernized engines showed an altogether phenomenal capacity for hard continuous steaming, and an excellent front-end design that enabled large volumes of steam to be freely and effectively passed through their cylinders. But Gresley's main development had been towards the three-cylinder simple locomotive, and his large 'Pacific' engines of 1922 were in some way a synthesis of the lessons learned with the superheated 'Atlantics' and the new three-cylinder designs.

In one very important respect the new 'Pacifics' were greatly inferior to the modernized 'Atlantics' and that was the arrangement of the front end. The 'Pacifics' had the clever mechanical arrangement of the valve gear that enabled the valve motion of the inside cylinder to be regulated by a conjugated gear coupled to the valve spindles of the outside cylinders, and thus to dispense with any motion between the frames. But in the design of the valve gear as a whole certain restrictions to steam flow were introduced, which made the 'Pacifics' as first designed inferior to the old 'Atlantics' in this respect. This deficiency made itself apparent in high coal consumption, and a reluctance to run freely, which was emphasized in an unfortunately public manner after a friendly interchange of locomotives between the GWR and LNER in the spring of 1925. Technical details which were intended for private discussion between the two companies were, by unilateral action, unhappily made public, and the immediate result was acrimony rather than exchange of useful information. But the fact emerged that the GWR 'Castle' class 4-6-0, a development of the basic Churchward 'Star' of 1907, was able to make considerably faster time on a lower coal consumption than the Gresley 'Pacific' on similar duties both between Paddington and Plymouth and between King's Cross and Doncaster. Before these interchange trials were run Gresley was aware that improvements to the valve gear of the Pacifics were desirable, and an investigation was in progress at Doncaster Works, but it was not until two years later that the results became apparent.

In the meantime a very important committee had been set up to investigate the effects of different types of locomotives on underline bridges. In chapter 11 reference was made to the beneficial results of co-operation between the civil and mechanical engineers in Holland to enable larger locomotives to be introduced, and how the lack of such understanding on Britain's premier railway, the London and North Western, placed unnecessary restrictions upon the Chief Mechanical Engineer when large new locomotives were projected in 1911. Now, in the technical sessions and fieldwork of the Bridge Stress Committee the effects of badly balanced locomotives were laid bare, and the advantages of multi-cylinder types emphasized. The outcome was a general trend towards three- or four-cylinder designs for fast express passenger work, on all four of the grouped railways. The Great Western was, of course, set in its development of the four-cylinder 4-6-0 type, though the Bridge Stress Committee pointed out ways of improving the balancing. Also, on the London and North Eastern Railway, Gresley was in this respect confirmed in his preference for the three-cylinder simple type. It was on the London Midland and Scottish Railway that policy remained somewhat confused for a few years.

The one time pre-eminent position of the London and North Western Railway, through the remarkable work of C. J. Bowen-Cooke's superheater 4-4-0s of the 'George the Fifth' class, and the high maximum power outputs of the

One of the original Gresley 'Pacifics' of 1923 modified only in respect of the valve gear, on a maximum tonnage King's Cross–Leeds and Bradford express: engine No. 4477 *Gay Crusader*.

A gigantic American three-cylinder 4-12-2 freighter, of the Union Pacific, including the Gresley conjugated valve gear for the inside cylinder. Built in 1926 by ALCO.

four-cylinder 4-6-0 'Claughton' class, had proved no more than transient. It has previously been mentioned how the chassis design of the 4-4-0s was not strong enough to sustain their high power output; but a more cogent factor at the time of the grouping was that the LNWR had lost by death or retirement the services of several of its most eminent and influential men, including Bowen-Cooke, and in the greatly enlarged company formed by the grouping the major influences passed to men of the former Midland Railway, whose policy on locomotive design and utilization differed greatly from those of the North Western. The merger was accompanied by much controversy, and it was some little time before a definite plan of development began to emerge. The only immediate outcome as a result of dynamometer car trials between Leeds and Carlisle (Midland route) was a decision to build many more three-cylinder compound 4-4-0s of the Midland type, and although no answer to the need for large modern locomotives these moderate sized 4-4-0s did much excellent work, particularly over the heavily graded main lines in the north of England, and in Scotland.

The improved valve gear fitted to the Gresley 'Pacifics' of the LNER, and the results obtained from it, was one of the great 'moments of revelation' in British locomotive history. Hitherto many experienced engineers had been inclined to look askance at the long valve travels that had been standard for many years on the Great Western Railway; but long valve travels permit of generous port openings, both to admission and exhaust, and on the Gresley 'Pacific' resulted in a reduction in coal consumption from around 52 lb. per train mile to something less than 40 lb. on duties requiring fast and heavy work. It was the kind of improvement that had been made with the introduction of high degree superheating, and the reduced consumption of the LNER 'Pacifics' made possible the spectacular development, in the summer of 1928, of non-stop running between King's Cross and Edinburgh, 392¾ miles. It is remarkable, in passing, to realize that this, by far the longest run made non-stop anywhere in the world, should have taken place in so small a country as Great Britain! Technically, it would not have been practicable without the marked reduction in coal consumption of the locomotives concerned. Moreover the engines ran more freely, and maximum speeds which previously had not greatly exceeded 80 mph now began to top the '90' on occasions.

On the continent of Europe some notable developments were to be seen by the mid-1920s with the French railways at first taking a strong lead. A distinguished British manufacturer, the late Edgar Alcock, Chairman of the Hunslet Engine Company, had been deeply impressed with the prowess of the German locomotive industry on a visit he made in 1914 and had stressed the point that German locomotive builders would soon become a most serious competitor to Great Britain in the locomotive export trade. But he also noted that they were copyists rather than original designers, despite the notable contributions that German engineers had made to the development of the locomotive. In the 1920s it was certainly the French who were making the running and, at first, particularly the Northern Railway. During the war the Ministry of Public Works had ordered 400 of the 'Pacific' type used on the État system with the general intention that this should possibly be developed as a national standard. But the Northern Railway preferred to design its own post-war 'Pacific', and after early teething troubles the new locomotives of the '3, 1201' class proved extremely successful. It was through the performances of these engines on the very heavy boat expresses between Calais and Paris that many British observers became aware of the quality of French locomotive work. The '3, 1201' class were four-cylinder de Glehn compounds, and one Englishman who was most deeply impressed was Sir Henry Fowler, Chief Mechanical Engineer of the LMSR from 1925. As a former Midland man he was a supporter of the compound system, and his first proposal for a new heavy main line passenger engine was a four-cylinder compound 'Pacific', based upon studies made of the best contemporary French practice.

One of the most important features of the new LMSR organization, based on the policy of the former Midland Railway, was to separate the responsibility for locomotive running from that of the Chief Mechanical Engineer; and the running department of that time were not prepared to accept a compound locomotive for the heaviest main line duties. As an alternative a three-cylinder simple 4-6-0, the 'Royal Scot', was hastily produced, and after certain detail features of its design had been amended the class of seventy locomotives did very good work. It was nevertheless a time when many engineers were seeking greater thermal efficiency even beyond that which high degree superheating and long-travel long-lap valves could give, and three experimental locomotives must be mentioned:

(a) the Ljungstrom turbine locomotive, run experimentally on the LMSR;
(b) Gresley's water-tube boiler 4-6-4 compound on the LNER (No. 10000);
(c) Sir Henry Fowler's high pressure 4-6-0 No. 6399 on the LMSR.

None of these was in any way successful. The Ljungstrom engine showed no advantage over the standard Midland three-cylinder compound 4-4-0s on the St Pancras–Manchester route. Gresley's No. 10000 came the nearest to any degree of success, but the Yarrow water-tube boiler gave much trouble, and the locomotive did little revenue earning

Northern Railway of France: the final development of the de Glehn four-cylinder compound passenger engine, by Collin, here seen on the Simplon–Orient express near St Denis.

service. The Fowler engine did not get beyond the experimental stage, and was withdrawn after a disastrous explosion that killed one of the testing staff.

The last years of the decade witnessed some interesting and significant developments in British practice. In 1926 on the Southern Railway, R. E. L. Maunsell produced a powerful new four-cylinder 4-6-0, the *Lord Nelson*, in response to a requirement from the operating department for a locomotive capable of hauling 500 ton trains at start-to-stop average speeds of 55 mph. The finer points of valve gear design were incorporated in this new locomotive, and an interesting feature was the arrangement of the cranks so as to give eight exhausts per revolution instead of four. The *Lord Nelson*, with a nominal tractive effort of 33,500 lb., was for a short time the most powerful passenger locomotive in Great Britain; but although very free running

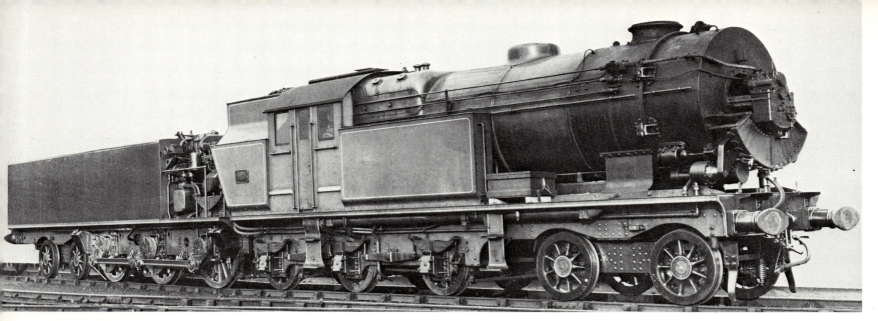

The Ljungstrom turbo-condensing locomotive, which did some experimental running between St Pancras and Manchester in 1926.

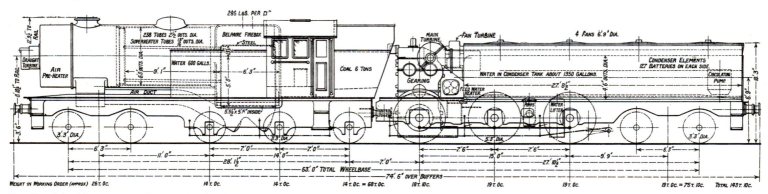

Details of the Ljungstrom turbo-condensing locomotive built by Beyer, Peacock & Co. and tested on the LMSR (Midland Division) main line.

182 Steam: moving towards the climax

LNER: the experimental high pressure four-cylinder compound 4-6-4 with Yarrow water-tube boiler, using a pressure of 450 lb. per sq. in.

Southern Railway: R. E. L. Maunsell's four-cylinder 4-6-0 *Lord Nelson*, built in 1926 and for a short time having the highest tractive effort of any British passenger locomotive.

Great Western Railway: one of the four-cylinder 4-6-0s of the 'King' class (40,300 lb. tractive effort) hauling the Cornish Riviera Express near Reading.

the steaming of locomotives of this class was not always reliable, and the distinction of maximum power was, one regrets to add, on paper only.

The ultimate development of the Churchward locomotive on the Great Western Railway came in 1927 with the production of the *King George V*. This splendid engine was, except in one detail, a direct enlargement of the 'Star' class, which had reached its final form with the production of the 'Prince' series in 1913. Table 15.1 giving basic dimensions shows the various increases, which resulted in the first British locomotive with a nominal tractive effort of more than 40,000 lb. It will be seen that by a pleasing coincidence the two locomotives were named after father and son in the British Royal Family.

The 'King' class locomotives were designed in the faith of an assured continuance of operating conditions that had prevailed on the GWR for the past twenty-five years, including ample supplies of picked grades of Welsh coal, and engine crews trained and supported by generations of dedicated locomotive running inspectors. To see a Great Western fireman at work, whether on a light or a heavy duty, was to appreciate what the footplate tradition of the line really meant. It was only by such firing, with first class coal, that the moderate degree of superheat provided could be truly effective. Boiler pressure was rarely allowed to fall more than 20 lb. per sq. in. below rated maximum. With such basic proportions, backed up by the fine workmanship for which Swindon Works was famous and such expertise on the footplate, the daily work of the 'King' class locomotives was magnificent, fully justifying all the laudatory claims that the publicity department of the GWR made for them. But in view of what was happening elsewhere on the railways of Great Britain, particularly in respect of fuel supplies, one questioned how long the halcyon conditions down in the West of England might last.

All over the world locomotive engineers were adopting higher boiler pressures. The *King George V* was the first British engine to have 250 lb. per sq. in. On the LNER Gresley had increased from 180 to 220 on his later 'Pacifics', and the 'Royal Scots' of the LMSR, which followed the 'Kings' by little more than a month, had 250. The history of the 'Royal Scots' throws a vivid light upon how a matter of detail can sully the reputation of an otherwise successful design. It was found that the coal consumption of these engines, which was most gratifyingly low upon their first introduction to the heaviest main line duties between Euston and Glasgow, rose alarmingly with increasing mileage. Careful and analytical studies eventually revealed that this was due to internal leakage of steam past the pistons, as the rings became worn. These engines originally had a built-up valve head, with the rather complicated

Table 15.1

Date	1913	1927
Engine name	Prince of Wales	King George V
Cylinders (4) dia., in.	15	$16\frac{1}{4}$
stroke, in.	26	28
Coupled wheel dia., ft in.	$6-8\frac{1}{2}$	6–6
Total evaporative heating surface, sq. ft	1,842	2,202
Superheater, sq. ft	263	313
Grate area, sq. ft	27·1	34·3
Boiler pressure, p.s.i.	225	250
Nom. tractive effort, lb.	27,800	40,300

LMSR: the 'Royal Scot' class three-cylinder 4-6-0 of 1927, here shown in its final style of livery before nationalization in 1948.

Schmidt type of ring, traditional from the early days of superheating. Solid valve heads with six narrow rings were substituted, and it worked like a charm. It was applied also to the LNWR four-cylinder 4-6-0s of the 'Claughton' class, which since grouping had been rather in eclipse. The fitting of the modified valves brought their basic coal consumption down by some 20 per cent which was an important factor in their successful use as first line units on the Anglo-Scottish expresses over the Midland route, on the difficult section between Leeds and Carlisle. By the end of the 1920s the basic coal consumption of the large modern British passenger locomotives of all railway groups was about 3 lb. per drawbar horsepower hour. Against this the ex-LNWR 'Claughtons', of 1913 vintage except for the modified valves, were returning about $3\frac{3}{4}$ lb. per drawbar horsepower hour.

By the end of the decade the centre of interest in locomotive development, which with the production of the 'Kings' and the working of the 'Royal Scot' train non-stop between Euston and Carlisle ($299\frac{1}{4}$ miles) all the year round, had been focused on Great Britain, now definitely moved to France. In 1925 both the Eastern and the Paris, Lyons and Mediterranean Railways had introduced very large 4-8-2 locomotives for passenger work. The Est machine, a de Glehn compound by M. Duchatel, was designed for high-speed work, but had suffered a little from a frame design a little too flexible. The PLM engines were designed for the hilly central section of the main line from Paris to Marseilles, where the line passes through the Côte d'Or mountains, and although they were also four-cylinder compounds the engine layout was the reverse of de Glehn's, with the high pressure cylinders inside. In fast running these great engines suffered from the shortness of their connecting rods; but the long boiler, on the other hand, was a great success, and formed the basis for subsequent development of the 4-8-2 type on the PLM Railway. From the outset however the original design of 1925 was successfully used on the very hilly coastal route between Marseilles and Nice, where high-speed running was not then being made.

It was however on the Paris–Orléans Railway in 1929 that there came the advance, little short of sensational, that was to have worldwide repercussions, and to be justifiably claimed as the greatest since the introduction of high degree superheating. The Engineer-in-Chief briefed André Chapelon, and his classic studies arose out of a disappointment with the results of superheating some of the original compound 'Pacifics'. It has been told in chapter 11 how the Orléans was the first railway in Europe to adopt the 'Pacific' type for passenger work, and in view of the success obtained elsewhere, it had been hoped to obtain outputs of around 2,400 indicated horsepower. In fact the performance was little better than that of the earlier de Glehn compound 'Atlantics', which were able to develop 1,800 indicated horsepower continuously. So Chapelon set out to lay bare the internals of the 'Pacifics' to find out where the hidden losses were occurring, and why – as indicator diagrams revealed – the low pressure cylinders were doing so little of the work. The result of a long and sustained investigation was a complete re-design of the steam circuit, providing enlarged and streamlined steam passages, free entry and exit from valves, a higher degree of superheat, a blastpipe giving improved draughting, and all accompanied by a strengthening up of the frames to sustain the anticipated increased power output. Engine No. 3566 was completely rebuilt in this manner at the Tours workshops of the railway, and when tested in heavy express work showed an increased maximum output of 50 per cent – *fifty per cent!* – from 2,050 to 3,120 indicated horsepower, with increased thermal efficiency. At the Liège Exhibition in May 1930 the Paris–Orléans Railway exhibited a graph of a run from Poitiers to Angoulême, 70·1 miles, start to stop, in 62¾ minutes, with a load of 567 tons. Some of the most experienced connoisseurs of locomotive performance who saw and studied that graph found it incredible; but in fact it was no more than the beginning of the astonishing Chapelon era.

For the final scene in the 1921–30 decade we must once again cross the Atlantic. Although the 4-6-2 type was still in extensive use for passenger work, and was indeed the standard type on so important a line as the Pennsylvania for many years afterwards, it was, by the year 1930, being superseded not only by the 4-6-4, but by 4-8-2 and 4-8-4 locomotives in express passenger service. In all the latest designs, in complete contrast to current British and conti-

Northern Railway of France: one of the Chapelon rebuilt 'Pacifics' purchased from the Paris–Orléans Railway. These epoch-marking locomotives were known on the Nord as the 'P. O. Transformations'.

nental European practice, only two cylinders were used. These naturally were rising to very large proportions in locomotives having a nominal tractive effort of more than 60,000 lb. The basic dimensions of typical examples of the four wheel arrangements are quoted in Table 15.2.

In view of the previously quoted performance of the Paris–Orléans 4-6-2 compound locomotive, the recorded work, with dynamometer car, of a 4-6-4 of the New York Central is of interest and importance. The class in question has a rated tractive force of 42,300 lb. derived from cylinders 25 in. diameter by 28 in. stroke, coupled wheels 6 ft 7 in. diameter and a boiler pressure of 225 lb. per sq. in. The trials were made over a section of line 140 miles long with heavy trains of around 1,600 tons of passenger stock. The

A great American development: one of the later 4-6-4s of the New York Central, used to haul the 'Twentieth Century Limited' and other crack trains.

The trend of American express locomotive development: a huge 4-8-2 of the Baltimore and Ohio, having a tractive effort of 65,000 lb.

Table 15.2 American express locomotives

Railroad	Reading	Boston and Albany	Baltimore and Ohio	Atchison, Topeka and Santa Fe
Type	4-6-2	4-6-4	4-8-2	4-8-4
Cylinders dia., in.	25	25	$27\frac{1}{2}$	30
stroke, in.	28	28	30	30
Coupled wheel dia., ft in.	6–8	6–3	6–3	6–1
Total evaporating heating surface, sq. ft	3,045	4,484	5,506	5,672
Superheater, sq. ft	745	1,920	2,451	2,250
Grate area, sq. ft	95	81·5	92·3	108·0
Boiler pressure, p.s.i.	230	240	250	210
Nominal tractive effort, lb.	40,200	44,800	65,000	66,000
Booster, lb.		10,600		

average speed was 44 mph. The indicated horsepower was 2,500, and the drawbar horsepower 1,900. These results were obtained with good economy at a coal consumption of about 3 lb. per drawbar horsepower hour. The maximum indicated horsepower was 2,986, from a locomotive having a weight, without tender, of $152\frac{1}{2}$ tons. It is always difficult to make direct comparisons in fairness to different types of locomotive, as conditions can vary so considerably; but the French compound engine which was found capable of developing 3,000 indicated horsepower continuously had a weight without tender of 98 tons, while the English four-cylinder 4-6-0 of the LNWR which in 1913 developed between 1,400 and 1,650 indicated horsepower continuously for 35 minutes had a weight of 77 tons. The ratios of indicated horsepower to weight in tons are 19·5, 30·5 and 20, which measure for measure gives some indication of the advance that Chapelon had achieved. In all three countries still greater advances were to be recorded before development was again halted by war, in 1939.

16 Inception and early development of the diesel

The application of the diesel engine to railway traction took place in an interesting variety of ways, including direct gearing of the diesel engine to the road wheels, or through various means of mechanical and hydraulic transmission. But one of the most attractive propositions in early days was to couple the diesel engine direct to an electric generator to deliver power to traction motors on the train. It was claimed that a diesel electric train, while eliminating costly electric transmission lines, sub-stations and track work, retains the advantages of electric traction and at the same time gives the flexibility of steam working. It was claimed that the diesel-electric system extends considerably the scope of railway electrification, the main handicap of which, as previously discussed, is the high capital outlay involved in power stations, sub-stations, transmission lines and such like.

One of the first and very interesting early applications was made on the Buenos Ayres Great Southern Railway, where suburban traffic at the great city terminal of Plaza Constitution was reaching saturation point with steam working. The brilliant but somewhat explosive Chief Mechanical Engineer, P. C. Saccagio, conceived the idea of a multiple-unit electric train that would receive its power from a mobile generating station attached at one end, in which the power would be generated by diesel engines. In collaboration with Sir W. G. Armstrong-Whitworth & Co. Ltd of Scotswood-on-Tyne, a 1,200 brake horse-power diesel-electric power unit was designed and built, and entered service in the Buenos Ayres suburban area in 1929. The train itself was a five-coach set, with a power house on wheels attached to it.

On the continent of Europe diesel power was being applied in a number of ways by the year 1930. There was considerable experimenting with different forms of transmission.

As long previously as 1925 the eminent Polish steam locomotive engineer Professor Lomonossoff had designed a 1,200 horsepower diesel locomotive with electrical transmission. It was put into service by the Soviet Railways on the line between Moscow and Kursk, and gave thoroughly reliable service. It was probably the first diesel-electric locomotive in the world to enter regular railway working. By way of contrast however a rival form of high power diesel locomotive was delivered to Russia in 1926 by the Hohenzollern A. G. of Düsseldorf, which had a direct geared drive. Some trouble was experienced with damage to the gears, which was partly attributed to the inexperience of the operators. This locomotive, which was also of 1,200 engine horsepower, had four gears, but a criticism was that the 'steps' in power output that they represented did not provide the flexibility of control inherent in a steam locomotive.

A development that was currently thought to contain the greatest promise was the German Railways' introduction, in 1929, of a locomotive with a diesel engine as prime mover, and transmission by compressed air. This remarkable machine showed the evident desire of early pioneers in diesel traction to avoid electrical transmission, if at all possible. The view of German engineers of the period was that electrical transmission, while offering no particular technical difficulties, was costly, heavy, and yielded no more than moderate overall efficiency. Despite the experiments in Russia, the German Railways themselves rejected direct gear transmission, chiefly because of the lack of any simple means of changing gear without interrupting the continuity of the drive. Hydraulic transmission had been tried on a number of small shunting locomotives, but at that stage in the development it was considered that space restricted this system to power units of 500 horsepower or less. In the German view at that time there remained the

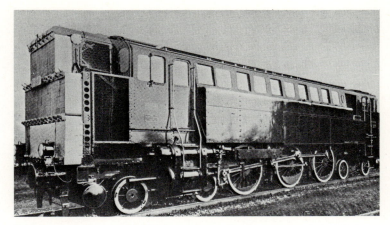

German State Railways: 1,200 horsepower diesel-compressed air 4-6-4 tank locomotive.

system of transmission by compressed air, which seemed to offer the advantages of lower cost and weight, simplicity, and the possibility of reproducing most closely the cherished characteristics of the steam locomotive. All that was necessary, it was argued, was to replace the steam boiler by an air compressor driven by a diesel engine.

So eventuated the interesting locomotive shown in the accompanying illustrations. By steam standards of wheel notation it was a 4-6-4 tank engine, with $27\frac{1}{2}$ in. by $27\frac{1}{2}$ in. cylinders, 5 ft 3 in. coupled wheels, and a working air pressure of about 100 lb. per sq. in. It was calculated to have a horsepower of about 1,200. From the illustrations and the cross-sectional drawing it will be seen that the diesel engine, directly coupled to the air compressor and mounted on a common bedplate, extended to a point roughly level with the rearmost pair of coupled wheels. The compressor was at the forward end just behind the driver's cab, and so

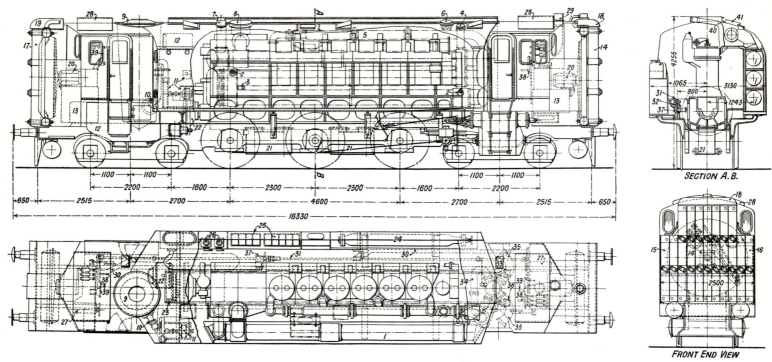

1 Air heater.
2 Safety disc, bursting in the event of abnormal pressure rise.
3 Safety valve.
4 Ackermann safety valve to control the working pressure.
5 Exhaust header.
6 Exhaust safety valve.
7 Motor exhaust.
8 Safety valve on compressor header.
9 Oil-fired heating boiler.
10 Oil burner.
11 Blower with 5-H.P. electric motor and starter.
12 Fuel tank.
13 Water tank.
14 Water cooler.
15 Cooler for lubricating oil.
16 Cooler for injection water.
17 Cooler for piston circulating oil.
18 Equalising water tank.
19 High-level tank for injection cooling water.
20 15-H.P. electric motor and fan.
21 Tank for lubricating oil for Diesel motor.
22 Petersen generator with friction coupling and driving gears.
23 Fuel supply pump.
24 Starting-air bottles.
25 Electric storage battery.
26 Lubricating pumps (Bosch-Reichsbahn pattern).
27 Fan starter.
28 Roof resistances.
29 Locomotive cylinder exhaust.
30 Water connection.
31 Regulator shaft.
32 Reversing shaft.
33 Schmidt and Wagner valve regulator.
34 Fresh air in front of the valve regulator.
35 Fresh air behind the valve regulator.
36 Air suction valve (Knorr pattern).
37 Compression control valve.
38 Reversing hand wheel.
39 Regulator lever.
40 Air intake for Diesel motor.
41 Air intake for compressor.

Elevation, plan and sections showing arrangement of 1,200 horsepower diesel-compressed air locomotive.

situated to supply compressed air to the locomotive cylinders by the shortest route, as it were. A great number of problems in detail design arose in the construction of this locomotive, and the apparatus for regulating the working of what could well be regarded as three separate machines: the diesel engine, the compressor and the locomotive engine. In all contemporary accounts great emphasis was laid on the similarity of its road operation to that of steam. One report, of a test on heavy gradients, read: 'Every start, particularly on sharp curves and gradients, demonstrated the advantages of the compressed air transmission and showed the machine to possess exactly the characteristics of a steam locomotive.' After the initial publicity however this notable experimental machine dropped completely out of the picture, and in Europe at any rate little was heard of diesel main line locomotives again for some years.

It was from the USA that the most important and influential development came in the 1930s. It was in 1922 that the Electro-Motive Engineering Corporation was founded, with H. C. Hamilton as President. He had been a salesman in the heavy lorry business, and by reason of exceptional administrative ability he had risen rapidly. He was a man who had great skill in gathering able men around him and in drawing forth their talents. Two such men were C. F. Kettering and Richard Dilworth. Kettering was a natural inventor, and with a string of innovations to his credit he then threw his whole energies into the development of the diesel engine. His son Eugene W. Kettering was in the same mould, and between them they produced the famous '567' diesel engine. Theirs was no exciting game of moving from one thing to another as successively attractive projects lured them on. Having designed a good lightweight diesel engine they concentrated on perfecting it – literally perfecting it – in every single detail, with a view to marketing a completely standard and immutable product. This became the unshakeable policy of the firm so well known today as 'General Motors', even though at times it meant turning down orders from customers who wanted something a little out of the ordinary.

It was Richard Dilworth, who was Chief Engineer of the corporation from 1934 onwards, who built the nigh-perfected Kettering '567' engine into a successful main line diesel-electric locomotive, and an equally successful shunter. Built up unit-wise, with 8, 12 or 16 cylinders and all components completely standard, it was used to equal advantage in 2,500 horsepower heavy freight locomotives, 1,750 horsepower express passenger units, and so on. It will be told later in this chapter how railways in many parts of the world rushed to introduce specialized streamlined railcar sets powered by diesel engines and a variety of transmissions. But Dilworth saw the greatest field for development was in production of standard locomotives that could take the place of steam; that could be coupled in multiples, giving locomotives with an engine horsepower of 5,000 or more that could be run by a single engine crew, and thus eliminate the multiple manning necessary when heavy trains required the services of three or four steam locomotives.

Dilworth was thinking of freight as much as high-speed spectacular passenger services, and in this respect the diesels had a distinct operating advantage over steam. Two locomotives, one steam and one diesel-electric, may have an almost identical tractive effort from a speed of 25 mph and upwards, and in express service the choice between the two forms of motive power will have to be made on grounds of relative thermal efficiency, maintenance costs, and availability – for in the last instance a diesel-electric needs far less in the way of day-to-day servicing than a steam locomotive. But in the speed range from

Union Pacific Railroad: General Motors diesels in multiple: a four-unit 6,000 horsepower combination on the 'San Francisco Overland Limited' near Green River, Wyoming.

0 up to 20 mph the otherwise identically powered locomotives differ greatly. In the case of a 3,000 horsepower diesel and a 4-8-4 steam locomotive the respective available tractive forces at 8 mph are 24 tons with steam, and no less than 45 tons with the diesel, while at 15 mph the figures are 22 tons with steam and 28 tons with the diesel. At 25 mph they have equalized at 18 tons each. The very high available tractive force of the diesel at low speed gives it a great advantage when starting a heavy load, or slogging up a steep gradient, like those found in the Rocky Mountains.

The Electro-Motive Corporation of General Motors never had any doubts about the kind of transmission to use; it was electric from the outset, and nothing else. In the 1930s the economic conditions in the USA were at first not favourable to large capital investment in new locomotive power, and success came slowly. For similar reasons the Big Three among American steam locomotive builders, Baldwin, Lima and ALCO, showed little inclination to take

The familiar form of the standard General Motors 'first generation' unit, on the Ontario Northland Railway, at Moosonee, Canada.

interest in the new form of power, despite the wealth of publicity it received in the technical press and elsewhere. It was the Baltimore and Ohio that put into service the first General Motors 1,800 horsepower main line passenger diesel, in 1935, to be followed in the same year by a pair coupled in multiple to make a 3,600 horsepower locomotive on the Atchison, Topeka and Santa Fe. The rush to change over to diesels had barely started, while one American railroad after another purchased units in small numbers and made careful appraisals of their capacity. But one thing was sure at that time, General Motors virtually had the field to themselves. It was a situation that had a very important bearing on future development when the USA became involved in the Second World War at the end of 1941. Then the War Production Board decided to allocate all orders for road diesels to the largest and most experienced builder, and General Motors had the field to themselves for a critical four years.

In Europe during the earlier 1930s it was Germany that was setting the pace, and in 1932 the epoch-marking 'Flying Hamburger' diesel-electric railcar train was put into service. Quite apart from any technical features the positive audacity of the train service provided fairly caught the imagination. It was a time when British and French steam hauled express trains were beginning to advance beyond the standards attained before the First World War. It was a gradual advance, but none the less gratifying, and then into the international arena came the 'Flying Hamburger'. Table 16.1 can give some idea of the surprise and sensation that was caused. Apart from those noted all the trains concerned were steam hauled; and then came the 'Flying Hamburger', covering the 178·1 miles from Berlin to Hamburg in 138 minutes at a start-to-stop average speed of 77·4 mph!

This German train was a two-coach articulated set with engines and generators mounted on the leading and trailing bogies while the centre bogie carried the two force-ventilated axle-hung traction motors. The two 12-cylinder diesel engines were of the Maybach type giving a combined output of 820 engine horsepower. As the tare weight of the complete two-car unit was only 76 tons

Table 16.1 Fastest express trains, summer 1933
Great Britain

Railway	Route	Distance, miles	Time, min.	Average speed, mph
Great Western	Swindon–Paddington	77·3	65	71·4
LMSR	Crewe–Willesden Junction	152·7	142	64·5
LNER	Grantham–King's Cross	105·5	100	63·0

France

Railway	Route	Distance, miles	Time, min.	Average speed, mph
Alsace-Lorraine	Mulhouse–Strasbourg	67·3	61	66·2
Nord	Paris–Jeumont*	147·7	134	66·1
Est	Bar-le-Duc–Paris	157·5	150	63·0
Orléans	Les Aubrais–St Pierre†	69·5	67	62·2
État	Paris–Deauville‡	136·2	120	68·1

*Time to passing Belgian frontier at slow speed.
†Electrically hauled.
‡Bugatti railcar.

German State Railways: diesel-electric high-speed motor coach train, the 'Flying Hamburger', leaving Berlin.

there was ample power for traction. The application of the driving power in the middle was interesting, because it meant that the end bogies, though loaded with the weight of the diesel engines and generators just above them, were virtually idlers. But very great care had been taken in the design and suspension of the bogies, and the general impression of British travellers was that the riding was excellent. The maximum speed of 100 mph was sustained for long distances. The power units on the centre bogie were quite independent of each other, and if one should have been out of action for any reason the other was capable of driving the two-car unit at about 75 mph on straight level track. The unit provided seats for 102 passengers and the only criticism from British travellers was that the accommodation on such an obviously prestige train was rather cramped. The seating was arranged to provide for three abreast on one side of the gangway and one on the other, and while it was claimed that three out of every four passengers had a 'corner' seat there was not a great deal of elbow room, in a coach width internally of 8 ft 11 in. In the ordinary way this book is concerned only with traction, and not directly with passenger comforts. But the rather restricted accommodation on the 'Flying Hamburger' had some interesting repercussions later. In view of the importance of coach suspension at high speed detailed drawings are reproduced of the end and central bogies of this train (see page 198).

The Germans were certainly first in the field with a really high-speed diesel propelled railcar train, but the Americans followed quickly after, and with the railways being privately owned, there was soon rivalry between some of them as to which could operate the fastest and most spectacular services. This was particularly the case with the railways radiating westwards from Chicago. The Union Pacific was first off the mark with their advance publicity, but the Chicago, Burlington and Quincy had the first train in operation, and on a demonstration run on 26 May 1934 the lightweight streamlined 'Burlington Zephyr' made the remarkable time over the 1,015 miles from Omaha to Chicago of 13 hours 5 minutes – an average speed of 77·6 mph. This was easily the fastest railway journey made up to that time over so long a distance. It was, of course, a demonstration, rather than a trial of a new train service, and the most elaborate precautions were taken to ensure a safe and clear road. The maximum speed attained was $112\frac{1}{2}$ mph. As a demonstration of what

Inception and early development of the diesel

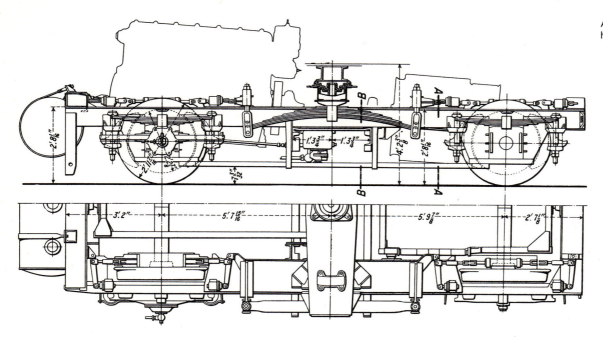

Arrangement of end bogie of German high-speed diesel train.

a lightweight diesel railcar train could do, it was certainly impressive.

The 'Burlington Zephyr' differed from the 'Flying Hamburger' by having all the power plant at the leading end. But it was streamlined throughout to a shape determined by experiments at the Massachusetts Institute of Technology. Again, unlike the 'Flying Hamburger', a considerable proportion of the coach space was given up to mail and baggage accommodation, while the facilities for serving meals on the long American runs were necessarily far more elaborate. In fact in this highly specialized three-car train, articulated throughout, there was seating accommodation for no more than 72 passengers. The rear end of the train was formed into an observation lounge. The total weight of an entire three-car assembly was only $87\frac{1}{2}$ tons, so that the power plant for driving the train at the high speeds intended consisted of a single eight-cylinder two-stroke diesel engine with a total rated horsepower of 600. The Union Pacific took delivery of its first diesel-electric railcar train about the same time as the 'Burlington Zephyr' made its sensational début, and further trains consisting of six- and nine-car formations were forecast before the end of the year 1934. The potentialities of the diesel engine were certainly being utilized to attract attention to the American railways. It was a time when their financial position and their public image were at a

Inception and early development of the diesel

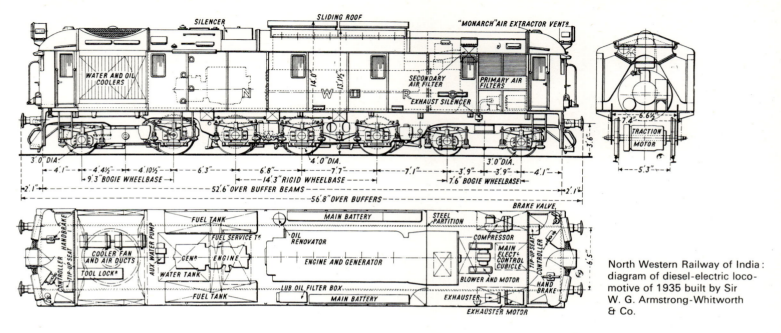

North Western Railway of India: diagram of diesel-electric locomotive of 1935 built by Sir W. G. Armstrong-Whitworth & Co.

low ebb, and the introduction of these fast services, with attractively styled trains, was taken as some evidence of a forward looking attitude, even though the number of passengers they carried at first was of course very small, in proportion to the total numbers travelling at that time.

Although in actual service the 'Burlington Zephyr' was not at first permitted to run at more than 85 mph on its regular run between Lincoln and Kansas City, it attracted so much business that an extra car had to be added to the formation. It was yet another instance however of traction stepping ahead of what the permanent way could carry. In the 250 miles of the run just mentioned no fewer than 198 miles was laid with nothing heavier than 90 lb. rails, much of it on softwood timbers in cinder ballast. There were no less than 175 unprotected level crossings on the route. In 1935 the total of 250 miles was scheduled to be run in $5\frac{1}{2}$ hours, inclusive of three intermediate stops totalling 41 minutes between them. The fastest start-to-stop run was over the 130 miles from Council Bluffs to St Joseph, in 136 minutes. With two further trains of the 'Zephyr' type put into service in the winter of 1934–5, the 'Burlington' was able to schedule a non-stop run between Chicago and St Paul, 431 miles, at an average speed of 66 mph. In this case some substantial overhauling of the track was undertaken beforehand to permit of regular running of this standard.

Inception and early development of the diesel

Great Western Railway: the first diesel lightweight railcar, with mechanical transmission. Introduced 1933.

Apart from lightweight trains one of the most interesting developments with which British industry was concerned was the supply in 1935 of two large main line diesel-electric locomotives to the North Western Railway of India, especially interesting in that the manufacturers were Sir W. G. Armstrong-Whitworth & Co., who supplied the power units for the Buenos Ayres Great Southern diesel-electric train of 1929. The new Indian locomotives were of 1,200 engine horsepower with an eight-cylinder Armstrong Sulzer engine. But the builders rated the locomotive at 1,300 horsepower because a 100 horsepower Armstrong-Saurer high-speed oil engine is included in the equipment to provide power for most of the auxiliaries, which latter absorb some of the main engine output on other diesel locomotives and thereby reduce the power available for traction. As will be seen from the accompanying diagram (page 199) these were large locomotives of the 2-Do-1 type, having an overall weight of 113 tons.

The reasons behind the experimental introduction of these locomotives has a bearing upon later diesel developments elsewhere. There was a long standing project in British India to construct a new direct line between Bombay and Karachi. It would have run over arid, waterless country where provision and servicing of steam locomotives would have involved many problems. The diesel with its relatively small consumption of water seemed a likely answer. The two locomotives supplied by Armstrong-Whitworth were at first put on to the Karachi–Lahore mail trains, which run for part of their journey across the Sind Desert, where conditions likely to occur on the still longer run to Bombay, if it ever materialized, would to some extent be simulated. Unfortunately these locomotives were pioneers in India, and at long range it was not easy to find remedies for teething troubles. With some smaller units supplied five years earlier giving far more serious trouble, this first experiment with diesel-electric traction was prematurely abandoned, and these two fine locomotives were withdrawn after a relatively short life. But they pointed the way, and are deserving of more attention than they received in their working life.

Elsewhere the adoption of diesel traction mostly took the form of small lightweight railcars, which in many areas were hailed as the answer to the branch line passenger service problem; but for the future it was the work of Dilworth and the Ketterings at General Motors that contained the germs of subsequent world development. Mention must be made however of the introduction in Great Britain of diesel shunting locomotives. These small, unobtrusive units, in their economical fuel consumption and elimination of standby losses, gradually made a considerable impact upon the operation of a service that constituted an essential, and sometimes wasteful proportion of British railway working, at a time when a large amount of 'flat' shunting had to be undertaken, involving much waiting time.

 The zenith of steam: 1935—45

The results of Chapelon's remarkably successful rebuilding of the de Glehn compound 'Pacifics' on the Paris–Orléans Railway became generally known at a time when many railwaymen were beginning to think that steam traction had reached its limit, and that the future lay in more modern forms of motive power. But when success with the 'Pacifics' was followed by the equally brilliant conversion of the original smaller wheeled 4-6-2s into 4-8-0s specially for the heavily graded sections of the line to Toulouse, the steam locomotive entered upon a period of development and enhanced performance the like of which had scarcely been matched at any time in its earlier history. To take Chapelon's own work first, the conversion of 'Pacifics' into 4-8-0s was a move of some significance in itself, without the epoch-marking improvements in boiler, cylinders and valves that had so characterized the early conversion. The line south of Vierzon passing across the western flanks of the Massif Central includes such continuous heavy grading and curvature that a locomotive with ample adhesion was needed. The running conditions were made more difficult through the heaviest trains running at night, or in the early morning, when low cloud or ground mist often made for a bad rail. British locomotive engineers were reluctant to forego the physical advantage of a two-wheeled trailing truck, in allowing use of a wide firebox; but Chapelon designed an extremely efficient, deep, narrow box, and gained the advantage of the extra adhesion from eight coupled axles.

These 4-8-0s produced even more astonishing results than the 'Pacifics' – generally about 50 per cent greater maximum output than even Chapelon himself expected. An exceptionally fine feat of hill climbing on the Toulouse line may be recalled, on the northbound run climbing from Souillac to Gignac, where the gradient is 1 in 100 for 10

Paris–Orléans–Midi Railway: Chapelon's outstanding four-cylinder compound 4-8-0 rebuilt from a 'Pacific' of 1907.

miles, with continuous curvature. As the gradient is uncompensated for this curvature the equivalent inclination from the traction point of view is 1 in 87. At the foot of this difficult gradient the train was slowed to 18½ mph over a viaduct under repair. Then the locomotive was opened out, to attain 50 mph in 4¼ miles. The load being hauled was 530 tons, and this very rapid acceleration required an equivalent *drawbar* horsepower of almost 3,000. The indicated horsepower would have been at least 3,700. Such performances as these, which became typical of these locomotives, were superior to anything the much larger 4-8-2s of other French railways were achieving at that time.

In the midst of references to work by these large French locomotives mention must be made of an interesting new English design that proved an unexpectedly striking success. Enhanced locomotive power was needed for the Hastings line of the Southern Railway. Between Tonbridge and St Leonards it is steeply graded with much curvature, but also subject to structure gauge restriction in certain tunnels. The robust and successful two-cylinder 4-6-0 'King Arthur' class was not acceptable to the civil engineer, so R. E. L. Maunsell produced a three-cylinder 4-4-0 equivalent, using a shortened version of the same boiler, and three cylinders to secure better balancing and a reduced hammer blow. These locomotives, named after English

Southern Railway: a three-cylinder 4-4-0 of the 'Schools' class, by R. E. L. Maunsell, 1930.

public schools, fulfilled their original function so well, that from being a special purpose type for one awkward route, more were built for the Portsmouth line; and after that area was electrified and the 'Schools' working there would otherwise have been redundant, they were transferred to Bournemouth to do work that was altogether outstanding in relation to their size. Though having a total weight of only 67 tons (109½ tons with tender) they hauled loads of 500 tons between Waterloo and Southampton, 79¼ miles, in 87 minutes.

Despite the striking developments in France, however, and the notable British progress in design in the later 1920s, the record for the fastest daily start-to-stop run in the world, in 1931, was held by the Canadian Pacific Railway. At that time there was intense competition for the traffic between Montreal and Toronto. The Canadian National had the easier route, and to run on equality the CPR had to make very fast time where they could. The 'Royal York' express was booked to cover the 124 miles from Smiths Falls to Montreal West in 108 minutes, an average speed of 68·9 mph. The loads were very heavy, and in 1929 some huge 'Hudson' type locomotives were introduced. So far as tractive effort was concerned, with 45,300 lb. they were not so very much more powerful than the Great Western 'Kings', but they had enormous boilers and fireboxes, designed for continuous very heavy steaming. The tenders of the Canadian engines, when fully loaded with coal and water, weighed almost as much as the 'King' and its tender! The total weights were 288 tons CPR, and 135¾ tons GWR. The acceleration of the 'Cheltenham Flyer' in 1932 to a 65 minute run from Swindon to Paddington recaptured the daily start-to-stop record for Great Britain, 71·3 mph; but there was a great difference in the load. The 'Cheltenham Flyer' rarely loaded to much over 250 tons, whereas the Canadian expresses often scaled over 600 tons.

It was on the London and North Eastern Railway that French influence was at first apparent in Great Britain. Gresley had a traction problem in Scotland. The introduction of third-class sleeping cars had increased the loads of the night expresses, and on the East Coast route north of Edinburgh sharp intermittent gradients and many speed restrictions put the haulage of the principal trains beyond the capacity of the standard 'Pacific' engines. Gresley decided on a 2-8-2, and from his friendships and technical discussions with French engineers he incorporated the principles of internal streamlining and twin orifice blast-pipes into the new design. The first engine of the new class, the *Cock o' the North*, had poppet valves actuated by rotary cam gear, and Gresley's standard three-cylinder engine layout. The second engine, the *Earl Marischal*, had Walschaerts gear actuating piston valves, with the LNER arrangement of two outside sets of motion, and conjugated gear driving the inside piston valve. Gresley, who was a persistent advocate of a stationary locomotive testing plant, sent the *Cock o' the North* to France for tests on the plant at Vitry-sur-Seine, because at that time there was no British plant of the capacity needed. Later, the engine was tested on the Paris–Orléans line between Paris and St Pierre des Corps (Tours).

These tests with the *Cock o' the North*, which were carried out in 1935, created much interest among French engineers. They followed a period of great comparative testing activity instigated by the Nord. That company was always seeking to improve its locomotive practice, and in 1933 arrangements were made for one of the newly rebuilt Chapelon 'Pacifics' of the Orléans to be tested against a standard Nord 'Pacific'. To make the comparison still more comprehensive two different designs of 4-8-2 were also included: a standard Est de Glehn four-cylinder compound, and a new express passenger compound of the PLM. The four engines were tested in heavy express duty between Paris and Calais. The results were fascinating. The giant new PLM 4-8-2 produced the greatest output of power, whereas the corresponding Est locomotive overtaxed her strength and cracked her frames. The Nord 'Pacific' put up a characteristically good performance, but was quite outclassed in power output by the Chapelon. The Nord authorities responded quickly to the results of these trials by ordering twenty of the rebuilt 'Pacifics' from the Orléans company. The first of these engines were in service by the spring of 1934. The Nord also tested one of the Chapelon 4-8-0s and in no half-hearted style either. Not only was a test train of 650 tons made up, but for the purposes of this test the traditional speed limit of 120 km. per hour was waived. On one 20 mile section of level track, between Noyelles and Étaples, the speed was continuously 87 mph. Actual drawbar horsepowers of 2,100 and 2,600 were recorded on steep rising gradients, with equivalent values on level track exceeding 3,000, while the net running times on the four successive start-to-stop stages gave the remarkable results shown in Table 17.1, which, it must be emphasized, were made by a locomotive weighing 109 tons without its tender and hauling a load of 650 tons. Railway traction history was certainly made in France on 18 and 19 February 1935.

Table 17.1   Dynamometer car runs: P.O.–Midi 4-8-0 No. 240.707

Section	Distance, miles	Time, min. sec.	Average speed, mph
Paris–Amiens	81·2	67·20	72·4
Amiens–Calais (Maritime)	103·1	85.00	72·7
Calais (Maritime)–Amiens	103·1	85.32	72·3
Amiens–La Chapelle	80·2	68.55	69·8

In Germany the performance of the 'Flying Hamburger' diesel railcar train made such an impression on H. N. Gresley of the London and North Eastern Railway that he furnished the makers with full details of the route between London (King's Cross) and Newcastle, and asked them for an estimate of a schedule they could guarantee. The result was disappointing. While in Germany their train was maintaining a start-to-stop average speed of 77·4 mph between Berlin and Hamburg, the gradients and intermediate speed restrictions of the English route were such that they could not promise better times than 4 hr. $15\frac{1}{2}$ min. northbound nor 4 hr. 17 min. southbound, respective average speeds of 63·1 and 62·7 mph. The Chief General Manager of the LNER, Sir Ralph Wedgwood, suggested that better times could be made with a standard Gresley 'Pacific' engine, and a train of ordinary coaching stock, and on 5 March 1935 this was shown convincingly to be the case. The 'A3' locomotive No. 2750 *Papyrus* with a six-coach train reached Newcastle in 3 hr. 57 min., despite 7 min. lost by a signal stop *en route*, while on the return journey made the same day, but with a different engine crew, the overall time was 3 hr. $51\frac{3}{4}$ min. The net average speeds on the two journeys were 70 and 70·7 mph. Not only were the speeds considerably higher than those the German manufacturers could promise, but they were achieved with a train providing much more extensive and lavish passenger accommodation.

In the light of this demonstration, which had included the making of a new world record speed with steam traction of 108 mph, authority was given for the construction of a new train to provide a four hour service between London and Newcastle. Four new 'Pacific' engines were included in the authorization, and these embodied all the principles of internal streamlining that had been so successful on the 'Cock o' the North' 2-8-2s; but they were also externally streamlined to most spectacular effect. In honour of the twenty-fifth anniversary of the reign of His Majesty King George V the train was named 'The Silver Jubilee', and locomotives and rolling stock alike were finished in 'silver'. Making a brilliant demonstration run three days before commencing public service on which a maximum speed of $112\frac{1}{2}$ mph was attained, the train was a great success, and its seven-coach formation was loaded to capacity daily.

By this year of 1935 new records for high-speed railway travel were being set up in many parts of the world. The Great Western supremacy did not last for long. The streamlined 'Hiawatha' of the Chicago, Milwaukee, St Paul and Pacific surpassed it with a run from New Lisbon to Portage, 43·1 miles in 35 minutes, and then the 'Detroit Arrow' of the Pennsylvania was scheduled over the 64·2 miles from Plymouth to Fort Wayne in 51 minutes. These fast spurts gave average speeds of 73·9 and 75·5 mph, but it was extraordinary that both these high speed trains were originally run by 'Atlantic' type engines. The American philosophy of express locomotive operation was to provide large steaming capacity, but relatively low cylinder volume. This involved driving with a short range of expansion, since the point of cut-off in the cylinders had to be late in order to obtain the requisite cylinder horsepower. The 'Detroit Arrow' was originally a train of about 350 tons, and for its very fast running the Pennsylvania used their 'E6' class Atlantics of 1915 vintage. They were certainly powerful engines of the type, with a tractive effort of 31,300 lb., but they nevertheless had to be worked hard to run the 'Detroit Arrow' to time.

For the 'Hiawatha' the Milwaukee designed some new 'Atlantics'. They were streamlined, and painted in gay colours. It is interesting to compare their basic dimensions with those of the Pennsylvania 'E6', as indicating what was considered desirable for a high-speed locomotive in the 1930s (see Table 17.2). The principal differences lay in the smaller diameter cylinders and longer stroke of the Milwaukee engine, but perhaps most notable of all the vastly higher boiler pressure of 300 lb. per sq. in. All the same, 'Atlantics' did not last long on the 'Hiawatha'. With its load of only six cars (310 tons) it had to be run in two sections daily, and at the busiest periods there were often seven sections. To avoid this expensive daily duplication a class of large streamlined 'Hudson' engines was introduced in 1938, having a tractive effort of 50,300 lb. and enabling trains of twice the weight to be worked to the same schedules.

American steam locomotive performance was at a very high level in the years 1935–9. On the 'Hiawatha' the Milwaukee 4-4-2s could keep time with loads up to nine cars (420 tons) and details of one trip show the fastest section from Portage to New Lisbon run start-to-stop in 32 min. 20 sec. at an average speed of 78·4 mph. Maximum speeds frequently exceeded 100 mph. The new 'Hudsons' of 1938

Table 17.2 American high-speed 'Atlantics'

Date	1915	1935
Railroad	Pennsylvania	Milwaukee
Cylinders dia, in.	23½	19
stroke, in.	26	28
Coupled wheel dia., ft in.	6–8	7–0
Total evap. heating surface, sq. ft	2,867	3,245
Superheater, sq. ft	810	1,029
Grate area, sq. ft	55·8	69·0
Boiler pressure, p.s.i.	205	300
Total engine wt., tons	107	127·5
Nominal tractive effort, lb.	31,300	30,700

were designed to haul sixteen of the lightweight cars used on the 'Hiawatha' – about 750 tons. For really heavy passenger train loads the New York–Chicago services of the New York Central were rarely surpassed, at the speeds then scheduled. With loads of 1,500 tons speeds of 75 mph had to be maintained on level track, and the basic dimensions of the NYC and the Milwaukee 'Hudsons' make an interesting comparison (see Table 17.3). It is a comparison made between one locomotive habitually used in very heavy 'moderate' speed services, and the other on 100 mph 'lightweight' trains.

In Great Britain there was at first no response from the London Midland and Scottish to the high-speed enterprise of the LNER. To meet a programme of steady acceleration of ordinary services, and the need for increased utilization of the locomotive stock, W. A. Stanier introduced an

Chicago, Milwaukee, St Paul and Pacific Railroad streamlined 'Atlantic' locomotive built for the 'Hiawatha' high-speed train.

entirely new range of locomotives, from large 'Pacifics' with a tractive effort of 40,300 lb. down to medium powered mixed traffic units; but the most interesting development at this stage was a high power non-condensing turbine locomotive. In the previous ten years several attempts had been made to improve the low overall efficiency of the steam locomotive by using turbine, instead of the traditional cylinder and piston drive. All previous attempts had included the use of condensers, as in marine propulsion practice. Illustrations of some of the most interesting of these experimental locomotives are included, as listed in Table 17.4. A locomotive of the Ljungstrom type was also built by Beyer, Peacock & Co. and run experimentally on the London Midland and Scottish Railway. Stanier's locomotive of 1935, which was built to compete with his large 'Pacifics' of the 'Princess Royal' class on the London–

Table 17.3 American 4-6-4 'Hudsons' of 1938

Railroad	New York Central	Milwaukee
Cylinders (2) dia., in.	22½	23½
stroke, in.	29	30
Coupled wheel dia., ft in.	6–7	7–0
Total evap. heating surface, sq. ft	4,187	4,166
Superheater, sq. ft	1,745	1,695
Grate area, sq. ft	81·5	96·5
Boiler pressure, p.s.i.	275	300
Total engine wt., tons	163	163
Nominal tractive effort, lb.	43,400	50,300

Table 17.4

Country of origin	Maker	Type	Total weight, tons	Tractive effort, lb.
Great Britain	Reid-Ramsay	Turbo-electric	154	22,000
Switzerland	Krupp-Zoelly	Condensing turbine gear drive	179	27,500
Germany	Maffei	Condensing turbine gear drive	169	30,000
Sweden	Nydquist & Holm	Ljungstrom condensing gear drive	141	32,800

Glasgow service, was non-condensing and was designed to try and secure some of the advantages of turbine propulsion without the complications arising from the use of condensers and all their attendant equipment. With all the locomotives previously mentioned, the additional maintenance work so reduced the availability of the locomotives in service as to outweigh completely any reductions in fuel consumption arising from increased thermal efficiency. Stanier had the co-operation of Metropolitan Vickers, and Ljungstrom, and the resulting locomotive, No. 6202, came near to being a great success. At its best

Attempted departure from conventional steam. The Ramsay turbo-electric condensing locomotive of 1923. The six-coupled drive units beneath the boiler and condenser sections were powered by 600-volt direct current electric motors.

208 The zenith of steam: 1935–45

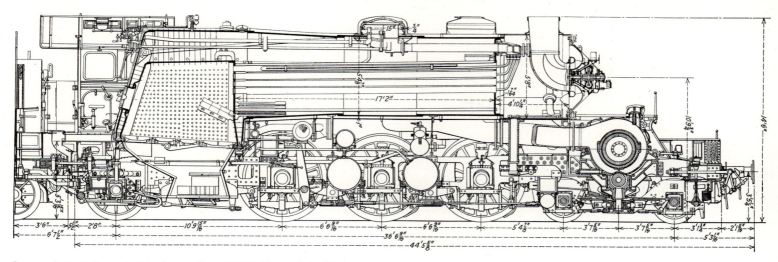

German State Railways turbine locomotive of 1926. The main turbine, which was situated above the bogie centre, transmitted its power by means of a double reduction gear through connecting rods to the six-coupled driving wheels.

the work of this engine was so good as to suggest that any amount of time and trouble was worthwhile, to secure maximum reliability; but unfortunately the outbreak of war in 1939 meant that the individual attention that the locomotive needed could no longer be given. Some serious failures occurred, and although it continued intermittently to give good revenue earning service, in the heaviest express duty, it was decided after the war to bring the experiment with non-condensing turbine propulsion to an end.

The nearness to complete success that Stanier and his men had attained before the war however was reflected in the decision of the Pennsylvania Railroad to have a huge 6-8-6 type locomotive built by Baldwin, on similar lines, in 1944. The French National Railways also contemplated a turbine-driven version of the de Caso 4-6-4 of 1940. The Pennsylvania, in anticipation of the westward spread of its electrified network, had delayed the development of its express passenger steam locomotive stud, relying on the 425 units of the 'K4' 'Pacific' class, which had the high tractive effort, for the type, of 44,000 lb. But in 1939 a four-cylinder non-articulated, streamlined 6-4-4-6 was built and displayed at the New York World's Fair, and this was followed in 1942 by the new standard design of the 4-4-4-4 type, with four cylinders $19\frac{3}{4}$ in. diameter by 26 in. stroke, 6 ft 8 in. coupled wheels, which with a boiler pressure of

LMSR: the Stanier non-condensing turbine locomotive No. 6202 of 1935, which did much excellent work.

below
The Pennsylvania 6-8-6 non-condensing turbine locomotive.

Backbone of the Pennsylvania high-speed passenger services in the later 1930s: the 'K4' 'Pacific' of which there were 425 in service.

300 lb. per sq. in. gave a tractive effort of 65,000 lb. These locomotives, of which fifty were built, though somewhat addicted to slipping could haul a load of 1,000 tons at 100 mph on level track. The turbine engine worked on the same duties as these 4-4-4-4s; but the life of neither was very long, because of the onset of the diesel-electrics after the end of the war.

By the end of the 1930s the era of the eight-coupled express passenger locomotive had definitely arrived, and some outstanding examples of the 4-8-2 and 4-8-4 type were produced for service in Canada, Australia, and for the 3 ft 6 in. gauge South African Railways, as well as for the USA. Details of five representative classes are set out in Table 17.5. The South African 4-8-2 is limited by reason of the 3 ft 6 in. gauge to a maximum speed of 55 mph, and the South Australian is primarily a mountain climber. The Canadian National 'U-2-g' was engaged in heavy and fast work between Montreal and Toronto, as well as on the long transcontinental runs at moderate speed; but both the Santa Fe and the New York Central 4-8-4s also had very severe assignments. The former, oil-fired, regularly worked through over the 1,234 miles from La Junta, Colorado, to Los Angeles on fast and heavy duty, manned successively by nine different crews, while the latter operated, without change, between Harmon and Chicago, 928 miles. Further reference to this latter duty is made in chapter 19 of this book.

In Great Britain, during the last years before the Second World War, it was a time of much record making. The demonstration run of 'The Silver Jubilee' train in September 1935, was followed a year later by the attainment of a maximum speed of 113 mph by the engine *Silver Fox* on a dynamometer car test with the southbound train. This was the highest speed ever reached by a British steam locomotive when hauling a service passenger train. Preparation for the high-speed Anglo-Scottish trains to be introduced in the coronation year of 1937 included a remarkable round trip from Euston to Glasgow, in which the 401·4 miles were not only run non-stop in both directions, but on the southbound run on 17 November 1936 the record average speed of 70 mph was made over the full journey. On both runs the locomotive was the Stanier 'Pacific' No. 6201, *Princess Elizabeth*. For the new 'Coronation Scot' train this design was developed into the 'Duchess' class, with many notable improvements, which, as will be told in chapter 19 of this book, came to make the record for the highest sustained power output of any British passenger locomotive. The first of the class, No. 6220, *Coronation*, attained a maximum speed of 114 mph on a demonstration run on 29 June 1937. For a year this remained, by a slight margin, the British railway speed record, but it was substantially beaten on 3 July 1938, when, in the course of some brake trials, the

Table 17.5 Eight-coupled passenger locomotives

Type	4-8-2	4-8-4	4-8-4	4-8-4	4-8-4
Railway	South African	Canadian National	South Australia	Santa Fe	New York Central
Rail gauge	3 ft 6 in.	4 ft 8½ in.	5 ft 3 in.	4 ft 8½ in.	4 ft 8½ in.
Class	'23'	'U-2-g'	'500'	'3771'	'Niagara'
Cylinders (2) dia., in.	24	25½	26	28	25½
stroke, in.	28	30	28	32	32
Coupled wheel dia., ft in.	5–3	6–1	5–3	6–8	6–7
Total evaporating heating surface, sq. ft	3,415	4,080	3,648	5,313	4,819
Superheater, sq. ft	661	1,835	835	2366	2,073
Grate area, sq. ft	62·5	84·3	66·6	108	101
Boiler pressure, p.s.i.	225	250	200	300	275
Weight – engine only, tons	111·2	178·5	144·5	227·5	210
Engine & tender, tons	216·2		222·3	428·5	360
Nominal tractive effort* (engine), lb.	49,000	56,800	51,000	80,040	65,000
Tractive effort booster, lb.			8,000		

*At 85 per cent boiler pressure.

LNER streamlined 'A4' 'Pacific' No. 4468, *Mallard*, was pressed to a maximum of no less than 126 mph and this remains a world record for steam traction.

In just over a year from these exciting and spectacular events railway traction in Europe was involved in equally vital, but vastly different matters. So far in this book I have been concerned mainly with the development of express passenger designs, because the service is at one and the same time the most spectacular and most demanding.

opposite above
South African Railways: the '23' class 4-8-2 express passenger locomotive (3 ft 6 in. gauge).

below
LMSR: the Stanier 4-6-2 No. 6201 *Princess Elizabeth*, maker of the record non-stop London–Glasgow runs of 1936.

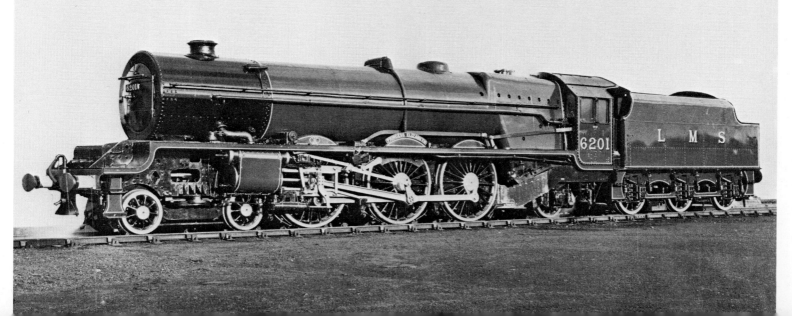

LNER: the Gresley 'A4' streamlined 'Pacific' No. 4468 *Mallard*, maker of the world's maximum speed record with steam traction, 126 mph on 3 July 1938.

But the war years demanded the availability of large studs of general purpose units, of good average tractive ability, but needing the minimum of day-to-day servicing. Before the war two designs, one British and one German, were already meeting this need, the Stanier 'Black Five' 4-6-0 of the LMSR and the Reichsbahn, class '50' 2-10-0. Construction of the 'Black Five' continued, but in Germany an austerity version was produced in 1942 designed with great skill to effect a maximum saving in materials and production time. The class '50' was not heavy for its high power – 85 tons for a tractive effort of 50,000 lb.; but in the so-called 'Kriegslokomotiv', class '52', by dispensing with everything not essential in a purely wartime locomotive, no less than 26 tons was saved, and the total weight in working order was 117 tons, as against 144 tons on the class '50' – still with a tractive effort of 50,000 lb. Eventually more than 10,000 of them were built, many in Austria.

While the war was still at its height, the thoughts of engineers responsible for railway traction were frequently turned towards post-war development. Two noteworthy designs, one British and one Franco-American, must be specially mentioned. In Great Britain, while long established and successful methods of maintenance in certain areas favoured the retention of old time orthodoxy, such as inside valve gears on outside cylinder locomotives, the general trend was to follow the Maunsell *dictum* 'make everything get-at-able'. Yet it was Maunsell's successor as Chief Mechanical Engineer of the Southern Railway, O. V. S. Bulleid, who went to the opposite extreme in his three-cylinder 'Pacific' engines of the 'Merchant Navy' and 'West Country' classes. The valve gear for all three cylinders was not only placed inside the frames, but totally

Striking example of a handsomely styled American 4-8-4 built by LIMA for the Southern Pacific 'Daylight' service between San Francisco and Los Angeles: tractive effort 64,760 lb., with an additional 13,000 lb. with the booster in action.

One of the German 'Kriegslokomotiv' 2-10-0 type, of which more than 10,000 were built: a post-war photograph at Vienna of one working on the Austrian Federal Railways. This example is fitted with the Giesl oblong ejector, which improved combustion and steaming.

enclosed in an oil bath – the idea being that thus ensconced it would need no attention. Very careful attention was given to the boiler design, to ensure free steaming on poor or variable quality coal. At their best the locomotives of both the passenger and mixed traffic variety were free running and developed a high output of power. But the concept as a whole was more ambitious than the detailed design could sustain, and they proved troublesome engines in service.

In November 1944, while the liberation of continental Europe was in progress, a French mission was sent to the USA to arrange for bulk supplies of new locomotives. At that time destruction of railways was so extensive that only one line remained open between Paris and the south, and the daily train by a circuitous route to Bordeaux, via Lyons, Nîmes and Toulouse, was worked by locomotives of the Chapelon P.O.-Midi 4-8-0 type, which were then about the only locomotives in the country still in reasonable working order. In consultation with the Baldwin Locomotive Works a design of two-cylinder 2-8-2 was worked out, and orders were given to the leading American and Canad-

One of the remarkable 1-4-1R mixed traffic locomotives, of which more than 1,300 were built by North American firms for the rehabilitation of the French Railways after the Second World War.

ian builders for 1,340 locomotives. They were a massive, characteristically American job, designed for hard thrashing, and maximum availability; and although so different from the traditional French designs they won universal acclaim from their free steaming, and trouble-free service under the most strenuous conditions. They worked passenger, freight, and along the Côte d'Azur were regularly assigned to real express work. Many of them were fitted for oil firing. They were the very antithesis of the Bulleid engines in England, which latter, of course, represented no more than a small and transient phase. In France, the 1-4-1R class, 'L'Americaine', showed the true trend of steam traction everywhere, which was resumed in full measure after the nationalization of the British Railways in 1948. By that time however the 'Zenith of Steam' had passed. Only the 'St Martin's Summer' remained.

18 The ultimate in articulation

Up to the year 1930, if one excepts a few locomotives of the Beyer-Garratt type introduced for medium-speed passenger service, the articulated locomotive generally was a slow-speed, heavy load hauler, and questions of riding stability did not enter the field of design problems. But the need to run faster freight services in the USA brought also the need for more powerful freight locomotives that could operate at 50 mph or even more. The non-articulated freight locomotive had virtually reached its limit in the three-cylinder 4-12-2s of the Union Pacific introduced in 1926, with a tractive effort of 96,600 lb., but the drawback to the use of articulated locomotives in faster service was the instability of the leading end due to its carrying less weight than the rear engine unit carried on to the main frames. One has only to look at broadside views of some of the largest articulated freight locomotives built around 1930 to appreciate how this might be so.

The Northern Pacific 2-8-8-4, of 1928, was not only the first four-cylinder simple of this wheel arrangement, but had what is believed to be the largest firegrate ever fitted to a steam locomotive, 182 sq. ft. It was designed to burn Rosebud lignite coal, which it had been found burned best on table-type grate bars with circular air openings. The mechanical stoker fitted had a capacity of 40,000 lb. per hour, and no difficulty was experienced in keeping that huge grate adequately fed. The dimensions of this locomotive, which had a tractive effort of 140,000 lb., are given in Table 18.1. They may be compared with those of the Southern Pacific locomotives of the same wheel arrangement, built for the mountain division of that railway, between Roseville, California, and Sparks, Nevada. This includes a steeply adverse stretch of 80 miles where the ruling gradient is 1 in $37\frac{1}{2}$, with 10 deg. curves, frequent tunnels and snowsheds. Even though all locomotives were

Northern Pacific RR: the 2-8-8-4 'simple' articulated locomotive type of 1930.

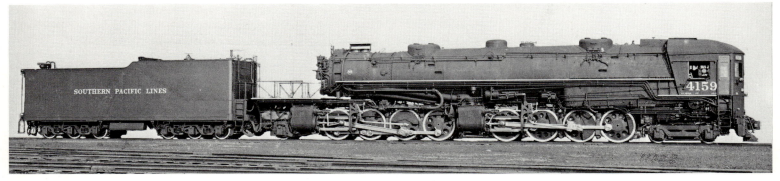

The Southern Pacific cab-in-front type of 'articulated' 2-8-8-4 type, oil-fired, 1937 design.

oil-fired, conditions in some of the long single line tunnels were so bad that the crews wore gas masks. Taking advantage of the oil firing a series of 2-8-8-4 articulateds, initiated in 1938, were turned back to front as it were, with the cab at the leading end, and a four-wheeled centre pin truck under the cab instead of the usual radial truck, so as to give more positive guiding. The radial engine unit however was just as unstable in its reversed position and crews were forbidden to ride on the open deck over the two-wheeled radial truck at any speed above 25 mph.

The era of the express articulated locomotive in the USA can be said to have originated with the 4-6-6-4 type first built by ALCO for the Union Pacific. Its success was due in large measure to an even weight distribution between the front and back engine units, and the superior guiding qualities of the four-wheeled truck at the leading

Table 18.1 Large 2-8-8-4 articulateds

Railroad	Northern Pacific	Southern Pacific
Cylinders (4) dia., in.	26	24
stroke, in.	32	32
Coupled wheel dia., ft in.	5–3	5–3½
Total evaporated heating surface, sq. ft	7,666	6,468
Superheater, sq. ft	3,224	2,601
Grate area, sq. ft	182	139
Boiler pressure, p.s.i.	250	250
Wt., engine only, tons	323	285
Total engine and tender, tons	503	459
Tractive effort, lb.	140,000	123,400

A fine example of the fast freight 4-6-6-4 on the Denver and Rio Grande Western.

end. A further refinement was to have front boiler supports with flat bearing surfaces together with no more than working vertical clearance on the single articulation pin. The stability in riding enabled these engines to be safely run up to 70 mph. A disadvantage of the 4-6-6-4 type, which is seen in the broadside illustration of the Western Maryland example, was that the grate was generally blocked off at the rear of the firebox throat plate to provide clearance for the rearmost pair of driving wheels. The firebox was relatively shallow, but it had an extended internal combustion chamber that provided good firebox volume for the available grate area. The combustion conditions were not so good as those obtainable on 2-6-6-4 and 2-6-6-6 engines like those of the Norfolk and Western, and of the Chesapeake and Ohio; but these latter were not considered to be such stable riders as the 4-6-6-4 type. The basic dimensions of all three are given in Table 18.2.

The climax so far as the American articulateds were concerned came in 1941 with the construction by ALCO of the Union Pacific 4-8-8-4 class, the largest and heaviest steam locomotive ever built. With an all-up weight of 534 tons they surpassed the previous maximum, which was held by the Northern Pacific 2-8-8-4s previously referred to. These latter were designed for slow heavy freight duties, whereas the new Union Pacific giants were designed to operate at speeds up to 80 mph. They were special purpose locomotives, designed to haul the heaviest freight trains over the Wasatch Mountains between Green River, Wyoming, and Ogden, Utah, where the ruling gradient is 1 in 88. To enable them to run steadily at maximum speed special attention was paid to the equalizing and spring rigging, so that despite their exceptional length, they could traverse not only horizontal curves easily, but also negotiate the vertical curves consequent upon marked changes of gradient, without undue shifting of the weight from one part of

Western Maryland 4-6-6-4.

Table 18.2 Fast freight articulateds

Railroad	Western Maryland	Norfolk & Western	Chesapeake & Ohio
Type	4-6-6-4	2-6-6-4	2-6-6-6
Cylinders (4) dia., in.	22	24	22½
stroke, in.	32	30	33
Coupled wheel dia., ft in.	5–9	5–10	5–7
Total evap. heating surface, sq. ft	5,770	6,650	6,794
Superheater, sq. ft	1,735	2,703	2,922
Grate area, sq. ft	118·8	122	135·3
Boiler pressure, p.s.i.	250	275	260
Wt., engine only, tons	268	255	336
Total engine & tender, tons	419	424	491
Tractive effort, lb.	95,500	104,500	110,200

the wheelbase to another. The basic dimensions show a general increase in size from earlier articulated locomotives, but one needs to study the accompanying drawing (page 222) to appreciate something of the immense proportions. The dimensions were:

Cylinders dia., in.	23¾
stroke, in.	32
Coupled wheel dia., ft in.	5–8
Total evap. heating surface, sq. ft	5889
Superheater, sq. ft	2466
Grate area, sq. ft	150·3
Boiler pressure, p.s.i.	300
Engine wt., tons	340·2
Engine & tender wt., tons	534·2
Tractive effort, lb.	135,375

The men nicknamed them the 'Big Boys' and their performance was in keeping with their size. Such was the wartime traffic over their appointed route however that one of them was not enough. One of our illustrations

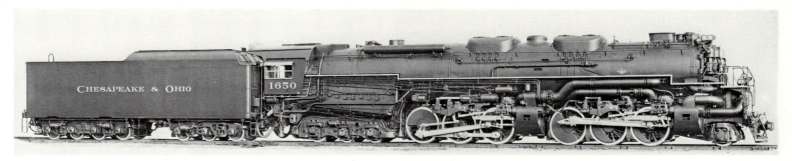

One of the highest developments of the American 'articulated': one of the 1948 series on the Chesapeake and Ohio, 2-6-6-6 type.

shows two of these monsters double-heading a very long and heavy train. One of their most important duties was to run the fast fruit trains, which were limited to a maximum load of seventy refrigerator cars, about 3,200 tons. The 'Big Boys' worked them over the mountains from Ogden to Green River, and for these, for the flatter grades eastward, the 4-6-6-4 articulateds were used. The mountain section usually took about $6\frac{1}{2}$ hours, for 200 miles, with intermediate stops for servicing and refuelling at Echo, Evanston and Carter. It was certainly significant of the work they had to do that although the tenders of these great engines carried 25 tons of coal they had to be refuelled twice in the $6\frac{1}{2}$ hour trip.

While the USA was developing the four-cylinder simple articulated to these vast proportions Great Britain was exporting ever larger examples of the Beyer-Garratt, mostly for use on rail gauges less than 4 ft $8\frac{1}{2}$ in. Because of these physical limitations the tractive effort of the largest designs did not reach the magnitude of the American locomotives, but even so 83,000 lb. represented a mighty big engine on the metre gauge. The physical conditions that in so many cases dictated design had arisen because many of the railways had been built to open up the countries concerned. There was no anticipation of any need for fast running; the sole aim had been to establish communication where nothing had previously existed. Originally there had been little prospect of heavy traffic; sharp curves, and steep gradients did not matter. The overriding consideration was to get some sort of a line through, at minimum cost. When heavier loads had to be moved, the problem of securing adequate fuel supplies was added to the natural complexities of the routes themselves, while in many of these virgin territories water was an even more difficult matter. The way in which a variety of awkward circumstances, in many one-time remote parts of the world, were successfully met is really the mid-twentieth century saga of one English firm, Beyer, Peacock & Co. Ltd.

The development of the Garratt type of articulated locomotive was not merely one of size. The basic principle of articulation was extremely simple and, as related in an earlier chapter, it permitted the use of a boiler of ideal proportions. But the very nature of the country through which these railways ran called for the highest standards

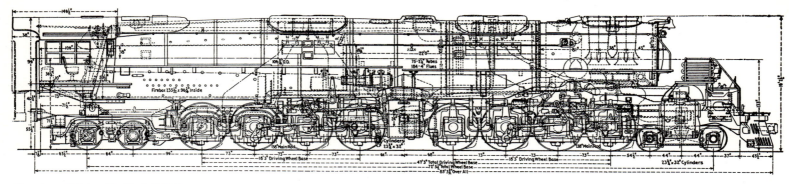

Drawing of Union Pacific 4-8-8-4.

of reliability in all the working parts, particularly in the jointing of steam pipes to suit the articulation, and in the design and lubrication of bearings, motion pins and such like which had to withstand extremes of climate and a terrain varying from desert to tropical jungle. Every detail was constantly under review in the drawing office and works of the builders, with the result that Beyer-Garratt locomotives put into service from 1935 onwards worked long mileages with little intermediate attention. It was equally the aim to make every detail as simple as possible bearing in mind that many of the crews were non-European. To the honour of these men it can also be added that they made an excellent job of handling these large locomotives.

Conditions in three African territories show clearly the kind of railways on which the Beyer-Garratt type was successfully introduced. In the Sudan the problems arose from the desert and lack of water. There were severe sandy conditions; in certain areas the watering stations were as much as 150 miles apart. Much of the track was laid with rails no heavier than 50 lb. per yard, which imposed a maximum axle load of 12 tons. Within these parameters a powerful locomotive of 38,400 lb. tractive effort was designed, in which economy in coal and water consumption was increased by use of feed water heaters. What can be achieved by scientific application of this principle will be recalled from the results F. H. Trevithick obtained on the Egyptian State Railways just before the First World War. An incidental distinction of these Sudanese Garratts was that they were the first anywhere of the 4-6-4+4-6-4 type.

On the west coast two separate railways in Angola introduced Garratts. The Luanda Railway is a relatively short metre gauge line, extending for no more than 265 miles inland, but nevertheless including gradients as steep as 1 in 33, curves of 5 chains radius, and attaining an altitude of 380 ft at Malanje. The Benguela Railway, on the other hand, extends from Lobito Bay for nearly 850 miles to the frontier of the former Belgian Congo, and, forming part of a continuous line of railway through Zambia and Rhodesia to South Africa, is 3 ft 6 in. gauge. Both railways in Angola purchased Beyer-Garratt locomotives of advanced design,

A tremendous power combination: two Union Pacific 'Big Boys' (4-8-8-4) type with a load of 101 cars on the 1 in 67 gradient of Sherman Hill, Wyoming.

A remarkable high-speed Beyer-Garratt: the Algerian 4-6-2+2-6-4 at Calais Maritime during dynamometer car trials on the Northern Railway of France.

of the 4-8-2+2-8-4 type, and having tractive efforts of 43,520 lb. (Luanda) and 52,360 lb. (Benguela). The Luanda engines are oil-fired, but the penetration of the Benguela Railway through many hundreds of miles of undeveloped jungle would have presented many difficulties and high cost in furnishing supplies of the more conventional forms of locomotive fuel, and the Garratts are fired with wood. In the early days of the railway, land was acquired on either side, and eucalyptus forests planted. These are maintained and progressive planting by mechanical means has ensured a steady supply of wood fuel alongside the line. The Garratts carry a crew of four, with two labourers in the fuel bunker passing the logs forward in addition to the driver and fireman.

In total contrast to the rate of travel on what, in the geographical sense, could be termed 'colonial' railways, a remarkable design of Beyer-Garratt locomotive was introduced for first-class express passenger service on the Algerian Railways in 1936. This followed the successful working of a prototype built in 1932, to the order of the Paris, Lyons and Mediterranean Railway, for its Algerian system. This locomotive, of the 4-6-2+2-6-4 type, was designed for really fast running. It was a four-cylinder simple, with the Cossart valve gear, then much in favour in France. The production batch of twelve included various improvements in design, and were remarkable in their steadiness at high speed. The prototype had been tested up to no less than 82 mph in Algeria, and one of the most spectacular tasks set to one of the later engines, before going to Africa, was the haulage of a fast English boat train from Paris to Calais and back, over the Nord system.

The design of the locomotive was the result of close collaboration between Beyer, Peacock & Co. and the French builders, the Société Franco-Belge, of Raismes (Nord). In view of what has been written earlier in this chapter about the difficulty of obtaining stability in riding with the large American Mallet engines, the weight distribution on this Algerian double-Pacific was interesting. The total weight on each engine unit was 106·2 tons, and of this 33·4 tons was carried by the four-wheeled bogie and 18·2 tons on each of the remaining axles. The proportion of 1:1·8 had been found to provide good stability on Beyer-Garratt locomotives with a leading bogie, and this was certainly confirmed on the high-speed French runs. Having a nominal tractive effort of 58,102 lb., which was practically double that of a Nord compound 'Pacific', no difficulty was experienced in hauling the boat trains to time. It was a case of observing the behaviour of the locomotive in continuous high-speed running conditions. French opinion was enthusiastically summarized by the *Revue Générale des Chemins de Fer*, in June 1936, translated thus:

> All these investigations and trials have confirmed the remarkable suitability of the double Pacific type GARRATT locomotives for the haulage of heavy trains at high speeds. Their perfect stability should permit the regular attainment of speeds in the neighbourhood of 140 km. (87 miles) an hour without difficulty on heavy, well laid track. This is the ideal type of locomotive for service on varied and difficult profiles.

Difficult profiles were certainly evident on the Kenya and Uganda Railway, which by the end of the 1930s seemed to be developing into an all-Garratt railway. From sea level at Mombasa its main line climbs to an altitude of 7,700 ft in 365 miles, with much bad curvature, gradients as steep as 1 in 50, and an axle loading limit over the 550 miles between Nairobi and Kampala of only 11¾ tons. With the slow running inevitable in such a territory and the long distances between crossing loops the carrying capacity of the line was becoming saturated. The only solution, other than the expensive alternative of putting in many additional loops, was to run longer and heavier trains. The 'EC1' and 'EC2' classes of Garratt, with the 4-8-2+2-8-4 wheel arrangement, and each with a tractive effort of 40,000

The largest Garratt ever on the metre gauge: one of the East African 4-8-2+2-8-4s of the 59th class.

lb., were doing excellent work; but something larger was needed, and at that time it was desired to have locomotives capable of operating over the entire main line between Nairobi and Kampala. Any new design was therefore subject to the maximum axle load restriction of $11\frac{3}{4}$ tons.

The answer was found in the remarkable 'EC3' class, the first ever to have the wheel arrangement 4-8-4+4-8-4, and the largest Garratt ever built to run on rails no heavier than 50 lb. per yard. These enormous engines, with a tractive effort of 46,100 lb., were however no more than a lead up to the ultimate in East African steam power. After the Second World War, with traffic still increasing, it was decided to take advantage of the more substantial road between Mombasa and Nairobi, laid with 80 lb. rails, by introducing still larger locomotives that would be confined in their operation to this section, and thus permit of greatly increased loads over the most congested section. The outcome was the colossal '59' class. Improvements in the track allowed an axle load of 21 tons, and the comparative proportions of the 'EC3' and the '59', shown in Table 18.3, are truly startling. I have had the privilege of riding on the '59' class and it is indeed an experience to go pounding up a 1 in 50 gradient, hauling more than 1,000 tons, round a curve so severe that at one time the rear of the train is running parallel to the head end, but in the opposite direction.

Ever since the classic tests in Natal in 1921–2 the South African Railways have been increasingly large and appreciative users of the Beyer-Garratt type, though not on the principal main line between Cape Town and the Transvaal. In the years after the Second World War powerful new varieties were introduced for the line between Johannesburg and Mafeking, for the 'Garden Route' along the south coast of the Cape province, and for further duties in Zululand and Natal. These are all relatively slow running routes, and it is on this account that the use of the Garratt type in Rhodesia has been of special interest. Shortly after the outbreak of war in 1939, Beyer, Peacock & Co. delivered four mixed traffic locomotives of the 4-6-4+4-6-4 type, known as the 15th class; these proved so outstandingly successful that the design was greatly multiplied after the war and is now the standard locomotive for both passenger and freight traffic on all the main steam operated routes. The coupled wheels are 4 ft 9 in. diameter, but the engines have a remarkable turn of speed, attaining the maximum permitted, 55 mph, with ease.

On these locomotives, except when looking directly ahead through the cab glasses, it is difficult to believe one is travelling on a 3 ft 6 in. gauge track. The overall width is 10 ft and the cab far more spacious than on the majority of British and European steam locomotives; but one's most lasting impression is that of the steadiness in riding. To be on one of them as it is approaching a curve at more than 50 mph and experience the way in which it glides

Table 18.3 East African Beyer-Garratts

Class	'EC3'	'59'
Wheel arrangement	4-8-4+4-8-4	4-8-2+2-8-4
Max. axle load, tons	$11\frac{3}{4}$	21
Cylinders (4) dia., in.	16	$20\frac{1}{2}$
stroke, in.	26	28
Coupled wheel dia., ft in.	4–6	4–6
Boiler pressure, p.s.i.	220	225
Total weight, tons	186·3	252
Tractive effort, lb.	46,100	83,350

Rhodesia Railways: one of the stoker-fired 20th class, 4-8-2+2-8-4, on a heavy freight from Bulawayo to Salisbury near Kombo.

South African Railways: one of the large 'GM' class Beyer-Garratts, with auxiliary water tank, for operating through near-desert country.

smoothly round, with no lurching or induced oscillation, is indeed an object lesson in the production of a locomotive that is well nigh perfect as a vehicle.

No less impressive is the freedom of steaming, though in this respect they are fortunate in having a good locomotive coal from Wankie readily at hand on the line. Before dieselization of the main line south through Botswana these engines worked through, on the caboose system, between Bulawayo and Mafeking, 484 miles. The various aids to running maintenance, such as the hopper ashpan and rocking grate, were used to good advantage on this long duty, which formed only one half of the complete round trip of 968 miles worked by the same two engine crews, manning and resting in the caboose alternately.

For purely freight duties of the heaviest kind these fine engines are surpassed by the 20th class, which, with a tractive effort of 69,330 lb., are fitted with mechanical stokers. The 15th class are hand fired, and carry an extra man, for getting coal forward and other duties. The com-

Table 18.4 Rhodesian Beyer-Garratts

Class	15th	20th
Wheel arrangement	4-6-4+4-6-4	4-8-2+2-8-4
Cylinders (4) dia., in.	17½	20
stroke, in.	26	26
Coupled wheel dia., ft in.	4–9	4–3
Total evap. heating surface, sq. ft	2,336	3,024
Superheater, sq. ft	494	748
Grate area, sq. ft	49·5	63·1
Boiler pressure, p.s.i.	200	200
Total weight, tons	179·5	225
Tractive effort, lb.	47,496	69,330

The ultimate in articulation

parative dimensions of the two classes are shown in Table 18.4. The 20th class handled loads of 1,600 and 1,700 tons on the hilly road leading north from Thompson Junction to the Victoria Falls. Although a new alignment has replaced the original, exceedingly severe gradients and curves of this projected 'Cape to Cairo' railway, the ascent is continuous at an average inclination of 1 in 150 for 20 miles with constant curvature. With one of the 15th class, and a freight train of 905 tons I have seen the 36 miles from Thompson Junction to Kasibi covered in 87 minutes start to stop. On the worst gradients the engine was working in 35 to 47 per cent cut-off with the regulator wide open, and the steaming perfect. A typical spurt by another of the 15th class, with a passenger train of 560 tons, was to run the 8·3 miles from Deli to Highfields in $12\frac{3}{4}$ minutes start to stop, with a maximum of 54 mph. These are good examples of the versatility of these excellent engines.

 The superseding of steam

By the end of the Second World War the standard nose-cab General Motors diesels were familiar sights on the railways of the USA. The spectacular peacetime trains like the 'City of San Francisco' carried heavier loads, but that merely meant putting an extra diesel unit at the head end. Diesels were attached to assist steam over difficult grades. The Great Northern, the Rock Island, the Southern were all early users of the diesels; but in those days it was perhaps the Santa Fe – a line on which steam had touched the topmost heights of its achievement in the USA – that the diesels began to make the biggest inroads. Eastern railroads like the New York Central, the Pennsylvania, and above all the Norfolk and Western at first resisted the challenge; but the gay new painting styles, and the American love of something new, were bringing in the diesels like an irresistible flood. And so far as the mountain divisions were concerned, they undoubtedly had the technical 'edge' on steam. Understandably, American influence was worldwide at the time. Servicemen, technicians and politicians too extolled the virtues of the new era that had dawned on the railways of the USA.

In Great Britain, whatever thoughts there may have been towards new forms of motive power, it had been a case of 'making do' and rebuilding existing steam units during the war years, but the immediate aftermath saw interesting moves towards new non-steam power on each of the four main line railways, despite the uncertainty caused by the general election of 1945, and the return of a Labour government pledged to railway nationalization. The LMSR and the Southern placed orders for prototype diesel-electric locomotives; the Great Western ordered two gas turbine electrics, while the LNER restarted work on the electrification of its severely graded main line between Manchester and Sheffield. Amid the post-war difficulties of obtaining adequate coal supplies the Great Western converted a number of its existing locomotives to oil firing. It was the LMSR project, pursued vigorously by H. G. Ivatt, the Chief Mechanical Engineer, that proved to be the most significant development. Construction of these two locomotives by the English Electric Company provided that firm with a design that with little adaptation was exported to many overseas railways. On the LMSR itself the intention was to carry out a series of exhaustive trials against standard steam locomotives to establish comparative running costs, availability and such like. The introduction of the gas turbines on the Great Western was backed by similar intentions except that in the latter case two different designs were involved, one built in Switzerland by Brown Boveri, and the other by Metropolitan Vickers.

The nationalization of the British railways, as from 1 January 1948, placed responsibility for all motive power development in the hands of the newly established Railway Executive, with R. A. Riddles as the member responsible for mechanical and electrical engineering. The economic situation at the time precluded any large scale importing of oil fuel for railway traction, and after a series of interchange trials between express passenger, mixed traffic and freight locomotives of the old companies, design work was started on a range of new standard steam locomotives embodying the best features of the regional types. Nevertheless, the excellent work done by the two LMS diesel-electric locomotives in regular express passenger service clearly provided a foundation for future building, when the time was more propitious. The design itself of the Co-Co arrangement was characterized by a robust simplicity in its details. The engine was a sixteen-cylinder, four cycle, turbo-charged unit having a 12 hour rating of 1,600 horsepower. The transmission was by six nose-suspended motors, with single reduction gear drive. By later criteria the complete locomotives, 61 ft 2 in. over buffers, and weighing 127·6 tons, were considered rather large and heavy for the power output; but Nos 10000 and 10001 were certainly milestones in British locomotive practice.

The new range of standard steam locomotives, of which the first appeared in 1951, were designed for the austere operating conditions of the day. They all had two outside cylinders, massive frames, ample bearing areas, and aids to maintenance such as self-cleaning smokeboxes, hopper ashpans, and all the running gear outside. They were designed to supplement rather than supersede the former company types, and in certain cases they worked in the same links. In view of this it was sometimes questioned why it should have been necessary to design a new range at all; but in 1948, and for some years afterwards, it was thought that steam would have to carry on for many years and that the new range would form the basis of necessary replacements. The majority of the smaller of the new types were developments of former LMS designs, which incorporated improved detail features, and only two of the British standard classes broke new ground. These were the '7MT' 'Pacific', known as the 'Britannia' class, from the name of the first engine, and the '9F' 2-10-0. The 'Pacific' had a somewhat mixed reception, particularly in areas where there was a strong loyalty to old traditions; but the '9F', which was the last of the range to appear, must be set down as one of the most successful classes ever to run the rails in Great Britain. Details of the design and its actual performance however belong to a later date in this particular theme.

In France, once the chaos of the 1944 and 1945 campaigns had subsided, railway engineers turned to a resumption of the motive power policies that had been interrupted by the war. Plans were prepared for further main line electrification, while the evolving of a unified programme of steam

British locomotive interchange trials of 1948: a Southern 4-6-2 'Merchant Navy' class working a London–Leeds express, with the ex-LNER dynamometer car.

The superseding of steam

A British standard class '7MT' 'Pacific' No. 70030 *William Wordsworth*, 'Britannia' type.

locomotive development, which had begun with the nationalization of the French Railways in 1938, proceeded under the master guiding hand of André Chapelon. Although, as told in chapter 17, a very favourable impression had been created by the American-built '141R' 2-8-2s there seemed no inclination to emulate the British example, and take the two-cylinder simple, with everything outside as the basis of future work. Compound expansion seemed likely to remain the sheet anchor of French practice. Orders had already been placed for many more of the successful four-cylinder compound '141P' 2-8-2, to bring the number of that class up to 358, but when it became apparent that a shortage of first line express passenger locomotives would develop soon, orders for the last forty of the '141P' 2-8-2s were cancelled, and a new design of four-cylinder compound 4-8-2 substituted. Because of the urgency this was, in part, based upon the original large-wheeled PLM 4-8-2 of 1932, then designated 241C1, which had done so well in the trials on the Nord in 1933. Because of the restrictions on materials construction of what became the '241P' class proceeded rather slowly, and it took four years – 1948–52 – to get the thirty-five engines built at the Le Creusot works. They were to do excellent work in the last years of French steam.

On the railroads serving the middle-west and western states of the USA the diesels made rapid headway, but in

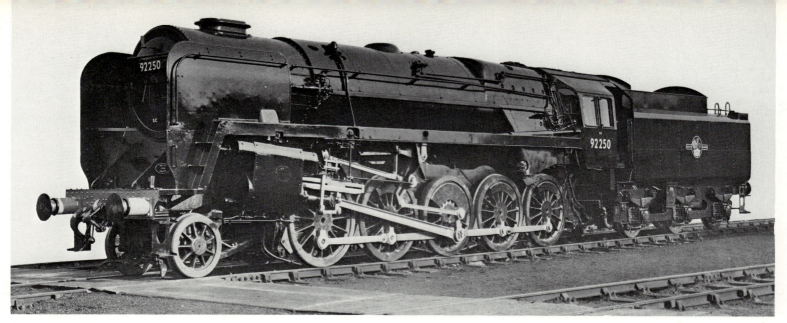

One of the British standard '9F' 2-10-0s.

areas where coal was readily available they were put to some searching tests, such as had been envisaged on the LMS in England when the prototype units 10000 and 10001 were introduced, in 1947. Of these American tests none were more comprehensive than a series conducted on the New York Central to compare the vital matter of availability. This was one of the factors on which a great superiority was claimed for the diesel. On the other side it was emphasized that in most cases comparison was being made between steam designs ten years old or earlier, backed up often by superannuated servicing facilities in the roundhouses. Accordingly the New York Central staged a long term trial of their latest 'Niagara' class 4-8-4s, built by ALCO in 1945. Six of these engines were set against six diesels of equivalent tractive power, on the New York–Chicago service, which involved hauling express passenger trains of around 1000 tons at sustained speeds of 80 mph on level track. The following remarkable results were obtained from a whole year's running of the 'Niagaras', in each case an average from the six engines. Of the total of 8,760 hours in a year, 672 were set aside for attention in shops and routine inspection, leaving 8,088 hours available to the running department. Of this total the locomotives on an average were unavailable due to servicing, and so on, for 1,435. Then of the remaining time the following analysis eventuated:

The superseding of steam 233

New York Central Railroad: one of the large 'Niagara' class 4-8-4s working an express freight train.

Hours available	6,653
Hours available but not used	573
Hours used	6,080
Per cent availability	75·9
Per cent utilization	69·4

During the year of observation the average mileage per locomotive reached the enormous total of 314,694, equivalent to 862 miles per day. It is fairly safe to suggest that never previously had such performances been achieved by steam locomotives. The availability was equal to that of the competing diesels though the latter showed a slightly higher daily mileage. Dimensional details of the 'Niagara' class locomotives are given in chapter 17.

This trial went some way towards demolishing the argument that the higher initial cost of the diesels was justified by their increased availability; but in the USA as elsewhere factors other than straight technical comparison hastened the superseding of steam. The 'Niagaras' had a shorter life than might otherwise have been expected. To keep down the weight an alloy steel with a silicon content had been used for the boiler plates, and after a distressingly short time these developed cracks. It would have been an expensive matter in any case to replace the boilers with new ones of the conventional carbon steel; but in view of impending dieselization it was out of the question. It would have been interesting to know how the '3771' class 4-8-4s of the Santa Fe would have fared in a similar comparison of availability.

In France post-war reconstruction included extensions

of the electrified system at 1,500 volts d.c. on the Paris–Orléans–Midi line, and conversion from steam of the main line of the PLM southwards from Paris. Electrification of the Orléans road as far south as Tours was completed in 1933, and the heavy express traffic had been successfully worked by locomotives of the 2-Do-2 type. They were found capable of running up to 90 mph and developing over 4,000 horsepower at the drawbar. For the post-war extensions to the electrified system, a locomotive of slightly greater power capacity was at first contemplated, with improvements in detail design found desirable from the twenty years' experience with the 2-Do-2 on the Orléans road. Then however a surprising factor supervened.

As soon after the end of the war as May 1946 an enormous new steam passenger locomotive took the road in France. André Chapelon had taken an experimental three-cylinder simple 4-8-2 delivered to the État system in 1932, and entirely rebuilt it as a three-cylinder compound 4-8-4. Chapelon will always be renowned for his rebuilds of older engines, but this one could have brought him the greatest fame of all. The features that had contributed to the success of the P.O.–Midi 'Pacifics' and the subsequent 4-8-0s were all present on a magnified and improved scale; the Kylchap blastpipe was of triple orifice, but the most interesting feature was the use of three rather than four cylinders. In this respect Chapelon, with some deliberation, had followed the Smith-Johnson system on the English Midland Railway. Having only one high pressure cylinder, inside, enabled him to have enormously stronger crank webs on the driving axle. This was a necessary provision seeing that the power developed in that one inside cylinder sometimes exceeded 2,000 indicated horsepower. It was an outstandingly successful engine – probably the most powerful steam express passenger unit to run outside North America, often producing equivalent drawbar horsepowers exceeding 4,000. Unhappily however it did not last long, though its influence was profound.

Unlike its unlucky contemporaries on the New York Central, its herculean feats of load haulage were not achieved at the expense of subsequent mechanical failure. '242A1' was a singularly trouble-free locomotive; but the edict had gone forth, 'no more steam', and this noble engine remained the only one of its kind. At the time it was making its remarkable runs, however, the electrical engineers were designing the new locomotives for the PLM line, a moderate advance in power capacity upon the Paris–Orléans 2-Do-2 type. But when the test results from '242A1' became known it was realized that Chapelon had produced a steam locomotive fully equal, if not a little superior, in power to the largest high speed electric locomotives, and which could equal their finest performances. The design of the new electric locomotives was then hurriedly changed to incorporate the maximum possible power, and the new '9100' class, which appeared in 1951, had a capacity of about 1,000 horsepower more than was originally intended – thanks to the stimulating competition of Chapelon's '242A1'. The development of the high speed electric loco-

The giant Chapelon three-cylinder compound 4-8-4 locomotive No. 242A1 : the most powerful locomotive to run in Europe.

The superseding of steam 235

Culmination of Canadian Pacific steam locomotive development: the '5921' class 2-10-4 'Selkirks', for service in the Rocky Mountains.

motive, from this indirect starting point, is discussed in all its fascinating detail in the next chapter.

At this stage the diesel locomotive was not making much headway in France. The conditions of long sustained high speed running on lines like the Nord, PLM, and the Orléans favoured steam as much as diesel, and it was to large scale electrification that the French railways were turning. In Canada however conditions strongly favoured the diesel. The principal traction problem there was with freight, and in many areas over very severe gradients. The working of heavy trains through the Rocky Mountains in British Columbia provided a feast for the photographers, with three and sometimes four great steam locomotives pounding up the severe inclines of the Kicking Horse Pass, and the Beaver Hill on the Canadian Pacific main line to the west; but it was not efficient rail roading, and it was on the divisions west of Calgary that the General Motors diesels made their first impact. Their traction characteristics gave them an immediate and pronounced advantage over the great 2-10-4 'Selkirks'. And from this beginning their use spread rapidly all over Canada. They could be used in multiple on the great transcontinental passenger and freight trains, without the duplication or triplication of engine crews that was needed when two or three steam locomotives were used. At this early stage the standard General Motors nose-cab locomotives were purchased, the type that became known later as the 'first generation' diesels.

Meanwhile in Great Britain, for the first ten years after the end of the war, steam still reigned supreme. The main line diesels could be counted on the fingers of one hand, and the widespread introduction of the new standard types infused a healthy competition, where regional loyalties remained strong. One very important feature of this period in British locomotive history was the establishment of new and wholly scientific methods of testing on the modernized stationary plant at Swindon, and on the new plant at Rugby. The principle of testing at constant steam rates was followed, eliminating the variable factors inevitably associated with dynamometer car testing at variable speed out on the line. The testing of a locomotive in a laboratory, as it were, enabled features of design to be studied, and those contributing to indifferent performance eliminated. Certain locomotives of pre-war design, the performance of which had deteriorated in the austere running conditions of the post-war years, were closely studied, and improvements made that restored their performance to its former levels of efficiency.

Examples of adjustment with locomotives of pre-nationalization origin will give an insight into the ceaseless quest for greater efficiency in steam locomotive performance, at a time when, on a worldwide basis, it was generally considered that the days of steam traction were nearly over. In the Western Region the famous four-cylinder 4-6-0s of the 'King' class had their draughting arrangements in the smokebox modified to deal with inferior coal, and some were fitted with high degree superheaters. This enabled pre-war express train schedules to be restored despite the continuing variation in quality of fuel supplies. On the former London and North Eastern Railway wartime troubles with the Gresley conjugated valve gear had led to the introduction of new designs of 'Pacific' with a modified layout of the machinery, and boilers with larger fireboxes. But none of these new designs measured up to the best pre-war standards of the Gresley 'Pacifics' and the answer was found in greater precision of repair work, optical lining up of frames, cylinders and horn guides, together with a substitution of the de Glehn type of big-end for the inside connecting rod instead of the previous marine type. These changes worked like a charm, and in their last years the Gresley 'Pacifics' of both streamlined and non-streamlined varieties were doing work that surpassed their pre-war finest. The haulage of the 400 ton 'Elizabethan' express non-stop over the $392\frac{3}{4}$ miles between King's Cross and Edinburgh at a booked average speed of 60 mph was an outstanding piece of steam locomotive working.

In the Southern Region much study was made to try and eliminate the many unreliable features of the very powerful Bulleid air-smoothed 'Pacifics'. Ultimately however it was concluded that nothing short of a drastic rebuild would suffice. The air-smoothed casing was removed, and the front-end completely reconstructed on orthodox lines, removing the totally enclosed valve, and substituting three sets of standard Walschaerts motion. While in this modified form the locomotives did not surpass their best achievements in the original form, they became good, reliable traffic units, still capable of very speedy running. One of the larger variety, *Clan Line* of the 'Merchant Navy' class, attained a maximum speed of 104 mph when hauling the 'Atlantic Coast Express'. So far as maximum recorded sustained power output is concerned the record for a British steam locomotive was attained by one of the Stanier four-cylinder 4-6-2 'Duchess' class in the course of some controlled road tests following a trial session on the stationary plant at Rugby. With a load equal to 900 tons behind the tender the long 1 in 100 gradient between Settle Junction and Blea Moor, on the former Midland line to Carlisle, was climbed at a steady 30 mph with the boiler steamed at the record rate of 38,500 lb. per hour for 30 minutes on end. In Great Britain there have been many transient outputs of power greater than this, but none steadily maintained for so long. The equivalent drawbar horsepower was 2,225 – a remarkable figure at so relatively low a speed; with such an output from the boiler the power output at 60 mph would have been over 3,000 *drawbar* horsepower. The engine concerned was the *Duchess of Gloucester*, No. 46225.

The British standard '9F' 2-10-0 proved a remarkably versatile high-power mixed traffic engine. The original intention had been to make it a 2-8-2, as a direct variant of the 'Britannia' class 4-6-2; however, to provide greater

The superseding of steam 237

British Railways: the ex-LMSR 4-6-2 No. 46225 *Duchess of Gloucester* climbing the Beattock Incline, with a Glasgow express. It was this engine that achieved the record output in trials on the Settle and Carlisle line.

adhesion the ten-coupled arrangement was finally decided upon, and with 5 ft coupled wheels and a boiler pressure of 250 lb. per sq. in., the tractive effort was 39,667 lb. But the surprising feature of these locomotives was their freedom in passenger train running in addition to their ability to handle maximum tonnage freight trains. Several instances were recorded of maximum speeds of 90 mph when these engines were used on express passenger trains.

A total of 221 was built. The last one, the No. 92220, completed at Swindon Works in 1960 and specially named *Evening Star*, was the last steam locomotive to be built for service on British Railways.

While the steam locomotive was enjoying its St Martin's Summer in Great Britain it was only in India and South Africa that steam was envisaged as a first line form of railway traction for some years to come. In South Africa the role of the Beyer-Garratt articulated locomotives has already been described; but for heavy and fast main line work in non-electrified areas a new non-articulated type of maximum proportions was introduced in 1951. The increase in loading of passenger and freight trains crossing the High Veldt between Kimberley and De Aar Junction, and southwards over the Great Karoo desert, was providing a problem in haulage, particularly in view of the scarcity of natural water, and the new locomotives were arranged to condense their exhaust steam and thus use the same water over and over again. They were a development of the '15F' class 4-8-2 but with a large firebox having a grate area of 70 sq. ft and mechanically fired. Although very large and of the 4-8-4 type, the tenders containing the condensing apparatus were even longer, and the ensemble had a total length of 111 ft over the couplers, of which the tender accounted for 60 ft 5 in. The arrangements for condensing are very interesting. Exhaust steam from the cylinders is passed into a turbine which drives a fan blower in the smokebox. This replaces the normal draught created by the action of the blastpipe. From the blower turbine the exhaust steam passes in a large pipe along the side of the locomotive, and then through an oil separator to another turbine in the tender. This latter turbine drives a series of intake fans. Finally the steam passes to the condensing elements mounted on both sides of the tender, and the condensate is collected in a tank fitted underneath the tender frame whence it is fed back to the boiler. These great locomotives often run over 600 miles without taking water. Their basic dimensions are, cylinders 24 in. diameter by 28 in. stroke; coupled wheels 5 ft diameter; boiler pressure 225 lb. per sq. in.; tractive effort 51,000 lb.

In the rapid spread of diesel traction all over the world, the main tendency has been to use the slow running marine type of engine, of which the American '567' Kettering

Eastern Railway of India: one of the standard semistreamlined 'WP' class 'Pacifics'.

and the Swiss 'Sulzer' are excellent examples, with electric transmission. Notable variations are the German hydraulic drive, which, in addition to its adoption by the Deutsches Bundesbahn, was used on the Western Region of British Railways for its express passenger units of the 'Warship' and 'Western' classes. In practically every early example the external styling of the locomotives was designed to provide a degree of streamlining effect, with the casing built out to the normal limit of the loading gauge, and so presenting a continuity of outline between the locomotive and the coaching stock. This has continued in later British and continental European designs. In the USA, however, what are sometimes referred to as the 'second generation' diesels are more functional in their external design. The body casing only encloses the machinery and a walkway is provided in the open, outside the engine casing. This provides much more ready access for servicing, because once the casing doors are opened there is ready ingress

The superseding of steam

South African Railways: one of the '25' class 4-8-4s of 1951 with the condensing tender.

right
One of the most numerous and successful of British diesel-electric designs: the Brush Type '4' 2,750 horsepower, class '47'.

far right
'Second Generation' type diesels in the USA: a group of 3,000 horsepower units in service on the Chicago, Milwaukee, St Paul and Pacific Railroad.

from outside, instead of through the relatively narrow passage inside the early types of locomotive. An outstanding exception to the general trend of diesel-electric design, and one equally outstanding in its record of successful service, is the English Electric 'Deltic' type which uses the Napier quick running aero-type delta engine. Twenty-two of these locomotives, having an engine horsepower of 3,300, have for some years been operating the high-speed express passenger service on British Railways between King's Cross and Edinburgh, at maximum speeds of 100 mph.

An important trend in the transition from steam traction has been the adoption in many countries of the self-contained unit train. It was a natural development in England when the Southern Railway began to extend its electrified suburban network to the nearer coastal towns; but it has been adopted for longer distance services of the luxury type, incorporating many pleasant amenities for travellers paying supplements above the basic fares – British examples were the 'Blue Pullmans', while numerous high-speed European trains of relatively limited accommodation owe their inspiration to the success of the original German high-speed railcar trains of the 'Flying Hamburger' type introduced before the Second World War. To a motive power department and to traffic operators alike, a train that requires no separate locomotive can be a great convenience, except of course that a defect in one of the motors can put the whole train out of action. In Holland today practically the entire internal passenger train network is provided by fast multiple-unit trains, either electric or diesel. It is only the international express trains and the freights that require separate locomotives.

This chapter concerns mainly the period up to the year 1960, but by way of a prelude to the remarkable events I have to record in the last three chapters of this book, some mention must be made at this stage of the process of the

The superseding of steam 241

British Railways: one of the 3,300 horsepower diesel-electric locomotives, Deltic type, with the high-speed Napier aero type engine, here shown working a northbound Pullman express, on the East Coast Route.

evolution that characterized the railways of Japan in the years after the Second World War. The original 3 ft 6 in. gauge network, built at a time when speed of travel was of no consideration, and minimum cost of construction was important, had become hopelessly out of date, and congested with much slow-moving traffic in the 1930s. The steam locomotives employed were of good design and were well maintained, but were unsuited to the needs of a swiftly expanding nation. Even before the Second World War plans were being formulated for an entirely new high-speed network, that would be electrically operated; and although no final decisions had been taken by 1939, it was generally felt that the existing 3 ft 6 in. gauge was too narrow for the high speeds felt to be essential in the future. At that time the fastest running in the world on the 3 ft 6 in. gauge was being made on the electrified sections of the South African Railways; but 60 mph was far below what was envisaged on the new railways of Japan. The war, and the havoc caused to railway properties by bombing in its concluding stages, greatly delayed the implementation of these plans for development, and it was not until the mid-1960s that the first section of the New Tokaido Line, was opened, using the 4 ft 8½ in. gauge. By then experience elsewhere in the world with high-speed electric railways had been carefully studied with beneficial effects.

20 High-speed electrics

The scene now moves to the short, but magnificent Lötschberg line. It is remarkable that the motive power practice of a railway with so little facilities of its own for really fast running should have come to exercise so striking an influence not only in Western Europe, but in Great Britain and very much farther afield. It would be the merest platitude to state that adhesion is of vital importance on a line with long sections of 1 in 37 gradient! In 1926 a locomotive class having the 1-Co-Co-1 wheel arrangement, 'Ae 6/8', was introduced. They were powerful and successful, of 5,300 horsepower, though rather heavy by later standards, weighing 140 tons. They were nevertheless followed in 1939 by an improved version, of 6,000 horsepower. Then in 1944 came the epoch-marking 'Ae 4/4I'. It was primarily an express passenger design, with a rated performance equal to haulage of a 390 ton train up the mountain ramps at the maximum permitted speed of 75 km. per hour (47 mph). While the later 'Ae 6/8' class of 140 tons had a capacity of 6,000 horsepower, the new 'Ae 4/4I' class, developing 4,000 horsepower, had a total weight of no more than $78\frac{1}{2}$ tons. This represented an improvement in the power–weight ratio of 19 per cent.

In the new locomotives the entire weight was available for adhesion. For the first time on a powerful main line electric express locomotive the non-powered 'carrying' wheels had been dispensed with, and this innovation was accompanied by all-round attention to weight reduction. The bogies and superstructure were of all-welded construction, and light alloys were used in the fabrication of the body. Adhesion weight may be important, but every ton has to be lifted up those tremendous gradients, and for a basic power output any reduction in locomotive weight means that a proportionately greater pay load can be hauled. The 'Ae 4/4I' was a beautifully balanced design, and

at once began to do superb work. Its success was quickly appraised by the Swiss Federal Railways, and was developed at first in a rather surprising direction. Enhanced power was needed for the fast inter-city trains, which required a high average speed on routes including much curvature. To make practicable a high curve speed without causing excessive wear on both locomotive and track a maximum axle load of 14 tons was stipulated. The Swiss Federal Railway engineers had by that time become familiar with the excellent riding qualities of the Lötschberg 'Ae 4/4I' locomotives, and to secure high adhesion for rapid acceleration the same wheel arrangement was adopted for a new design of express passenger locomotive first introduced in 1946.

French National Railways: one of the post-war '2D2-9101' class electric locomotives entering Lyons with an express from Paris.

left
Bern–Lötschberg–Simplon Railway: one of the 'Ae 4/4I' electric locomotives hauling a southbound international express train descending the 'southern ramp' into the Rhone valley.

With a total weight of 56 tons, the horsepower rating was 2,580 – almost the same power-weight ratio as in the Lötschberg locomotives. Fifty of these 'Re 4/4' locomotives were put into service and between them the Lötschberg and the Swiss Federal Railways had, to use a colloquialism, fairly 'started something'.

At first the French railways were a little slow in taking up this line of development. In the previous chapter I have told how their plans for post-war electric motive power had to be changed to meet the challenge of Chapelon's latest steam locomotives, and the massive 2-Do-2 '9100' class was the result. In the meantime, however, experiments had been initiated to try and obtain an all-adhesion express passenger locomotive, which would have at one and the same time an increased adhesion weight and reduced individual axle loading. Two prototype locomotives of the Co-Co type built in 1949 had a one-hour rating of 5,000 horsepower, for a weight of 102 tons, and on early trials a speed of 100 mph was attained in good riding conditions. It is interesting to compare, in Table 20.1, the proportions of these locomotives with the more conventional '9100'

Table 20.1 New French electric locomotives

Class	'7001'	'9101'
Type	Co-Co	2-Do-2
Length over buffers, ft	62	59
Total weight, tons	100	147
Max. axle load, tons	16·1	22·6
Rated horsepower, 1 hr	5,000	4,880
Horsepower, per ton	50	33

High-speed electrics 245

French National Railways: a 'CC-7101' class high-speed electric locomotive on a Toulouse–Paris express at Brive. It was No. 7107 of this class that attained a maximum speed of 206 mph in 1955.

ents and ever-increasing traffic had always presented a major problem in motive power, and in 1952 new locomotives of the Co-Co type were introduced. These had a one-hour horsepower rating of 5,820, and a total weight of 120 tons. In service they have proved very successful, taking 600 ton trains up the 1 in 38 gradients to the Gotthard tunnel at the maximum permitted speed of the line, 47 mph.

In France both the '9101' class and the prototype '7001' did first-class work. The rebuilding of the former PLM from the fearful destruction wrought in the last months of the war was accompanied by great improvements in the junction layouts and it became possible to run at the line maximum speed without any intermission from the outskirts of Paris through to Dijon. Both classes of locomotive hauled loads of 600 tons and more at speeds of 85 to 87 mph on level track and while so doing the 100 ton all-adhesion '7001' was as steady as the much heavier '9101' with a four-wheeled bogie at each end. Moreover the Co-Co was lighter on the track. The adhesion weights were the same, or nearly so, in both types with 90 tons in the '9101' against 100, but the maximum axle load of the '7001' was only 16·1 tons, against 22·6 tons. The power developed in actual service by the prototypes '7001' and '7002' and by the subsequent production batches numbered from 7101 upwards was so great that it was considered that a lighter locomotive could be introduced for general express service on the 1,500 volt d.c. electrified lines, and again with the Lötschberg 'Re 4/4I' as an example, the remarkable SNCF '9000' class was produced.

Such was the advance in electric locomotive design techniques that in this class a one-hour horsepower rating of 4,450 was obtained for an overall locomotive weight of only 78 tons. The following important features were included in these locomotives:

class, designed in readiness for the Paris–Lyons electrification. In comparison with the Lötschberg and the Swiss Federal locomotives the '9101' was rather heavy – on the Lötschberg the horsepower per ton was 51. But the SNCF was no more than feeling its way. The '7001', on the other hand, was the starting point for an astonishing development, which followed after two years of most comprehensive testing. While this was in progress the all-adhesion type of locomotive had been adopted for a further important Swiss assignment. The Gotthard line with its severe gradi-

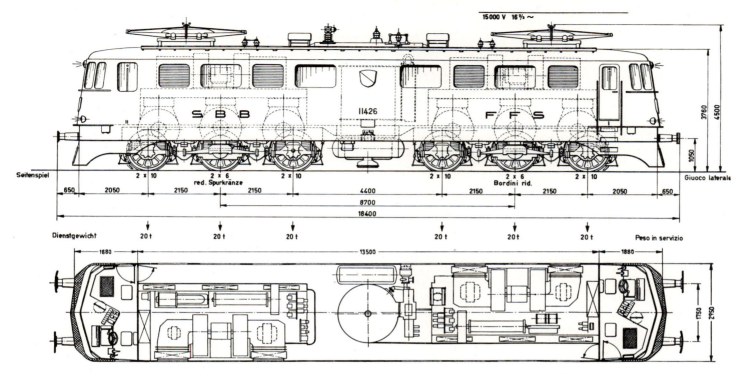

Swiss Federal Railways: diagram of the 'Ae 6/6' locomotive for the Gotthard line.

(a) The spring gear was of the carriage type on two stages of springs, the second stage between body and bogie being on the pendulum system.
(b) The motors were fully sprung, arranged in the centre of the bogies.
(c) The transmission of tractive force was through the body, the forces through the bogies being kept as low as possible.
(d) The two pairs of wheels of each bogie were coupled.

The total unsprung weight was only $12\frac{3}{4}$ tons, and this, in combination with the foregoing features, and a relatively long distance between the bogie centres of 30 ft $2\frac{1}{2}$ in. made an exceptionally steady and smooth-riding locomotive. In service on the former PLM line the Bo-Bo class were used turn and turn about with the larger and heavier Co-Co '7101' series, and to an observer in the train the performance

High-speed electrics

was indistinguishable. On the celebrated 'Mistral' express that I noted personally, locomotive No. BB 9276 had a load of 710 tons, and covered the 195·3 miles from Paris to Dijon in 142½ minutes, start to stop, while the average speed over the gradually rising 151·5 miles from Melun to the 1,325 ft altitude of Blaisy Bas was 88·3 mph. So far as maximum speeds are concerned, on special trials in 1955, south of Bordeaux, the following results were obtained:

  Co-Co No. 7107:   206 mph
  Bo-Bo No. 9004:   205·6 mph.

These spectacular results killed for all time the long-held conception that leading and trailing non-powered wheels in two-wheeled or four-wheeled trucks were essential to the smooth and safe running of a high-speed electric locomotive.

While results of a high excellence were attending the extensions of the 1,500 volt d.c. electrified system in France, some very important investigations were in progress with a system of alternating current traction at the commercial frequency of 50 cycles per second. The suggestion had come in the first place from a Hungarian engineer, K. Kando, and between the two world wars two lines had been equipped experimentally, one in Hungary itself and one in Germany. After the Second World War the German line, which connected the Rhine valley with a tourist region in the Black Forest, came into the French zone of occupation, and French railway engineers became closely acquainted with its operation. It had then been working successfully for about ten years, using a voltage of 20,000. One of the greatest deterrents in the path of widespread railway electrification is the high capital cost, particularly in the overhead line and its structures, and in the sub-stations; but the high tension 50-cycle system offered a substantial saving in this respect, even though the locomotives would be more costly. The French railways decided

French National Railways: one of the early 25,000-volt a.c. 50-cycle locomotives on the line between Dole and Vallorbe.

on a trial of the single-phase high tension 50-cycle system, and a stretch of 48½ miles on the Geneva–Chamonix line, between Aix-les-Bains and La Roche-sur-Foron, was equipped.

Because of the connection between the experimental 50-cycle line and the 1,500-volt system at Aix-les-Bains, the first locomotive built for the former was designed so as to be able to work also over the 1,500-volt system, though at somewhat reduced power; but in any event the 50-cycle line proved a great success, and it was estimated that the capital cost of equipping a main line with the system would be no more than two-thirds of that necessary with direct current. These conclusions, reached late in 1951, immediately faced both the French and the British railways with the need to make vitally important decisions.

Both administrations were then quite decided in their policy to use the 1,500-volt d.c. system. In France extensions to the existing equipment were rapidly being made; in Great Britain, a committee reporting to the British Transport Commission in 1951 confirmed two pre-war recommendations that the 1,500-volt d.c. system should be adopted. Yet the financial savings that the high tension 50-cycle system held out were so large that they could not be ignored, and in France a decision was taken to electrify the important north to south freight-carrying route between Thionville and Valenciennes, at 25,000 volts a.c. 50 cycles. Quite apart from the economy of installing this system, in preference to other systems of electrification, 105 new electric locomotives replaced no less than 304 steam locomotives. This pilot scheme, covering 188 route miles, came into operation in 1954; it proved so successful that the French railways decided that all future main line electrification should be on this system. In Great Britain on the recommendation of S. B. Warder, then Chief Electrical Engineer, a similar decision was made for the projected electrification of the London Midland main line from Euston to Liverpool and Manchester.

The first French lines radiating from Paris that were equipped on the 25,000-volt 50-cycle system were those of the Nord, from Paris through Amiens to Lille, and then the Eastern Region main line to Nancy and Strasbourg. The first named included the working of the English boat trains between Paris and Amiens, with change of traction from electric to steam at Amiens itself. The new express locomotives were of the Bo-Bo type, with a continuous horsepower rating of 4,920, and they were geared for a maximum speed of 100 mph. The mechanical part of their design was based on the successful direct current Bo-Bo locomotives of the '9200' class. The traction motors were direct current, working at 920 volts, fed from Ignitron rectifiers. When electric traction was first introduced the change south of Amiens was little short of sensational in the way the electric locomotives dashed away, attained the maximum permitted line speed of 87 mph, and sustained this unvaryingly uphill and down dale, irrespective of gradient and train load. Enthusiasts with nostalgic and historic leanings nevertheless found great enjoyment in the continued excellent performance of the Chapelon 'Pacifics' between Amiens and Calais, even though the running speeds were slower than those of the new electrics. The maximum permitted line speed north of Amiens was the old French standard of 120 km. per hour (74·5 mph).

While British Railways had decided to use the 25,000-volt 50-cycle system for all new electrification, the Southern Region was so far committed to the 660-volt direct current system, with third-rail pick-up, that when this was extended to Folkestone and Dover, special arrangements had to be made for certain of the continental train workings, such as express freights for the train ferry service, and the 'Night Ferry' passenger train, with its through sleeping cars for Paris and Brussels. Locomotives were needed of a mixed traffic character. Many problems were involved in the design, because the locomotives had not only to run fast, with the express passenger trains, but also to operate loose-coupled freights, picking up vehicles in sidings and yards where third-rail electrification would be impracticable. They were therefore fitted with pantographs for overhead current collection as well as with pick-up shoes. Another problem was that of the gaps in the conductor rails, over level crossings and such like. With multiple-unit trains there would always be sufficient collector shoes to ensure continuity of supply; but on the new locomotives a booster motor generator set was installed. The motor and generator shaft carry a heavy flywheel to provide the kinetic energy to maintain the

High-speed electrics 249

British Railways: Southern Region, 2,500 horsepower electric locomotive for the Kent Coast electrification, with third rail pick-up, on the 'Golden Arrow' Pullman boat express.

British Railways: two of the 25,000-volt a.c. 50-cycle electric locomotives at Crewe, in 1965.

speed of the set over breaks in the normal supply caused by gaps in the conductor rails. These locomotives which are of the Bo-Bo type have a rated horsepower (one hour) of 2,500, and a maximum speed of 90 mph.

For the London Midland main line electrification the basic design of the Bo-Bo general purpose locomotives was similar to that of the French 25,000-volt locomotives of the same wheel arrangement, though there were naturally many differences in detail. As in France the traction motors are direct current, fed through rectifiers, and the service was planned from the outset for regular running by all express passenger trains at 100 mph. The work of rebuilding the track and furnishing the overhead equipment began at the northern extremities, and it was extended southwards until the full electrified service from London (Euston) was inaugurated in April 1966. Then journey times of the inter-city express trains were greatly reduced, and the frequency of service increased to a rapid regular interval pattern. In general terms the new electric locomotives were required to maintain start-to-stop average speeds of 80 mph with twelve-car trains of about 430 tons. It was soon demonstrated that an ample margin of power existed for recovery of lost time, through incidental delays, and punctuality was of a high standard. On the busiest part of the line, the $82\frac{3}{4}$ miles between Euston and Rugby, the density of high-speed traffic was the greatest in the world. It has since been considerably increased, and individual train performance enhanced with an improved design of electric locomotive.

In the meantime the Japanese National Railways had brought into operation the first section of their Shinkansen network, or 'New Lines'. Reference has been made earlier in

Japanese National Railways: one of the 'Hikari', or 'Lightning', trains entering Kyoto before its 130 mph run to Tokyo.

this book to the physical handicaps imposed by the 3 ft 6 in. railway system of Japan, from the circumstances in which it was originally constructed; but for the new line, built to the 4 ft 8½ in. gauge, little expense can have been spared, and a magnificently straight and direct line, regardless of all obstacles, was built to permit of continuous running from end to end of the country at 130 mph. It is a completely self-contained railway, and while the original intention was to run some freight traffic at night, the development of the train service in response to popular demand has been such that it is now confined entirely to passenger trains. The Hikari, or 'Lightning', trains run at 15-minute intervals throughout the day from 6 a.m. to 9 p.m. They are all alike, consisting of sixteen cars with a passenger-seating accommodation of 1,400. Every axle of every car is motored, and with motors of 250 horsepower there is 16,000 horsepower available for the complete train. The traction system is 25,000 volts a.c. at 60 cycles per second, the Japanese commercial frequency. On a typical run that I noted personally we ran the 213·5 miles from Tokyo to Nagoya in 120¼ minutes, start-to-stop, an average speed of 106·7 mph. We then continued over the 84 miles to Kyoto in 48¾ minutes, a start-to-stop average of 103·7 mph.

The Shinkansen network is being extended in many directions now and the newer sections are being built to carry a regular service speed of 160 mph. I had the privilege of riding in the driver's cab on one of these very fast trains. The actual running was extremely smooth, particularly when accelerating and braking. I noted some very rapid starts from rest including the attainment of maximum speed, 131 mph, in 3 min. 57 sec. from a dead start. Safety

High-speed electrics

of operation is provided by continuous inductive train control from the track circuits, and while the driver has a continuous visual instruction in front of him indicating the maximum speed at which he may run, there are no signals along the line. If the driver should exceed the maximum speed indicated on his panel, the brakes are automatically applied.

In contrast to this highly standardized single-purpose railway, modern engineering techniques have been exercised to notable effect in dealing with the varied railway conditions on the continent of Europe. No fewer than four different systems of electric traction are currently in use in Western Europe, thus:

1,500 volts direct current	France, Holland
3,000 volts direct current	Belgium, Luxembourg, Italy, Spain
15,000 volts a.c. $16\frac{2}{3}$ cycles	Switzerland, Austria, Western Germany
25,000 volts a.c. 50 cycles	France (new electrifications), Great Britain

With the international express trains it had been traditional for many years that some inter-running took place. French steam locomotives used to work throughout on the non-stop expresses between Paris and Brussels. With the development of the Trans-European Express network an extension of this principle was desired, with electric traction, and French railway engineers, who had already built locomotives that would operate on two different traction systems, produced the celebrated quadri-current type of locomotive, which can run over any of the electrified systems in Western Europe. The traction motors are 1,500 volts d.c. but the locomotives are equipped with four different pantographs. These do not, in themselves, correspond to the four different traction systems, but to the physical details of the overhead line construction shown in Table 20.2.

Table 20.2

Pantograph no.	Used on	
	Railway	Overhead supply
1	France	1,500 d.c.
	Holland	1,500 d.c.
	Belgium	3,000 d.c.
	Luxembourg	3,000 d.c.
2	France	25,000 a.c.
	Luxembourg	25,000 a.c.
	Italy	3,000 d.c.
3	Switzerland	15,000 a.c.
4	Austria	15,000 a.c.
	Germany	15,000 a.c.

The design of the locomotives is such that change can be made from one system to another without stopping. There is a selector index on the instrument panel, with seven positions. These define automatically the choice of pantograph to be raised, and simultaneously interlocks the group of electrical controls corresponding to the system of overhead line power supply that will be used. None of the electrical circuits are energized, however, until a comprehensive routine of cross-checking has taken place. Not until all this has been done and proved correct can the driver resume control in the ordinary manner. It takes quite a time to describe in detail the various checks that have to be made; but in actual practice it is all done in a matter of seconds. I rode on the locomotive working 'L'Étoile du Nord', the luxury Pullman train, non-stop

French National Railways: one of the quadri-current high power electric locomotives, at Brussels Midi station, before leaving with the non-stop 'Étoile du Nord' TEE for Paris, in the course of which run the power supply is changed from 3,000 volts d.c. in Belgium to 25,000 volts a.c. in France.

High-speed electrics

French National Railways: one of the 1,500-volt d.c. 'CC 6500' class electric locomotives at the Gare d'Austerlitz, Paris, before leaving for Bordeaux with 'L'Étendard' – a train that involves much running at 125 mph.

from Brussels to Paris, and at the Franco-Belgian frontier power was shut off for a very short time and speed reduced to 56 mph while the change in pantographs took place. We covered the 192·3 miles between the two cities non-stop in 139½ minutes, an average speed of 82¾ mph.

The maximum speed on this interesting journey was 100 mph but on the former Paris–Orléans line there are lengthy stretches scheduled to be covered at 125 mph by the fastest trains. Equally one never ceases to be amazed at the loads carried. Certainly the French railway engineers have rapidly stepped up the capacity of their locomotives until now the maximum *continuous* horsepower rating of the latest and largest is no less than 7,400. The development may be appreciated from Table 20.3. The 'CC 6500' class are superb locomotives. My first experience of them on the footplate was working the 'Mistral'. Maximum speed on the PLM line is limited to 100 mph and with the precision that is required of the French *mécanicien* we did not once exceed it. Yet for 73·1 miles, from Montereau to Tonnerre, we averaged 98 mph and for 160 miles out of the 195·3 from Paris to Dijon we averaged 95·8 mph. While I read the various dials in the cab, and noted the high output of power continuously in evidence I was equally impressed by the wonderful smoothness of the riding. I cannot say, as I have felt on some high-speed journeys, that one tended to lose the sensation of speed, because the old PLM line has many curves, and it was supremely thrilling to ride elegantly round them at 100 mph! But three years later when I rode another of these locomotives at 125 mph I did begin to lose the sense of speed.

This time it was on 'Le Capitole du Matin', the supreme 'flyer' that leaves Paris for Toulouse at 7.45 a.m. We had a characteristically heavy load consisting of eleven of the huge *grand confort* coaches, 622 tons in all, and it was after passing Étampes that we really began to run. We had not

Table 20.3 French high-speed electric locomotives

Class	Traction system	Weight, tons	Max. continuous horsepower	Max. permitted speed, mph
CC 7100	1,500 v d.c.	105	4,700	125
CC 40101	quadri-current	106	5,950	150
CC 6500	1,500 v d.c.	114	7,400	135

exactly been dawdling up till then, keeping up 86–7 mph in the winding valley of the Seine; but once past Guillerval, on a straight track, in level open country speed mounted to the '125', and just stayed there. It was then that I began to lose the impression of speed, so much so that when we slowed down for the Les Aubrais junctions at Orléans we seemed to be crawling – yet the speedometer and my watches told me we were still travelling at 65 mph. On this train we made an average speed of $92\frac{1}{4}$ mph over the entire $248\frac{3}{4}$ miles from Paris to Limoges, the first stop. These locomotives also run 'L'Aquitaine' non-stop over the 360 miles from Paris to Bordeaux in exactly four hours, an average of 90 mph.

Before concluding this chapter I must refer to the expresses in West Germany that also run at 100 mph – some of them even faster. I was able to make a run in the locomotive cab of the northbound 'Rheingold' express on its fastest section, from Freiburg to Karlsruhe, and covered this stretch of 84·6 miles in three seconds short of 57 minutes, an average of 89 mph. We did exceed by a fraction the 100 mph maximum stipulated, although this train, like most of the really fast ones in Germany, carries loads that are light compared to the French. On the 'Rheingold' our electric locomotive was hauling only 350 tons. Regular running at 125 mph is now made on certain trains between Munich and Augsburg, with the 38·1 miles between these two cities scheduled in $26\frac{1}{2}$ minutes start-to-stop. The 'E-03' class electric locomotives allocated to this work originally are of 8,750 horsepower, even though the trains consisted of only seven coaches. But as will be told in the final chapter of this book, the West Germans are constructing a new high-speed railway network that is symbolical of the renaissance of railways as a means of passenger transport, and these courageous spurts between Munich and Augsburg will then seem no more than a preliminary – not even a dress rehearsal.

 The belt-conveyor railways

In Great Britain, France, Germany and Japan the resurgence of railways in providing fast and frequent inter-city passenger services that are now of a speed that even the internal air lines find difficult to surpass, when city-centre to city-centre travelling times are compared, represents only one aspect of the new railway age, evident in so many parts of the world. As the Industrial Revolution spread from Europe to the vast, newly settled continents overseas, industrial activity and expansion developed in areas that were near to sources of mineral wealth, and at first concentrated upon iron ore and coal. But such was the rate of subsequent expansion, and the demand for steel in two world wars, that in the USA in particular the indigenous resources in iron ore began to appear within measurable distance of exhaustion, and new sources of supply had to be found. In Japan also the phenomenal growth of industrial activities requiring steel far outstripped anything that local or nearby resources could satisfy, and in seeking supplies from across the oceans, in vast tonnages, a series of closely integrated transport activities became a vital factor in meeting the needs. Mineral deposits of unprecedented magnitude, as yet untouched, were discovered as a result of geological and mining explorations; but these, almost without exception, were in districts not merely remote, but beyond existing limits of population, and many hundreds of miles from the sea.

Passing from the general to the particular, the needs of the American steel industry may first be considered in the light of the approaching exhaustion of the great iron-ore deposits in Minnesota. Many years earlier geological explorations in the north-east of Quebec and in Labrador had suggested that the peculiar rock formations might contain iron ore, but with ample supplies nearer at hand this hint of mineral riches was not taken up. It was not until after the Second World War that further prospecting took place. Then indeed the existence of an enormous deposit was confirmed, 350 miles north of the St Lawrence estuary. It was located where it could be economically mined, if the necessary equipment and personnel were available, and the means could be provided to move it once the ore was mined. But the area was then a remote wilderness, devoid of any human habitation, while between it and the St Lawrence estuary lay hundreds of square miles of forest, stunted black spruce, innumerable small lakes, and vast areas of muskeg swamp. There was only one solution – a railway; and a railway moreover that could carry ten million tons of ore down to the coast every year. How the Quebec North Shore and Labrador Railway was conceived, surveyed and constructed is no part of the present theme. But unlike the great majority of railways that were built in the hopes of attracting and developing traffic, the QNS & L had a definite traction assignment from the outset.

The main line would be 350 miles long. Economic studies determined that the most efficient operating results would be attained by running loaded trains of 14,000 tons at 30 mph. Returning empties would run at 40 mph, and with the average gradient in favour of the loaded trains, the traction effort, if not equalized, would not be too dissimilar in the two directions. It went without saying that the new railway would have to be built to first-class main line standards, and from the start of the work in October 1950, the line was through to the northern terminus at Knob Lake by February 1954. By the early summer of that same year the ore trains were running. The motive power which alone made this great project a readily practicable proposition was the diesel-electric locomotive; the tough, reliable 'second generation' type, and all built by General Motors in the Canadian plant at London, Ontario. The first forty, with which the railway opened for business, were of the

Quebec North Shore and Labrador Railway: loaded ore train, 135 cars, 3 locomotives, one mile long, passing Tellier at 30 mph.

'GP9' model, of 1,750 horsepower, nicknamed 'Geeps'; but these, as on many North American railways, were later reinforced by a number of the much more powerful 'SD40s' of 3,000 horsepower. They can be coupled in multiple, according to the loads to be hauled. I shall not forget my first sight of one of these ore trains. I was going north on the leading locomotive of the thrice-weekly passenger and mixed train, and we were switched into the loop road at Tellier to await the passage of a loaded ore train – three diesel locomotives and 135 loaded wagons of ore, just about one mile long. The pay load was about 11,000 tons, and she thundered through under clear signals at a good 30 mph. There are now five or six of these trains running down to the coast every day – a veritable belt-conveyor movement.

While the diesels are handling these big long distance

The belt-conveyor railways 257

hauls traction by rail has solved another 'belt-conveyor' type of problem. In addition to its northern terminus at Knob Lake, where the new city of Schefferville has grown up, there is an important branch leading to Labrador City, where the QNS & L collects further vast tonnages of ore. The Mill and Crushing Plant of the Carol Division of the Iron Ore Company of Canada is located near to Labrador City, and on the shore of Wabush Lake, while six miles away are the bleak mountains that contain deposits of iron ore that are nearly 40 per cent solid iron. Here again was a major problem in transport, to convey 80,000 tons of ore daily from the loading pockets in the mountains to the crushing plant. To maintain the steady flow of crude ore necessary to keep the plant at the mill working in the continuous flow manner essential for maximum efficiency, the concept of an automatic railway was developed, in which the loading and unloading of the trains could be interlocked with the mechanized 'earth-moving' plant at each end. Since the project was first initiated the daily tonnage to be moved has increased to 150,000, and seven 20-car trains are kept automatically shuttling to and fro. There are no drivers. The trains are hauled, and propelled back empty, by 1,200 horsepower electric locomotives, controlled through coded track circuits in the same way as the automatically driven trains on the Victoria Line tube railway in London, England, are regulated. Being purely mineral trains there is no need to have a man in attendance, and when I had a trip over this fascinating six miles of railway, it was literally a case of, 'Look, no hands!'

The Quebec North Shore and Labrador and the Carol Lake automated line are entirely new projects, built as part of a definite commercial enterprise, with an assured traffic from the outset. But the potentialities of modern railway traction are shown no less strikingly on other railways which, however optimistic the promoters might have been, fell upon hard times long before the line was completed. There has been no more striking example of this than the Algoma Central which runs north for 300 miles from Sault Ste Marie, Ontario, intersecting first the Canadian Pacific, at Franz, then the Canadian National main line to the west at Oba, and finally making a junction with the former National Transcontinental at Hearst. Like the QNS & L it has an important branch, connecting with rich iron ore deposits at Wawa. How this railway struggled through a long period of bankruptcy and a receivership to emerge in the late 1950s as a profitable, and, indeed, very prosperous enterprise, was assisted by the decision to go 'all-diesel'; and although its present mineral operations are not on the scale of the QNS & L, it is, in its own way, very much of a belt-conveyor railway.

There is however a great difference in operating conditions. From its very inception the Algoma Central was working on a shoe string. In its curves and gradients, and in the light character of its timber trestle bridge work, it had more the character of a 'logging road' than of a main line railway. Even today, while the track, bridges and general construction have been fettled up to first-class main line standards the curves and gradients remain, and it is the capacity of the great General Motors' 'second generation' diesels that enable it to operate lengthy trains of iron ore, and general freight, loading usually up to about 5,500 tons. Furthermore, while the heavier traffic is southbound to Sault Ste Marie, there is no general trend of favourable gradient for the heaviest trains. I was very much aware of this one icy morning when I was called at 3.30 a.m. to ride the leading unit of a 'posse' of five 'GP7s' working a maximum tonnage freight, mostly of iron ore, from Hawk Junction to Sault Ste Marie. We had a load of 5,500 tons, and the combined roar of our five locomotives as they toiled up the long climb from the Agawa Canyon to Frater, amid snow-laden forests and frozen waterfalls, with speed little more than 10 mph, was something to remember.

The far inland regions of Western Australia, particularly the country round Kalgoorlie, are often associated with gold-mining; but today the insatiable world demand for iron ore has opened up great new mineral resources west of what is still called the Golden Mile, and as in Labrador special arrangements have had to be made to convey the crude ore to the refinery on the west coast near Fremantle. The old 3 ft 6 in. gauge line with its awkward gradients and severe curvature could not have coped with the traffic the planned output of iron ore demanded, so a new line, on 4 ft 8½ in. gauge, was driven clean through the rough mountain country of the Darling Range, with such mighty engineering works as to avoid any gradient steeper than 1 in 200, and to provide an alignment such that the 10,000 ton ore trains could run continuously at 50 mph. And what of the traction? – the most powerful diesel-electrics in Australia, 3,300 horsepower, and three of them to each train. This is indeed another belt-conveyor railway, but one that also runs some prestige express passenger trains. The diesel railcar 'Prospector' service between Perth and Kalgoorlie is the fastest train in Australia, while the transcontinental 'Indian-Pacific' luxury sleeping train runs the 2,461 miles between Perth and Sydney on standard gauge tracks throughout.

On yet another great Australian standard gauge line, however, there are, as yet, no passenger trains. This is the railway of the Hamersley Iron Pty. Ltd, in the north-west of Western Australia. This is purely a belt-conveyor system built to convey iron ore from the mines at Mount Tom Price and Parapurdoo down to the north coast at Dampier. As on the Quebec North Shore and Labrador Railway a planned traffic was envisaged from the outset, at first 75,000 tons of ore a day, and 15,000 tons per train.

In zero weather, or torrid heat, diesels carry on:
(a) Four GP7s of the Algoma Central, backing on to a tonnage freight train at Hawk Junction, temperature 20 deg. below freezing point.
(b) At 100°F., a loaded ore train leaving Mount Tom Price for Dampier on the Hamersley Iron Railway.

The belt-conveyor railways

Hamersley Iron Railway: ore train for Dampier leaving the loading tunnel at Mount Tom Price.

The route lay through near-desert country, subject to appalling heat in the summer months, but like the QNS & L it was found possible to build the railway with gradients favourable to trains in the loaded direction. For the latter the maximum adverse gradient, between Tom Price and Dampier, is 1 in 300, whereas the empties have to face ascents of 1 in 50. The respective trailing loads are 18,000 and 3,000 tons, and this provides a maximum peak effort for the locomotives in each direction. Each train, consisting of 150 cars, is hauled by two American-built diesels of the Goodwin-ALCO type having 3,900 horsepower each. Because of the easier gradients the total power needed is not so great as on the Western Australian Government Railway standard gauge line. On a visit to this remarkable new railway, which commenced operation in 1966, time unfortunately did not permit me to ride the trains. Instead the busy community up at Tom Price travel, as I did, by light aeroplane, a little five-seater, in a flight that added to the zest of the visit. Some day the Hamersley Iron Railway may run an occasional passenger train; but at present it is all freight, and one traffic only, iron ore.

Another new enterprise, the very name of which excites the imagination, is the Great Slave Lake Railway, running through northern Alberta into the Northwest Territories of Canada. The main purpose in the building of this 385 mile line, through sparsely populated remote country, is to haul lead zinc ore concentrates from Pine Point, on the Great Slave Lake, to Roma, where connection is made with the Northern Alberta Railway. The new line is not difficult from the gradient point of view though in such latitudes it will naturally be exposed to extremes of winter climate. There is, however, ample experience in Canada of diesel-electric locomotive operation in such conditions, and as a division of Canadian National it is being operated with well tried standard equipment. At present the traffic is only just beginning to flow; but it is yet another very striking example of the new railway enterprises that are presently being undertaken, with the solid backing of the modern diesel-electric locomotive to provide the motive power.

The railways of Great Britain are probably unique in the extraordinary diversity of traffic handled, and the disparity in speed between the fastest and the slowest. It is true that the old-fashioned local goods train, stopping interminably at every country station, shunted laboriously at the least provocation to allow faster trains to pass, has disappeared; but in its place, in addition to the fast liner trains, carrying consignments loaded into sealed containers, there are the 'nominated' freight trains, which in every way are a British equivalent of the belt-conveyor type of traffic on the overseas railways already described. The difference in Great Britain is that these special freight trains have to be woven into an already crowded timetable. There is the remarkable example of the special trains run by the London Midland Region for the Ford Motor Company, conveying car components from the plant at Halewood on Merseyside to the great assembly plant at Dagenham, on the Thames estuary. This is veritably a link in the assembly line of automobile production. The rail distance between the two plants is about 200 miles, and the journey time six hours. The section from Halewood to Willesden is electrically hauled, at an average speed of 40 mph over a line swarming with 100-mph express passenger trains, after which the diesels take over for the negotiation of the crowded lines round the northern perimeter of London. Still more within the belt-conveyor concept are the merry-go-round coal trains run between certain collieries and the major generating stations of the Central Electricity Board. These run on a continuous circuit, with fully mechanized loading and unloading, in unchanged 'block' formation. The diesel-electric locomotives used for their haulage remain coupled to the train throughout.

In Southern Africa there are two great new mineral railway projects, one already in operation and the other constructing. Once again the freight is iron ore. This precious mineral was found to exist in large quantities at Ngwenya near Ka Dake on the borders of Swaziland and South Africa, and yet another entirely new railway was built to carry it to the east coast for shipment from Lourenço Marques. Swaziland is an extremely rugged and sparsely populated country, and the main deposit of ore lay in a mountain top more than 5,000 ft above sea level. No railway could be built to reach the mine itself, and special arrangements had to be designed to convey the ore to the railway loading point, 1,000 ft below. The line itself is no more than 140 miles long, but what a line! It includes a gradient 57 miles long, continuously at 1 in 50, though fortunately this is in favour of loaded trains. For once however the motive power is not diesel-electric, but trusty old 4-8-2 steam locomotives, purchased from the Rhodesia Railways, and used in pairs on the ore trains. It was a question of alternative investment. With new diesel locomotives used in multiple it would have been possible to work longer and heavier trains, operating on the train order system. But the Swaziland Railway chose instead to install full colour light signalling with centralized control from the depot station of Sidvokodvo, and to run lighter trains and more of them, with locomotives that could be purchased cheaply. They are now equipped, control-wise, for when the traffic increases, and existing service needs to be run with much heavier trains, no doubt by diesel-electrics. In contrast to this the second new line, now under construction, will run from Sishen, in Bechuanaland, south-westwards for 500 miles to a new ore-loading station on the west coast about 70 miles north of Cape Town – yet another manifestation of the new railway age.

It is perhaps fitting that the most spectacular use of modern diesel-electric power should be on one of the most historic railways in all the world, the Canadian Pacific, and in the most sublime mountain setting. The voracious appetite of Japanese heavy industry for coal is being met, in part, from the very large deposits in the Canadian Rockies, just north of the United States border in the Crowsnest Pass, British Columbia. This area lies some considerable distance to the south of the main transcontinental route, on a subsidiary line, built largely to block railway invasion from the USA at the time of fiercest aggression from the Great Northern Railway. At its western end the Crowsnest line connects with another route of the Canadian Pacific running up the Columbia valley to join the principal transcontinental route at Golden. Thence runs the coal train route from the Crowsnest almost to Vancouver, before reaching which, however, it turns south to an entirely new coal-shipping port at Roberts Bank. Again the pattern of operation is to run trains of gargantuan length, 105 cars with a gross trailing load of 12,400 tons. In this operation geography is certainly not on the side of the locomotive department.

The basic objective was to export about seven million tons of coal a year, and this would require six trains constantly shuttling backwards and forwards over a 'belt-conveyor' $701\frac{1}{4}$ miles long. In that distance there are tremendous variations in the physical nature of the route. Much of it is on relatively easy gradients, but intermediately there is the gruelling section through the Selkirk Mountains, the 90 miles between Golden and Revelstoke, with the fearsome obstacle of the Beaver Hill, nearly 15 miles inclined at 1 in 45. Now from what I have written earlier in this chapter, it will be appreciated that quite a lot of power is needed to get these lengthy mineral trains up the steep gradients, and with trains of 105 cars, 12,400 tons, little more than simple arithmetic showed that thirteen diesels of 3,000 horsepower would be needed to maintain the required speed of 15 mph up the Beaver Hill. Thirteen locomotives! How could such an assemblage of power be disposed in the train? Even if the track were perfectly straight one could not line them all up at the head end; the combined pull would be far too great for the draw-gear of the leading cars to withstand.

From an early stage in Canadian railroading it had been the practice to cut in locomotives intermediately when three or more had to be used to haul a train up a severe incline. On the original alignment of the Field Hill, on the CPR main line, where the gradient was 1 in 25, one often saw three steam 4-6-0 locomotives, one leading, a second about one-third of the way down the train, and a third pushing in rear. The theory was that while the whole train was coupled together each locomotive was taking about one third of the load. The same principle was applied to the working of the 105-car coal trains on the Beaver Hill. The 'lead' combination is of four 3,000 horsepower locomotives; a 'posse' of five more is cut in rather less than half way down the train, and then there is a pusher unit, of four more diesels, not at the extreme rear end, but leaving about 20 cars and the caboose trailing behind the last set of locomotives. A good deal of experimenting had to be carried out in arriving at the ideal disposition of the locomotives, but before discussing this manning must be mentioned.

Modern engineering science has enabled the group of locomotives in the middle of the train to be remotely controlled from the head end, thus avoiding the need for an additional engine crew. A robot unit is marshalled ahead of the mid-train locomotives, and this robot obtains its instructions by radio from the head end. The instructions are duly de-coded and passed on to the group of mid-train locomotives. In this way the driver's actions on the leading

CP Rail, Crowsnest operation: in the cab of the lead unit of a coal train, showing the electrical control panel by which the robot unit and slave locomotives in the middle of the train are controlled.

locomotive are echoed on the 'slave' through the interaction of the robot. On the pusher unit, near the rear end, there is a separate engine crew, in two-way voice radio communication with the head end. Last of all, in the caboose at the extreme rear end is the train conductor who is in two-way voice communication with both the lead and pusher locomotive crews. In finally determining the position of the robot unit and attendant slave diesels, it was appreciated that a lengthy moving train is like an accordion; it expands and contracts. After much experimenting and the occasional breakaway, it was found that

The belt-conveyor railways 263

left
CP Rail: freight working in British Colombia, a four-locomotive eastbound freight climbing the Field Hill, and just emerging from one of the spiral tunnels.

CP Rail: the same train photographed seconds later, with the lead unit crossing over its own tail end, with the intervening consist passing through the spiral tunnel.

CP Rail: mechanized unloading of one of the Crowsnest coal trains at Roberts Bank port, near Vancouver. The train is being 'inched' round the unloading circuit. One of the slave locomotives is seen in the foreground.

left
CP Rail: maximum tonnage coal train from the Crowsnest crossing Stoney Creek Bridge, near the summit of the Beaver Hill. There are four 3,000 horsepower locomotives at the head, but the robot, five slave locomotives, and the four pushers are far out of sight.

the answer was to have the robots pushing several cars ahead, as well as pulling those behind. It was necessary to ensure that the point of zero drawbar pull, which would move backwards and forwards in the train according to conditions, was always ahead of the robots.

It is only in mounting the Beaver Hill, $14\frac{3}{4}$ miles out of the entire $701\frac{1}{4}$ from the Crowsnest to Roberts Bank port, that thirteen locomotives are required. For a little over 500 miles only four are needed: $223\frac{3}{4}$ miles from Sparwood mines, in the Crowsnest Pass to Golden, and for $294\frac{1}{2}$ miles from Chase to Roberts Bank. Over the first named section the robots are not used. Four locomotives at the head end can provide all that is necessary, but on the latter stretch, with some sharp intermediate gradients, there are two locomotives in the lead, and two robot-controlled cut in at the pre-arranged point in the train. Through the mountain sections, apart from the altogether exceptional length of the Beaver Hill, six or eight locomotives are used, though on certain stretches the multiplicity of units is a matter of balancing, to work the locomotive to staging or divisional points where they would be needed to provide maximum power for trains returning in the opposite direction. The locomotives themselves are of the MLW 'M.630' type of the familiar 'second generation' type, and of ALCO design, with 3,000 engine horsepower, of the Co-Co wheel arrangement, and having an all-up weight of 175 tons. They are certainly doing a mighty job in the mountains of British Columbia, but the traffic is now reaching such proportions west of Golden, where the Crowsnest coal trains have their paths amid all the freight and passenger trains of the principal Canadian Pacific transcontinental main line, that investigations have reached an advanced stage towards the changing of the traction over from diesel to electric.

The belt-conveyor railways

The Great Anniversary and a look ahead

Viewing the developments described in the preceding three chapters one cannot doubt that the hundred and fiftieth anniversary of railway passenger transport is falling in a time of intensely dynamic activity in transport generally. On such an occasion it is natural enough to look back and salute the memory of those who laid the foundations of the railway industry; but it would be quite contrary to the spirit and personalities of those great men to muse nostalgically upon past events, and in a time that is undeniably full of many extreme difficulties to sigh, '*Eheu fugaces labuntur anni.*' Nevertheless, lapsing a little into the poetic for a few sentences, we can, at this time of so significant an anniversary, imagine ourselves surrounded by a cloud of witnesses, observing how the torch that they lighted has been carried forward; and in addition to Trevithick, Blenkinsop, Hackworth and the Stephensons, we think of other great men whose names have been writ large in this chronicle: Matthias Baldwin, Crampton, McConnell, Allan, Mallet, Westinghouse, for if the means of stopping had not been made safe and sure all other developments would have been of no avail. Then there were de Glehn and Schmidt; Churchward, Vauclain, Garratt, Gresley, the Ketterings, Dilworth and Stanier – not to forget perhaps the greatest of all steam men, André Chapelon, who is still happily with us.

But it is a time to look forward, not to look back, as emphasized by the prevalent theme of the international railway engineering conference held in London in the week preceding the actual anniversary date. In this book of course I am concerned only with traction, though nowadays permanent way design and signalling have become closely knit with locomotive practice, and not worlds apart as once they were. One of the most interesting trends at the present time is towards equipment for infusing greater precision into the actual handling of locomotives on the road. Throughout the steam era in most countries one could note considerable variations in the way individual drivers would set out to time a train. Some might immediately begin to accumulate minutes in hand as a contingency against incidental delays, while others would adhere more closely to their point-to-point schedules, and if delays occurred later, arrive at their destination a corresponding amount behind time. Others would run hard, seemingly for the sheer joy of it, while men in the same link would scrape along barely keeping time as though they grudged every lump of coal fed into the firebox. While this kind of working did not represent very good operation, it did not have widespread repercussions on the service as a whole, until it came to the running of closely timed, short headway commuter services. Even on multiple-unit electric trains, and on the older tube railways beneath London, one can detect variations in driving style, which are now eliminated by completely automatic driving as on the Victoria Line.

The French railways from quite early steam days set considerable store upon precision driving methods, and while British locomotives remained devoid even of a speedometer the French had not merely a speed indicator, but a recording apparatus, registering the speed on a continuous graph throughout the run. Today, when modern high-speed schedules require the trains to be run at or near the line maximum speed for lengthy stretches, some of the newest French electric locomotives have been fitted with speed selector devices. The driver selects the speed at which he desires, or is permitted, to run and the apparatus so activates the electric controls that the locomotive is rapidly accelerated to that speed, and subsequently held there regardless of gradient. Of course a pre-requisite of such working is a locomotive of great power, and I noted from the footplate in 1974 a remarkable instance of this on

French National Railways: one of the thyristor controlled 'BB 15001' class electric locomotives arriving at Strasbourg with the 'Stanislas' express from Paris.

one of the latest French 25,000-volt a.c. electric locomotives, with thyristor control, on the westbound 'Stanislas' express from Strasbourg to Paris. We had a heavy train of thirteen coaches, 660 tons in all, and ran at 100 mph on all the sections where that speed was permitted. Then, between Leronville and Nançois there is a 'gable' 8 miles rising at 1 in 125 followed by 6½ miles descending at the same inclination. Prior to passing Leronville there is a short stretch limited to 140 km. per hour (87 mph), but up the 1 in 125 and almost to Nançois the limit is 150 (92½ mph). Passing Leronville the driver set the selector to '150' but against such a gradient, with such a load, the acceleration was gradual, and the '150' was attained only about a mile from the summit. But then, without any action from the driver, it was maintained with complete precision as we topped the rise and began the corresponding descent – the controls bringing the regenerative brake into action for a time.

Even with conventional locomotive power, of which classification the French locomotives just referred to conform, if in a highly sophisticated form, the steep gradients that were found so trying even in the zenith of steam power are now being virtually ironed out. Of this there is no more striking example than in the northward extension of the British 25,000-volt a.c. electrification to Glasgow. The Shap and Beattock inclines, particularly the latter, needed special attention, in the provision of rear-end banking assistance; and when heavy trains were taken unassisted up these gradients of 1 in 75 the speeds on passing the summits were rarely more than 30 mph. Today the latest British electric locomotives of class '87' sustain speeds of 85 to 90 mph on these gradients, and it is only on occasions of bad rail conditions that anything less is customary with twelve-coach trains of about 430 tons gross weight. An instance has been recorded of an eleven-coach train being hauled over the complete ascent from little more than sea level at Carnforth, to the 915 ft altitude of Shap Summit, 31·4 miles in $19\frac{1}{2}$ minutes, pass to pass, at an average speed throughout of 96·3 mph.

From the developments on all the advanced railway systems of the world, however, it does not seem that the future for very high-speed passenger trains lies in further enlargement and sophistication of the conventional electric or diesel-electric locomotive hauling a train of coaches. Yet it is unlikely that the traffic elsewhere is likely to sustain such a frequent service of fixed formation super-speed trains as those now being operated on the Shinkansen lines of the Japanese National Railways. The traditional concept of a separate locomotive hauling a train of coaches was passed over from the outset, and the inflexibility of a fixed train formation overcome by the extreme frequency of these high-speed trains – one every fifteen minutes. My own journeys between Paris and Strasbourg in 1974 provided an example of the very opposite, when the normal formation of the 'Stanislas' express, seven cars, was increased to thirteen to meet heavy traffic demands. Instances of such wide fluctuation in the loading of individual trains are becoming less frequent, however, as the slogan 'lighter trains and more of them', raised more than forty years ago in Great Britain by certain far-sighted people, begins to become rather more of a reality than seemed possible only a few years ago.

The full potentialities of modern railway traction become evident when trains are run at such frequent intervals that regular travellers do not have to consult a timetable. The Japanese have done this on a single main line devoid of any branches, but the present day electric service of the London Midland, to and from Euston, is in many respects even more remarkable. There are four distinct traffic streams to be served, to Birmingham, Liverpool, Manchester, Preston and points north; and in every hour the 100 mph expresses are arranged in flights of six, leaving London at 40, 45, 50, 55 minutes past the hour, on the hour, and at 10 minutes past. This density is maintained for the first 83 miles north – the most intense express train service in the world. Its high standard of punctuality is maintained by the use of electric locomotives of ample tractive power, all having the same performance characteristics. This latter is a most important factor, but it is equally one that sometimes makes those responsible for advance planning reluctant to change, when such satisfactory results have been attained.

The introduction of still faster services always involves some disturbance. On a line like the London Midland route from Euston it would be the problem of finding suitable timetable paths. On French high-speed routes like

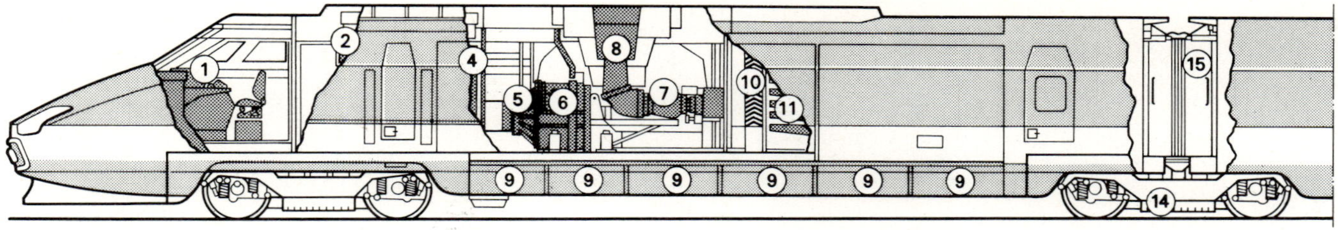

French National Railways: layout of the power unit of 'TGV 001'.

1 Control panel
2 Electrical unit-block
3 Rectifier group
4 Rheostatic brake
5 Generator for auxiliaries
6 Main generator
7 Turbo-motor
8 Exhaust
9 Includes air reservoirs, fuel bunkers, train heating and air conditioning apparatus
10 Louvres
11 Filters
12 Suction compartment
13 Baggage
14 Magnetic shoe
15 Gangway connection

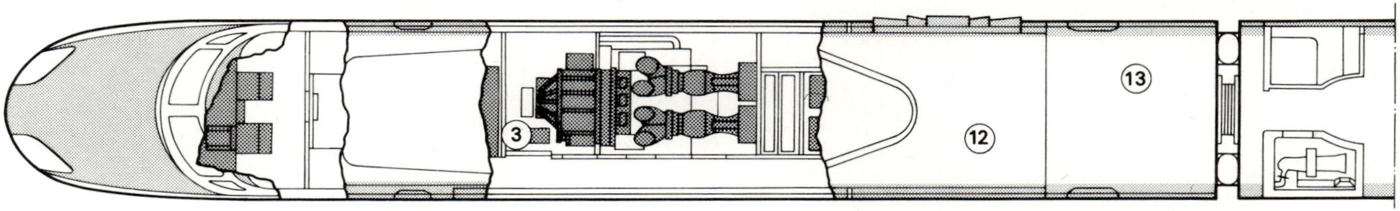

those from Paris to Lyons, to Bordeaux, or to Strasbourg, although there is not the same density of traffic, the track would require up-grading, and the super-elevation on curves that is suitable for 100 or 125 mph would certainly not be adequate for the speeds of nearly 200 mph now proposed. Like the Japanese, the French and the Germans are building entirely new railways, on which the average speeds from city to city will be about 150 mph. The SNCF has already carried out important tests with a prototype high-speed train, engineered by a consortium of the leading French manufacturers of electrical, mechanical and turbine railway traction equipment, and built at the famous works at Belfort renowned at the turn of the century for the products of Alfred de Glehn's designing genius. It was first shown to the Press on 23 March 1972, and before leaving its native Alsace had made a successful trial run at 240 km. per hour (149 mph).

The experimental train consisted of a power car at each end, both including also some passenger accommodation, and three trailer cars. The entire train was articulated, and carried on a total of six bogies. The motive power is gas turbine, with electric transmission, the first of its kind to be built for very high-speed service, and after its preliminary runs on the Alsace-Lorraine main line between Mulhouse and Strasbourg, it was transferred to the south-west, for *really* high-speed trials on the straight and level stretch of the former Midi Railway between Bordeaux and Dax, which had already witnessed the making of the world

The Great Anniversary and a look ahead

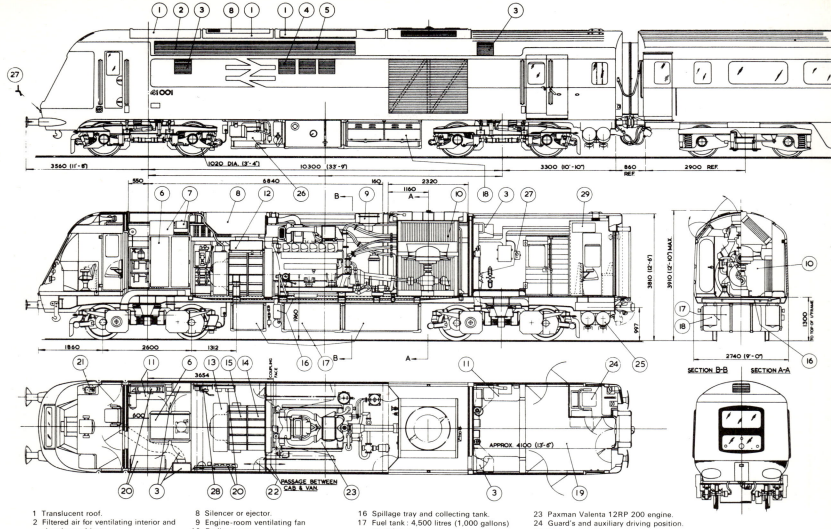

1. Translucent roof.
2. Filtered air for ventilating interior and electric machines.
3. Air for ventilating traction motors.
4. Air for ventilating engine room.
5. Filtered air for engine combustion.
6. Electric equipment cubicle.
7. Resistance unit and short-circuiter.
8. Silencer or ejector.
9. Engine-room ventilating fan.
10. Radiator group.
11. Flexicoil spring boxes.
12. Train supply and auxiliary rectifiers.
13. Exciter and traction rectifier.
14. Train supply and auxiliary alternators.
15. Traction alternator.
16. Spillage tray and collecting tank.
17. Fuel tank : 4,500 litres (1,000 gallons) capacity.
18. Battery.
19. Luggage accommodation (1 tonne).
20. Pneumatic and miscellaneous equipment.
21. Fire equipment.
22. Clean air compartment partition.
23. Paxman Valenta 12RP 200 engine.
24. Guard's and auxiliary driving position.
25. Main reservoirs.
26. Air compressor.
27. Emergency equipment.
28. Hydraulic parking brake.
29. Audio-navigator.

speed record for railway traction in 1935, by the standard electric locomotive CC 7107, at 206 mph. During experimental runs in July 1972 the maximum speed was pushed progressively higher, from 173 mph on 21 July to the full 300 km. (186 mph) on 27 July. Later, on 8 December, a maximum of 318 km. per hour was attained between Labouheyre and Facture. By this speed of 197 mph 'TGV 001', as this prototype is known, had not yet surpassed the earlier record of CC 7107; but the latter was pressed to its absolute limit, to such an extent that the heat generated on the overhead line caused the pantograph to burn out! On the other hand by 16 April 1973 'TGV 001' had completed its first 100,000 kilometres (62,000 miles) of successful running.

In its planned commercial version 'TGV 001' will provide accommodation for 300 passengers, of both first and second class, with a car having full bar facilities. At the speeds these new trains will travel there will be no time for full restaurant meals, served in the elegant style customary on French trains. With equipment of the 'TGV 001' type it is intended that the journey time between Paris and Lille, 156 miles, will be exactly one hour, and over the new line between Paris and Lyons, about 315 miles, the time will be two hours. On both these routes it is intended that the propulsion will be gas turbine. But the SNCF is also planning an all-electric 'TGV 001' which was to have run from Paris to London, through the Channel Tunnel, in two and a half hours. Journey times such as these, which are expected to be paralleled in speed on the new high-speed inter-city network in Germany, which is already being built, will give railways an advantage that the very fastest short distance air services will find difficult to surpass, particularly as the railway services will be able to run in weather conditions that can make flying impossible.

On the crowded network of British Railways, within the confines of a country of comparatively small geographical extent, a development towards ultra-high speed is not at present envisaged. The establishment of journey times of one and a half hours between London and Birmingham and two and a half hours between London and both Manchester and Liverpool by the electric London Midland trains has brought a gratifyingly large increase in passenger business; but the end-to-end average speeds of around 80 mph do not represent the limit of active present planning. In June 1973 the prototype high-speed diesel train made some spectacular runs on the East Coast main line, attaining a maximum speed of 143 mph between Northallerton and Thirsk, and on 2 August that year on a further demonstration run I had the pleasure of recording personally a maximum of 137 mph, and an average for 26 miles of 129·5 mph between Northallerton and York; 'HST' as it is known is diesel-powered, with Ruston-Paxman engines and Brush electrical equipment.

The trials have proved so successful that a number of these trains are now being built for use on non-electrified main lines of British Railways, and it is expected that the earliest of them will be entering service by the time this book is published. On the former Great Western line the anticipated timings, at the moment of writing, are 71 minutes for the 106·9 miles from Paddington to Bath (90·5 mph) and 82 minutes to Bristol; but on the longer non-stop runs north from King's Cross on the East Coast Route, the average speeds anticipated are 94·5 mph to Doncaster, 94·1 mph to York, 91·2 mph to Newcastle and 87·3 mph throughout to Edinburgh. The 'HST' is, of course, a departure from the traditional British locomotive and train; but its high-speed service and impeccably smooth riding is likely to make a strong appeal to travellers. Its maximum service speed will be 125 mph, and this does not by any means represent the present limit of British railway

British Railways: drawings of the HST power car, which attained 143 mph on trial, and will run at 125 mph in regular service.

Japanese National Railways: two views of the experimental magnetic levitation vehicle, basis of the new ultra-high-speed Tokyo–Osaka project.

traction planning. Behind the 'HST' is the gradually emerging development of the Advanced Passenger Train, the 'APT', which with new forms of suspension is designed to run safely at 155 mph on routes that now carry trains of the conventional type at 100 mph. The London–Glasgow run of 401·4 miles is now performed in five hours; with the 'APT' it is anticipated that the time will be cut to the level four hours – a city-to-city average speed of slightly over 100 mph.

The recession in railway business in the USA which has led to the bankrupting of several famous companies has naturally put a heavy brake upon any development that requires capital investment, and at a time when British, French and Japanese activities have been intensified, the USA has tended to fall out of the picture. But the formation of the National Railroad Passenger Corporation – Amtrak – has put a new drive and purpose into the revival of passenger train services, and one interesting step was the purchase of two French-built turbo trains, and their shipment from Le Havre to New York in 1973. These trains are of the earlier 'RTG' type, introduced on the Paris–Cherbourg line of SNCF in 1970. They are powered by an 820 k.w. (1,100 horsepower) aero-gas-turbine set in the driving units at each end of the five-car trains. The transmission is hydraulic, and the service speed is 125 mph. Whether this interesting importing into the USA of a French product will lead to extension of the high-speed gas turbine type of train remains to be seen; but it can only be recalled that the tremendous diesel-electric conquest of the American motive power world began in a similar way though on that occasion, nearly forty years ago, with an indigenous product.

As the time of the great anniversary approaches, there are experiments with still more revolutionary forms of traction, such as the 'hover train'. It would be rather

Nostalgic last look: 'The Flying Scotsman' in 1938, hauled by the Gresley streamlined 'Pacific' *Dominion of New Zealand*.

stretching the point to suggest that this is not really an instance of railway traction, because the operation is by what is termed magnetic levitation, a British invention, by Professor Laithwaite of Imperial College, London. But since rails are used to guide these remarkable vehicles, it is, in the broadest sense. In Japan it is thought that occupation of the Shinkansen line between Tokyo and Osaka will have reached saturation point by the year 1980, and already research work has started towards the construction and equipping of an entirely new line, on magnetic levitation principles, by which the journey time between the two cities will be no more than one hour – an average speed of about 280 mph. A test vehicle has already been built and is the subject of intensive research.

In coming to the end of this chronicle, and viewing the striking developments on the threshold of which we seem to be, it is impossible to approach this anniversary without once again looking back, and pondering over the astonishing strides in railway speed that have been made since Britain celebrated what was termed the 'Railway Centenary' in 1925. Then it was mainly a time of reflection. The British railway world was then in a state of flux, having recently experienced the disturbing process of company amalgamation on a vast scale. The fastest train in the world, the Great Western 'Cheltenham Flyer', then averaged no more than 61·8 mph over a very easy road. This was no more than a modest increase over the best booked speeds at the time of the Railway Jubilee celebration in 1875, when the Great Northern Railway could show one or two trains at around 50 mph from start to stop. It was however strangely enough in the depressed conditions of the 1930s that the real upsurge began, and by the time war broke out in 1939 six countries could claim start-to-stop runs at more than 70 mph. The German diesel railcar runs were perhaps exceptional, topped by an 83·3 mph run from Hamm to Hanover. It is remarkable however that the fastest European steam run was then made in Belgium, at 74·9 mph between Brussels and Bruges. It was beaten no more than narrowly for the world 'first' with steam by the 'Hiawatha' express of the Milwaukee Road at 75·8 mph, while the fastest electric run of the period was in Italy, at 72·5 mph, between Rome and Naples. In Great Britain the fastest run was that of the 'Coronation' between King's Cross and York, at 71·9 mph.

If a few rather special runs are left out of consideration one sees that the general average of fastest travel had, in fourteen years, increased from around 60 mph to a little over 70, and with the serious interruption caused by the Second World War, there was no significant increase again until about the year 1955. Now one can expect to travel from city centre to city centre at average speeds of more than 80 mph by quite ordinary express trains and at 90 mph by the élite. This leaves out of consideration the standards maintained for the last ten years on the Japanese Shinkansen lines, on which start-to-stop averages by the 'Hikari' trains are over 100 mph, on an exclusive special purpose railway. But the graph of booked speed is shooting skywards, with French prospects of city-to-city travel at 155 mph, and Japanese with magnetic levitation at 280 mph.

I hope I may be pardoned for ending on a lighthearted note. In 1895, at the time of the second great race to the north, the journey time from London to Aberdeen was cut, in six weeks, from $11\frac{1}{2}$ to $8\frac{1}{4}$ hours, and the great locomotive historian, E. L. Ahrons, wrote: 'By mid-August the Aberdonians were rubbing their eyes and wondering if at this rate the granite city was going to become a sort of northern suburb of London!' Perhaps at the present rate the commuters of Brighton may at last get the special high-speed railway that was projected in 1900, and hurtle up to London each morning in twenty minutes.

Nostalgia of steam: a triple-headed eastbound express on the Field Hill, British Columbia; Canadian Pacific Railway.

Bibliography

AHRONS, E. L., *Development of British Locomotive Design*, London, Locomotive Publishing Co., 1914.
AHRONS, E. L., *British Railway Steam Locomotive, 1825–1925*, London, Locomotive Publishing Co., 1927.
AHRONS, E. L., *Locomotive and Train Working in the Latter Part of the Nineteenth Century* (six volumes), Cambridge, Heffer, 1954.
AUSTRALIAN RAILWAY HISTORICAL SOCIETY, *A Century-plus of Locomotives, New South Wales Railways, 1855–1965*, Sydney, NSW, 1965.
BEYER-PEACOCK, *Beyer-Garratt Articulated Locomotives*, London, Beyer, Peacock & Co., 1947.
BOWEN-COOKE, C. J., *British Locomotives*, London, Whittaker, 1899.
BRITISH RAILWAYS, *Diesel Traction; a Manual for Enginemen*, London, British Transport Commission, 1963.
BRUCE, A. W., *Steam Locomotive in America*, New York, Norton, 1952.
CHAPELON, A., *La Locomotive à vapeur*, Paris, J. B. Baillière et Fils, 1938.
DALBY, W. E., *Steam Power*, London, Edward Arnold, 1915.
FERGUSON, T., *Electric Railway Engineering*, London, Macdonald & Evans, 1955.
GAIRNS, J. F., *Locomotive Compounding and Superheating*, London, C. Griffin & Co., 1907.
HINDE, D. W. and M., *Electric and Diesel-electric Locomotives*, London, Macmillan & Co., 1948.
JOHNSON, R. P., *The Steam Locomotive*, New York, Simmons-Boardman Publishing Corporation, 1942.
KAWAKAMI, Y., *A History of Japanese Railway Locomotives* (in Japanese), Tokyo.
NOCK, O. S., *Steam Locomotive*, London, George Allen & Unwin, 1957.
NOCK, O. S., *British Steam Railway Locomotive 1925–1965*, London, Ian Allan, 1966.
NORTH BRITISH LOCOMOTIVE COMPANY, *Manufactures during the War 1914–19*, Glasgow, North British Locomotive Co., 1919.
NORTH BRITISH LOCOMOTIVE COMPANY, *A History of the Company, 1903–1953*, Glasgow, North British Locomotive Co., 1953.
PALMER, A. N., and STEWART, W. W., *Cavalcade of New Zealand Locomotives*, Wellington (NZ), A. H. & A. W. Reed, 1956.
PETTIGREW, W. F., *Manual of Locomotive Engineering*, London, C. Griffin & Co., 1899.

SINCLAIR, A., *Locomotive Engine, Running and Management*, New York, John Wiley & Sons, 1885.

STEPHENSON, R., and HAWTHORNS, *Locomotives, Products of the Darlington Works*, Darlington, Robert Stephenson & Hawthorns Ltd, 1939.

VUILLET, BARON G., *Railway Reminiscences of Three Continents*, London, Nelson, 1968.

VULCAN FOUNDRY, *Vulcan Locomotive Works 1830–1930*, London, Locomotive Publishing Co., 1930.

WARREN, J. G. H., *A Century of Locomotive Building, 1823–1923*, London, Andrew Reid & Co., 1923.

WHITE, JOHN H., JR, *American Locomotives, an Engineering History 1830–1880*, Baltimore, Johns Hopkins Press, 1968.

YOUNG, R., *Timothy Hackworth and the Locomotive*, London, Locomotive Publishing Co., 1923.

Acknowledgments

The author and publishers wish to acknowledge the kind permission of the following to reproduce illustrations on the pages shown:

Science Museum, London: 3, 5, 8, 11, 13, 14, 16, 23, 25, 27; Crown Copyright, Science Museum: 19, 21, 26, 28, 29, 34, 37; British Railways: 30, 64, 72, 122, 126, 131, 136, 139, 182, 183, 186, 200, 202, 203, 210, 213, 214, 232, 233, 240, 250, 272; collection of the late E. C. Poultney: 58, 60, 65, 79, 88, 89, 128, 132, 133, 137, 144, 145, 146, 179, 188, 213, 215, 218, 220, 221; firms no longer in existence: (a) Robert Stephenson & Hawthorns Ltd: 20, (b) Beyer, Peacock & Co. Ltd: 95, 108, 134, 150, 152, 225, (c) North British Loco. Co. Ltd: 120–1, 147, 148, 241, 242; German Federal Railways: 41, 42, 191, 192, 197, 198, 209; French National Railways: 53, 90, 91, 216, 271; Swiss Federal Railways: 156, 157, 158, 162, 169, 170, 247; Bern–Lötschberg–Simplon Railway: 167, 244; Indian Railways: 174, 199; Canadian Pacific Rail: 143, 236, 263, 266; Canadian National Railways: 54; Norfolk and Western Railway: 165; Chicago, Milwaukee, St Paul and Pacific Railroad: 166, 207, 241; Union Pacific Railway: 222; Penn-Central: 171, 172, 210, 211, 234; Japanese National Railways: 274; Hamersley Iron (Pty) Ltd: 260; National Museum of Wales: 6; Swiss Locomotive Works: 159; E. J. Bedford: 78; the late C. A. Cardew: 64; C. R. L. Coles: 173; M. W. Earley: 184, 231, 274; G. F. Fenino: 181, 223, 245; E. Johnson: 264, 265; R. H. Kindig: 112, 113, 194, 219, 223; L. G. Marshall: 239; O. S. Nock: 75, 102, 114, 115, 117, 119, 155, 160, 164, 178, 183, 187, 195, 215, 227, 246, 248, 251, 253, 254, 257, 259, 267, 269; Rev. T. B. Parley: 85; P. Ransome-Wallis: 97, 136, 202, 235; the late G. H. Soole: 276; Bishop E. Treacy: 238; from documents, etc. in the author's collection: 2, 57, 62, 68, 74, 94, 106, 130, 139, 140, 141; original drawings by Mrs C. Boyer, from information in the author's records: 35, 36, 38, 39; from the 'F. Moore' collection of the Locomotive Publishing Co. Ltd: 44, 45, 49, 51, 52, 53, 59, 70, 71, 73, 82, 83, 84, 86, 98, 99, 104, 105, 125, 127, 138; Real Photographs Ltd: front endpaper, 17, 77; Keystone Press Agency Ltd: back endpaper.